" We have rapidly moved beyond islands of information technology implementation (e-commerce and Industry 4.0) towards total supply chain digitalization of the value stream and the organization. The authors are the first to provide thought pieces that help a new generation of supply chain leaders to effectively address digital transformation. **"**

PROF. DR. ARND HUCHZERMEIER

Professor in Production Management, WHU – Otto Beisheim School of Management and Co-founder Industrial Excellence Award Europe

" Digital supply chain has become a popular buzzword among industry executives, yet there has not been a clear picture of what exactly a digital supply chain is and how it can create value for a company. This book provides a very organized framework and journey for what constitutes a digital supply chain and how to make it possible. The book's rich examples showcase best practices as well as innovative developments, providing the reader with real-life insights. Digital supply chain indeed has great potential, and the book gives you a powerful guide to get there. I congratulate the authors for this insightful contribution. **"**

PROF. HAU L. LEE

The Thoma Professor of Operations, Information & Technology, Stanford University and Co-Director, Value Chain Innovation Initiative

" The future supply chain will be digital and powered by advanced analytics. While there are already some leading companies who set great examples of what digital supply chains can achieve, most companies are still at the beginning of the digital operations transformation journey. The authors in this book provide a great perspective for supply chain executives, where and how to begin this journey, with all its aspects ranging from technology to organizational change, enriched with frameworks and real-life case studies. **"**

DR. MARCUS EHRHARDT

Managing Director and Partner of Boston Consulting Group. Core member of the global operations practice and co-leader of the firm's work on digital and analytics in biopharma operations.

The Digital Supply Chain Challenge
Breaking Through

Ralf W. Seifert and Richard Markoff

Chemin de Bellerive 23
P.O. Box 915
CH – 1001 Lausanne
Switzerland
Tel: +41 21 618 01 11 – Fax: +41 21 618 07 07
www.imd.org

Typeset in Bliss® and Bliss Cap®. Bliss® and Bliss Cap® are trademarks of https://studiotype.com.

ISBN 978-2-940485-33-8

eISBN 978-2-940485-34-5

Designed by Yves Balibouse, BBH Solutions Visuelles SNC, Vevey, Switzerland, www.bbhgraphic.com.

*To all the supply chain executives who seek to separate
hype from reality, be champions for change and lead successful
digital transformations in their organizations*

TABLE OF CONTENTS

FOREWORD

After more than 35 years at the frontline of supply chain management, I have seen this discipline evolve from a business support function to a cornerstone of organizational strategy. Across industries, technological progress and digitalization have driven productivity, enhanced efficiency and reduced waste in supply chains around the world – unlocking enormous benefits for both organizations and society at large. It is no exaggeration to say that supply chain management has shaped the world we live in.

And while change has been a constant theme over the past four decades, today's operations are evolving faster than ever. A wave of digital technologies is transforming the very foundations and basic rules of supply chain management; conventional chains are increasingly being replaced with streamlined, connected and dynamic supply chain ecosystems. Organizations able to effectively seize these digital opportunities can level up their capabilities and performance; those that do not, face more challenging futures.

Yet, for all the technological possibilities and the pressing need for effective digitalization strategies, too many supply chain practices are unfit for purpose. In their defense, professionals in our discipline are faced with the difficult task of disentangling myth from reality, hype from facts, practical ideas from overused buzzwords. And even when you have a solid understanding of the truth, how do you formulate a winning strategy? Moreover, how do you successfully execute this strategy?

This book does much to bridge these gaps. By providing a comprehensive introduction to the challenges and opportunities of supply chain digitalization, it offers valuable insights for a wide range of supply chain professionals. In today's disruptive world, a solid understanding of the fundamental concepts –

as outlined in Chapters 1 to 3 – will empower supply chain executives to successfully navigate the complex landscape ahead of them. The case studies in Chapter 4 provide both inspiration and clarity in equal measure.

I congratulate the author team – Ralf W. Seifert and Richard Markoff – on their extensive research and the ambitious scope of this publication. Their work will serve to pave many a path toward an exciting new reality. Finally, I encourage readers to embrace the book's important learning journey on digital supply chain challenges. With many business leaders taking a close look at their supply chain resilience in the wake of Covid-19, its message is certainly more relevant than ever.

GUSTAVO GHORY

Chief Supply Chain Officer Kimberly-Clark

ACKNOWLEDGMENTS

There are many people we would like to thank, whose contributions were essential in bringing this book to life. First, we greatly benefited from personal exchanges with numerous supply chain executives, from many different industries, who were most generous with their time in sharing their stories and lessons learned. We are aware of the daily pressures these professionals are under to keep their supply chains running smoothly and appreciate the effort they made to carve out time for us. Without their insights and perspectives – articulated in interviews or fully developed case studies – our writing would not be up to date.

Second, we are grateful to IMD for supporting us in our supply chain research and granting permission to reproduce some of the articles and the case studies. Readers interested in obtaining individual case studies can order them from The Case Centre (www.thecasecentre.org).

Finally, we would like to thank the team at IMD for their dedication and help in completing this book project, for coordinating the whole process and keeping us on time. If there is one person we would like to mention by name, it is Lindsay McTeague, whose editing support was critically important, raising both the quality and clarity of our text. Her patience and skill were invaluable.

ABOUT THE AUTHORS

 Ralf W. Seifert is a recognized scholar and executive educator in the domain of supply chain management. As Professor of Operations Management at IMD business school for the last 20 years, Ralf has designed and directed numerous public and company-specific general management programs. He is currently director of the Digital Supply Chain Management program.

Based on his work with companies, Ralf has co-authored two books and more than 40 case studies, several of which have won international case writing awards. Ralf continues to actively research issues of supply chain strategy and execution and regularly publishes in both leading academic journals and practitioner-oriented outlets. He is also a tenured professor at the Swiss Federal Institute of Technology (EPFL) in Lausanne, where he has held the Chair of Technology and Operations Management (TOM) since 2003.

Prior to joining IMD, Ralf studied and worked in Germany, Japan and the US. While in the US, he consulted for Hewlett-Packard on its omnichannel strategy and served as teaching and research assistant at Stanford University.

Ralf earned his PhD and MS degrees in management science at Stanford University (US) specializing in supply chain operations. His dissertation back in 2000 focused on modeling internet-enabled opportunities in supply chain operation. He also holds a Diplom Ingenieur degree in mechanical engineering with specialization in production management from the Karlsruhe Institute of Technology (KIT) in Germany and a Master's degree in integrated manufacturing systems engineering from North Carolina State University. In addition, he spent one year as a Visiting Scholar studying operations research at Waseda University in Tokyo.

Richard Markoff has an extensive and varied supply chain background. His career includes 22 years with L'Oréal, starting in Canada in manufacturing before stints in Paris and New York, with ever-increasing supply chain responsibilities and scope. He completed his adventure at L'Oréal as the company's first global supply chain standards director, defining and promoting best practices in customer collaboration, distribution, demand planning and production planning.

Throughout his career, Richard has been a constant agent of change and innovation in supply chain. He has been a pioneer of supply chain digitalization, for which he was cited in the Wall Street Journal, among other publications.

He continues this spirit of innovation today as a supply chain strategy advisor, professor, author and board member based in Geneva, Switzerland. Richard is also a co-founder and partner of the venture capital firm Innovobot, where he advises startups on their road to success.

Richard holds a PhD in supply chain management from ESCP-La Sorbonne (France), where his research shed light on supply chain governance and its articulation with finance; an MBA specialized in supply chain from Northeastern University (US); and a bachelor's degree in chemical engineering from McGill University (Canada).

INTRODUCTION
STRONG CONVICTIONS IN A CHANGING SUPPLY CHAIN WORLD

The challenges facing supply chain professionals are changing rapidly. These executives used to be expected to deal with working capital, operating costs and first-order customer service. In many companies, supply chain worked in the background, trying to keep operations smooth and all the stakeholders happy.

But change has been afoot for many years – just think of the challenges of starting up a supply chain from scratch today compared with 25 years ago. The rise of contract manufacturing as a prevalent, viable option has made the make-vs.-buy decision for small companies a much easier calculation. The use of third-party logistics providers (3PLs) has exploded. In the United States, for example, the 3PL market increased *five-fold* from 1996 to 2014.[*]

These trends have quietly transformed the supply chain profession. There is now less emphasis on capital expenditures and traditional logistics skills like warehousing and transportation. Supply chain executives are finding that expectations of their role have moved to include more business-facing activities, particularly in the areas of planning and customer relations. Companies have begun thinking about end-to-end planning, becoming serious about demand planning and aligning different actors in the company such as sales and finance.

They have come to see customer care as an opportunity for competitive advantage in traditional distribution channels, rather than an order-to-cash

---

[*] "US and global third-party logistics market analysis is released." Press release. Armstrong & Associates, May 22, 2011. https://www.3plogistics.com/u-s-and-global-third-party-logistics-market-analysis-is-released-3/.

service department. Opportunities for differentiation have emerged in working deeply with external supply chain players to improve costs, satisfy end customers and make decisions in the interests of the entire chain.

At a time when business-to-consumer (B2C) companies might conduct 20% of sales through digital channels, the supply chain is now a key player in the definition of the go-to-market model.

The impacts of these evolutions are still playing out. Supply chain managers have risen in prominence in many industries and now have an opportunity to influence strategic decisions in novel ways. Companies are striving to rethink their organizations to enable end-to-end planning governance while maintaining sufficient local proximity to enact effective sales and operations planning (S&OP) models. Customer collaboration is now a prominent supply chain competence as companies realize that the most significant cost-to-serve improvements will come from working with downstream channel partners.

And, of course, the eternal supply chain preoccupations of working capital, cost and service remain, while other managers expect that these should become easier because of the fundamental changes taking place in the supply chain.

In the midst of this evolution come two more.

The first is the emergence of the e-commerce retail channel and its progression into omnichannel. The continued growth of e-commerce and its impacts on traditional brick-and-mortar retail are well known. Although this growth has been quick, the idea that consumers can interact with retailers and brands through multiple devices, order products through these devices, choose from multiple delivery options and expect a *seamless experience throughout* is now coming to the fore even more rapidly.

From a supply chain digitalization (SCD) perspective, this is putting pressure on traditional supply chains to improve their master data management, develop new data models for a customer base that is no longer "far removed," and manage a new magnitude of orders and product availability complexities. In the space of a few years, supply chains have been asked to transform from picking and shipping to a downstream client to being agile, last-touch ambassadors for their brand to the final customer and an engine for providing rich, valuable data that will drive future product offerings and promotions.

The final evolution is the growth of a web of technological innovations grouped together under the moniker Industry 4.0. The term "Industry 4.0" really entered the supply chain sphere in 2013. It springs from the idea that supply chain in the broadest sense (one that includes planning, distribution, manufacturing, sourcing and customer collaboration) is undergoing its fourth major reimagining in history. The first industrial revolution is the one taught in history books – the introduction of mechanization and steam power in the late 18th century and the social upheaval that came with it.

The second is electrification, the assembly line and mass production in the late 19th century. The success of Taylorism created the field of scientific management, which Ford employed in his auto plants, and manufacturing began a transformation to large factories and economies of scale.

The third industrial revolution is perhaps the toughest one to guess. It refers to the introduction of basic automation and computers in around 1970. The implementation of programmable logic controllers (PLC) allowed companies to use simple robots to perform highly repetitive tasks and captured the imagination with futuristic images of robot arms in automotive plants.

And, finally, there is the fourth industrial revolution – Industry 4.0. Industry 4.0 is an umbrella term that strives to describe a diverse mix of emergent digital technologies, each having a different value proposition to offer supply chain. There is no "normal" definition of Industry 4.0, and no formal list of technologies that it encompasses. But some of the most common elements that can be associated with Industry 4.0 are robotic process automation (RPA), collaborative platforms offered in the Cloud as software as a service (SaaS), machine learning (ML) and artificial intelligence (AI), big data, advanced analytics, cobots, internet of things (IoT), additive manufacturing and 3D printing, blockchain and augmented reality (AR). This is a very short list of examples – we have seen lists with *over 400 different* Industry 4.0 technologies.

To make matters more complicated, many consultants have begun to refer to supply chain digitalization (SCD). SCD has no universally accepted definition that we have encountered but refers broadly to the subset of Industry 4.0 technologies that impact the less physical parts of the supply chain. So SCD can be thought of as including tools like supply chain control towers, traceability, inventory management and order management systems, but excluding shop-floor level technologies like cobots or automated guided vehicles (AGVs). In this book we use the two terms interchangeably.

As a marketing strategy, the "Industry 4.0" framing has been a clear winner. It has helped catapult Industry 4.0 into a term many have heard – although not everyone will admit to not fully grasping the concept. We have received calls from small and medium-sized enterprise owners who would like to "do Industry 4.0," as though it were a piece of equipment or a new technique like lean manufacturing or design thinking.

All three evolutions are now intertwined and hard to untangle. It is difficult to talk about S&OP without slipping into advanced planning tools, supply chain control towers, big data, advanced analytics and even AI. Any examination of the role of customer collaboration risks entering into traceability technologies like smart packaging or blockchain-enabled smart contracts and provenance databases. It is impossible to define a business strategy for e-commerce without separating it from the supply chain capabilities needed to execute the strategy.

The result for supply chain executives today is a world that is completely different from what it looked like in 2005. It requires an understanding of all aspects of the business, an appreciation of the constraints and expectations of upstream and downstream partners, and sufficient technological savvy to navigate the bewildering array of options presented by Industry 4.0 and SCD.

THE DIGITAL SUPPLY CHAIN CHALLENGE

This book is for supply chain executives facing this new challenge.

It is *not* an attempt to systematically explore each of the principal technologies covered under Industry 4.0. This book is meant for supply chain executives who are constantly burdened not only with the classic balancing act between service, cost and working capital but also with more intense cycles of promotions, launches and customizations. And on top of these imperatives, they have been asked to formulate an Industry 4.0 and SCD strategy to transform their organization, which may have to compete with companies that are digitally native, with business models designed for this new era.

This book offers a way to separate the signal from the noise, the reality from the hype. The aim is not to provide a detailed exploration of the benefits and downsides of a laundry list of Industry 4.0 technologies. There are many resources for those who wish to find out more about a given technology. Rather, our ambition is to provide some perspective for the supply chain executive looking to understand *where* to begin on an Industry 4.0 or SCD voyage, *how* to think about organizing for change, *what* are the key success factors and *why* some technologies might be a better fit than others.

We hope that this book will serve as a source of inspiration for supply chain executives about to embark on a digitalization adventure. The topics included provide valuable benchmarks to help executives understand where their company stands compared with peers. It isn't enough to see the best-in-class success stories, it is important to be aware of the preoccupations and progress of other supply chain executives who find themselves in the same situation. It's hoped that along with inspiration comes a sense of clarity. The focus here is on tangible, concrete issues, free of the hype and noise often associated with consultants, vendors or technologists.

THEMES

The book is structured around four broad themes that strive to cover the whole of SCD transformation from a management perspective.

Separating hype from reality

In exploring the first theme, we share some views on the phenomenon of SCD in an attempt to keep things in perspective and avoid getting caught up in the overexuberance. There is a useful benchmark on the progress, or lack thereof, of Industry 4.0 and SCD transformation, plus a valuable framework for embarking on such a strategy. We examine the profitability challenges in the online grocery business as a reminder that exciting trends do not always yield business models with margins. There is also a look back at radio frequency identification (RFID), which at one time generated excitement as a revolutionary technology, similar to the enthusiasm for blockchain today. And we also provide a counterpoint to the buzz around AI as a breakthrough for demand planning.

Proof beyond the promise

The second theme looks for concrete wins brought by Industry 4.0 and SCD to help demonstrate where tangible value is to be had. We explore predictive maintenance, an Industry 4.0 application that might quietly serve as the pioneer for subsequent technologies. AI, too, has a role in SCD but in this respect it seems that "small is beautiful." We also look at how personalization is integrating supply chain and new value propositions and might surprisingly help reverse a decades-long trend of production concentration. Moving downstream, we explore how food waste can be tackled using digital supply chain tools. And although online grocery has profitability challenges, a comparison of digitally native online players like Ocado and traditionally offline retailers like Tesco will help illustrate how SCD is becoming an essential element of business strategy.

Successful execution of the basics

It would be a mistake to look at SCD as an opportunity to leapfrog the basic fundamentals of supply chain management. The evolutions that are shaping supply chain management do not mean that doing ABC analysis or understanding the right way to measure service no longer matter. They mean that these basics are prerequisites that are even more important today. "Simplify, standardize, digitize" supply chain processes has never been truer. This theme also looks at the changing definition of supply chain's core competency in fulfillment, and some novel insights into S&OP governance that must precede any investment in tools like supply chain control towers.

Leading a digital supply chain transformation

This book closes with some real-life cases of companies that faced the challenge of an SCD transformation, each with lessons and insights for managers. We also explore the human resources impacts of production concentration, impacts that could be undone by the growing trend for personalization, with clues about the next evolution in supply chain career opportunities.

HOW TO USE THIS BOOK

This book is a distillation of our 50+ years of combined supply chain experience, both at the coal face and in the classroom. During this time, supply chains and their design and management have been rapidly evolving – and continue to do so – not least spurred on by digital developments. We have regularly shared our insights and observations in short articles and best-practice case studies, mostly published by IMD business school. This book brings this work together in one place and in an easily accessible format to help address the concerns and possible questions of supply chain executives as and when they arise. Each stand-alone piece is short, to the point and jargon free.

We have updated some of the articles to reflect the current state of play, but as we have already mentioned, changes are happening so rapidly in some areas, e.g. e-commerce, that we are only able to *provide* a snapshot of a particular moment in time. Nevertheless, even if the precise facts change, the principles remain the same and provide food for thought.

By its very nature, this book is not designed to be read from cover to cover. We encourage readers to consult it at different times during their SCD voyage, to find benchmarks, relevant insights or even just to help formulate the right questions along the way. It is a sort of handbook to the essentials of digital supply chain transformation.

CHAPTER 1
SEPARATING HYPE FROM REALITY

Hearing and thinking about supply chain digitalization (SCD) can be intimidating at first. There are so many technologies, so many buzzwords and so few concrete examples to help solidify possibilities that it is hard to know where to start. The landscape is still embryonic and in flux, with a crowded and growing ecosystem of vendors, often with proprietary operating protocols. Consultants each come with their own frameworks and terminologies that, rather than providing clarity, further confuse what is meant by SCD, what it can offer and where to start.

A look at the 2019 Gartner Supply Chain Strategy Hype Cycle,[1] which represents the maturity, adoption and social application of specific technologies, points to how SCD has come to dominate the conversation about supply chain innovation:

- Seven supply chain enablers or capabilities are considered to be *on the rise*. All but one are within the scope of SCD. They are natural language generation, SCaaSA (supply chain as a service architecture), supply chain virtualization, artificial intelligence, data literacy and digital security. The lone outsider is circular economy.
- Six supply chain enablers or capabilities are *at the peak* of the Hype Cycle, four of them squarely within supply chain digitalization: blockchain, robotics/automation, social learning platforms and digital supply chain services. The other two are evergreen topics: customer intimacy and solution-centric supply chains.
- Even six of the eleven capabilities sliding *into the trough* are elements of SCD.

For supply chain managers balancing the day-to-day imperatives of service, cost and working capital management, as well as navigating internal stakeholders, it can be difficult to know how to approach the topic. It is likely that few supply chain managers are aware of the trends listed in the Gartner report, let alone able to sift through them and identify the best fit for their organization.

It is essential to separate the hype from reality before a digitalization journey can begin. This means engaging critically with new revolutions, benchmarking against others, understanding the right fit and developing the internal business case.

Looking at some pertinent contemporaneous and historical examples, there are lessons to be learned and warning signs to be heeded about the difference between hype and reality, or trend and profitability.

CHAPTER OVERVIEW

In this chapter there are five explorations of this theme, explorations that help set a reference framework and starting point for embarking on an SCD journey. The chapter begins with a helpful benchmark of the supply chain community, followed by a framework for starting to construct an SCD strategy that looks beyond the limited area of supply chain at the business as a whole. Then we look with a somewhat critical eye at two prominent SCD topics that perhaps warrant a more reality-based perspective that cuts through the hype. The chapter closes with a reflection on a notable supply chain hype of the past, where it is today and what it can teach us.

Topic 1: The voice of the supply chain community

The priorities of supply chain managers and the gaps they see in terms of achieving these priorities in their own organizations are revealed in the results of surveys undertaken in 2016 and 2019 by IMD business school in Lausanne. By looking at the evolution between the two surveys, we can see how perspectives towards SCD are changing and shaping the managerial vision of the supply chain community.

This is true not only for ascendant SCD technologies but also for those on the wane. In the space of four years, some technologies are already showing wear and beginning to fade. This is explored in the first section – "The Evolving Views of the Supply Chain Community."

Topic 2: Three key questions for Industry 4.0

Depending on the counting method, over 400 technologies are associated with SCD, also referred to as Industry 4.0. This can make it difficult for supply chain managers to know where to start, how to prioritize and finally how to choose which technologies are the right fit for the commercial and financial success of their company.

Any technology initiative can only succeed if it is part of a broader business strategy and addresses a key driver. Thinking only along economic lines in terms of return on investment both limits the universe of available choices and may serve as a cudgel to crush innovation altogether. Many benefits of SCD can be difficult or impossible to quantify properly or must be seen in the context of opportunities to support growth or new markets and not simply in terms of efficiencies.

In the second section – "The Real Industry 4.0 Challenge" – we try to offer a framework in the form of three key questions a supply manager should address when embarking on an Industry 4.0 or SCD program: finding the right technology fit with the business strategy, calculating the business case and overcoming barriers to implementation.

Topic 3: Is AI the answer for planning?

It can be useful when starting to reflect on SCD to recall that, on the whole, most companies start from modest beginnings in their use of data and tools. A *Supply Chain Quarterly* study[2] is helpful for positioning the current state of affairs. Some highlights are:

- Excel is by far the most common supply chain analytics tool
- Less than 5% of companies use advanced tools such as databases, structured query language (SQL) and control towers
- Only 10% of companies use a business intelligence tool

This is a good reflection of our experience in interactions with supply chain executives. Companies are struggling simply to keep up in data literacy and to exploit the tools available to them now, let alone take advantage of the proliferation of end-to-end planning packages and data analytics tools.

Almost every supply chain manager has a story to tell about spending time and money on a new demand planning tool with sophisticated statistical algorithms to provide accurate baselines, only to find that the demand planners are first downloading historical data into Excel, then using Excel as they did before all the money was spent, and finally uploading Excel into the new tool. If this sounds familiar, you are not alone.

In such a context, it is hard to imagine the potential of a technology like artificial intelligence to bring about a revolution in demand planning, as explored in the third section – "Demand for AI in Demand Planning."

Topic 4: E-commerce: Buying market share with supply chain

We are witnessing a historical restructuring of the world of retail. E-commerce is ascendant and changing the way consumers behave and interact with retailers and brands. This new order is triggering a retail apocalypse,[3] which also includes a revision of the expectation that the supply chain ends with getting products on store shelves.

Consumers are ever-more demanding in their expectations, and e-commerce players are rushing to meet them. For companies deciding to what extent they can compete with Amazon or Walmart.com, supply chain managers need to enter the discussion clear-eyed about the potential impacts on their cost to serve.

The supply chain cost dynamics of e-commerce are discussed in the fourth section – "The Emerging E-commerce Inflection Point."

Topic 5: Maybe we have been here before

A new emerging technology is going to revolutionize supply chains forever. It will improve traceability, limit fraud and waste, and provide instant visibility for all the actors from end to end. This is the promise we are hearing of blockchain. For those supply chain managers who have been around for a while, this may seem familiar. It has echoes of another revolutionary technology that entered the mainstream in the mid-2000s – radio frequency identification (RFID) tags.

There is a curious if incomplete analogy between the excitement surrounding blockchain and the buzz around RFID. The arc of the RFID story and where it sits today can offer insights into how new technologies can find their "sweet spot" and contribute to more efficient and high-performing supply chains, even if they do not live up to their initial expectations.

The story of RFID, and the analogy to blockchain, is told in the final section – "RFID: Yesterday's Blockchain."

1 THE EVOLVING VIEWS OF THE SUPPLY CHAIN COMMUNITY

In 2016, and again in 2019, IMD business school surveyed more than 300 supply chain executives from over 30 industries. The main industries represented included specialty chemicals, food & beverage, pharmaceuticals, industrial goods, fast-moving consumer goods (FMCG), oil & gas, and mining & minerals.

The objective was to understand which supply chain topics were considered of high importance to the community over the next three to five years, and also to develop an understanding of how well these managers felt their own organization or company was addressing these topics.

The survey results are shown in **Figure 1.1**. The responses were ranked on a scale from 1 to 7, with 1 being considered of very low importance and not well addressed and 7 being of very high importance and well addressed.

This approach provides rich insights into the priorities, preoccupations and self-assessment of supply chain executives, *and how this has evolved over time*. The survey results offer several takeaways for supply chain managers looking both to benchmark themselves and to develop a sense of strategic priorities.

The reality/hype gap of digitalization

The five supply chain topics deemed of highest importance in both surveys are not intrinsically supply chain digitalization (SCD) topics. They concern the fundamentals, also it is hardly surprising to find they are top of mind for supply chain managers.

The most important topic, *supply chain strategy/integration with business strategy*, is reassuring in that every other topic should naturally flow from this one. We will argue in the next section that this applies particularly to SCD initiatives, but it is also true in every dimension of defining supply chain strategy. Just as reassuring is that although the importance of this topic has not changed since 2016, the respondents feel they are addressing it slightly better.

There is an argument that the next four topics could be optimized or accelerated using digitalization. The second most important topic, *applying sales & operations planning (S&OP) throughout the organization*, is ripe for this perspective. However, it is doubtful whether a tool can help improve a managerial process that has not yet fully solidified. In Chapter 3 we explore how S&OP is more a function of process and policy than a topic of digitalization.

Figure 1.1: The voice of the supply chain community: IMD survey

Q1: Please indicate the relative importance between now and 2023 for your organization / your company

Q2: Please rate how well you think these items are currently being addressed in your organization / your company

● Importance 2019   ◯ Importance 2016
● How well addressed 2019   ◯ How well addressed 2016

Not important
Not well addressed
1

Very important
Well addressed
7

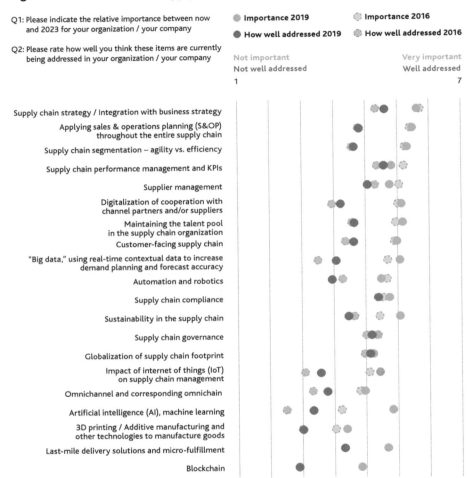

Digitalization is slowly gaining bandwidth

The first SCD topic mentioned is *digitalization of cooperation with channel partners and/or suppliers*. It has not increased in importance between surveys, but the perception of how well it is addressed has increased. It can perhaps be considered as a complement to *customer-facing supply chain*, just two ranks down. Both topics show the same evolution of profile. Customer collaboration – in the form of product data sharing, automation of orders and query management among others – is ripe for efficiency gains. This is truer than ever with the continued growth of omnichannel sales, which multiply the sources of orders and expose gaps in the information flow.

Looking down the list of topics and identifying those that fall into the broad category of SCD, there is an unmistakable trend that these topics are becoming more front of mind for supply chain managers.

Two of the three topics with the biggest increase in importance are SCD topics: *big data, using real-time, contextual data to increase demand planning and forecast accuracy* and *artificial intelligence (AI), machine learning.* (*Supply chain sustainability* is the third.)

These topics are truly enablers, capabilities that can drive deeper insights and improve many aspects of supply chain. It's a sign of the consistency and clear-eyed wisdom of the respondents that these two topics are increasing in importance, as they can help power many of the other topics on the list. A further demonstration of this coherence is that big data is needed to power the AI in the service of improved demand planning. We will address the potential of AI in demand planning later in this chapter.

2 THE REAL INDUSTRY 4.0 CHALLENGE

The true challenge of Industry 4.0 is that even though technological advances continue apace and early adopters reap the benefits of those technologies that fit their business context, executives at most companies are bewildered by the array of technologies and capabilities already available and do not always see an obvious entry point. Even after they have selected an innovation avenue, the business case is not easy to establish. And for those companies that do select an Industry 4.0 innovation, justify the economic case and get to implementation, there are still unique barriers to change that must be overcome. Taken together, this is a three-part problem that companies looking to innovate through Industry 4.0 need to solve: How will companies build paths to (1) select, (2) justify and (3) leverage the functionalities available to them? Each of the challenges is worth a closer look.

Finding the right Industry 4.0 fit

It isn't always clear for supply chain leaders which Industry 4.0 innovation initiatives to adopt. Industry 4.0 offers a host of exciting technologies, with a rich landscape of options and vendors attractive to senior management, but with high complexity risks for those closer to operations, who see a dizzying array of choices. Adding to the puzzle, there are both internal and external business drivers that might dictate which innovations have the greatest potential benefit and warrant prioritization.

External drivers

The external market forces that pull supply chains towards Industry 4.0 solutions could be linked to mass customization, agility in the face of ever more variable demand, using big data to understand and predict consumer behavior, and cloud collaboration networks with suppliers and customers.

There are prominent examples that show the potential of Industry 4.0. One is the use of 3D printing to produce customized hearing aids within hours,[4] leading the way to wider use of 3D printing in medical devices such as titanium knee or spinal prosthetics.[5] The potential is high enough that the Federal Drug Administration (FDA) has released guidance that establishes the path to regulatory approval for 3D printed medical devices.[6] Fast-moving consumer goods (FMCG) companies are now using predictive analytics fed by big data to understand how consumers may react to new product launches in order to better size demand plans.[7]

These are exciting opportunities that extend beyond supply chain and must be part of an overall definition of business strategy led by the CEO, with the participation of many different actors, including supply chain. And here Industry 4.0 is a key enabler. For example, investing in cloud-based order management tools that make it possible to leverage stores, warehouses and even third-party stocks to optimally fulfill e-commerce orders is a task for supply chains to solve. Even decisions on the configuration of the physical network are now dependent on the e-commerce order fulfillment strategy. However, the decision to use stores to fulfill e-commerce orders, either with stock or via click-and-collect, is clearly part of an overall business strategy. The business strategy must position the priorities of e-commerce, store traffic and order lead time, and weigh up staff training and complexity. Supply chains have a voice in the discussion to be sure, and the discussion must be had before rushing to implementation.

Going further upstream, deploying automation to increase the agility of line changeovers makes more sense if the business strategy is to have a larger product portfolio with smaller volumes and more promotional activity. The industrial strategy is a function of the business strategy, not the other way around. For example, adidas is innovating in the shoe market by deploying 3D printing to support a strategy of offering customized insoles and limited edition models.[8] Its competitor, Nike, announced an automation program to redesign the company's geographical production footprint – reducing the number of contractor factories by about 200 in four years – and bring increased agility to its supply chain.[9]

Internal drivers

In terms of internal business drivers, automation, transparent sales and operations planning (S&OP) suites, connected production sensors, predictive maintenance and shop-floor augmented reality can have immediate benefits for safety, quality and efficiency. These solutions are interesting because of internal performance ambitions, rather than external market influences, and they are more independent of the overall business strategy.

They may seem to lie purely within the domain of supply chain and operations, but in fact are often multidisciplinary. Even something like demand sensing – using big data and predictive analytics to "sense" short-term trends in consumer demand – is best done with the collaboration of commercial and category management teams. Without their support, it will be difficult for the supply chain to access, understand and leverage the data.

Once the challenge of identifying and prioritizing the most compelling possibilities of Industry 4.0 has been addressed, the next step is justifying the economic business case.

Calculating a business case

Adopting an Industry 4.0 technology, be it in response to internal or external business drivers, requires a uniquely challenging economic justification, since it goes beyond straightforward return on investment (ROI) scenarios.

This is partly because many Industry 4.0 technologies have not yet been widely deployed, and there may be reluctance to be the first adopter. New technology solutions are often met with skepticism, which can raise the bar for the ROI even though there are few demonstrable business cases available for comparison. When the proposed technology is truly cutting edge, the risks of failure are higher and the economic case is held up to greater scrutiny. Not every company has leaders ready to champion and sponsor innovation in the face of uncertain or less tangible outcomes.

One FMCG company we spoke to was an early adopter of automated guided vehicles (AGVs) to replace forklifts driven by humans. The pilot project showed a best-case payback of five years – just long enough for the project to be halted in its tracks for lack of a compelling return. However, the head of operations pushed forward, seeing the less tangible but critical value that investing in AGVs would represent. This would send a clear message that the company placed importance on safety, cleanliness and innovation. Today AGVs are widely deployed worldwide and their contribution is not questioned. How many companies have similarly visionary leaders ready to take risks on Industry 4.0? Indeed, most of the Industry 4.0 success stories we have encountered – some of which are included in this book – reached implementation through management's conviction that their company had to be an innovation leader rather than through an ironclad economic justification.

When Industry 4.0 solutions are due to external forces, this adds a layer of complexity. Supply chain managers are more used to justifying investments that provide efficiency or are required to meet a stated, projected demand. When the investments are part of a shift in business strategy, both the top and bottom lines in the economic model are moving, clouding the question even further. This is an opportunity for supply chain managers. They can now have a voice in shaping business strategy, rather than being uniquely a function of it.

An essential element to consider is scalability. A business case is more compelling when it is possible to pilot a new technology in a small, controlled environment before scaling up company-wide. Where possible, this can limit the size of the investment, but might discourage innovations that require high upfront fixed costs regardless of scale, such as a collaboration platform.

Overcoming barriers to implementation

Any technology deployment will inevitably encounter barriers to implementation. There are the usual hurdles of employee engagement, skepticism and fear of being unable to adapt that cannot be ignored. But Industry 4.0 entails other dimensions of implementation challenges.

The potential lack of a clear business case might undermine the motivation of key implementation actors, especially if the transverse nature of the transformation undermines their economic incentives.[10] For example, factory managers purely motivated around cost and efficiency may resist Industry 4.0 initiatives that promote connectivity, transparency and agility.

With so many companies looking to implement an Industry 4.0 strategy, finding qualified talent is becoming a problem. Similarly, the skill levels of current employees might not be adequate, raising the required training effort.

From a technology perspective, increased connectivity and cloud projects mean that issues like cybersecurity and data ownership must be addressed. Business continuity plans may no longer be suitable as new risk points and overall system threats emerge.

The big picture

Industry 4.0 advocates would do well to focus not only on the technology but also on the managerial implications. The technology is exciting and will undoubtedly change operations in the years to come. But companies that are looking to participate in and benefit from Industry 4.0 must prioritize projects that are consistent with an external business strategy, identify what the true benefits are, and understand how ready they are to make the change happen.

3 DEMAND FOR AI IN DEMAND PLANNING

Demand planning is starting to become the object of supply chain digitalization (SCD) attention. Tech giants like Amazon and Microsoft have announced artificial intelligence (AI) tools for improving demand planning, and several consulting companies are promoting their skills to bring AI to companies' demand planning processes. In fact, a 2019 survey by the Institute of Business Forecasting (IBF)[11] identified AI as the technology that will have the largest impact on demand planning in 2025.

It's not hard to see the fit between AI and demand planning. Demand planning involves lots of number crunching, data analytics and is repeated cycle after cycle. It is tempting to imagine that a self-learning AI application could do at least as good a job as a planner.

Taking a closer look reveals that there are serious challenges to AI successfully penetrating the demand planning market. These challenges are not so much technical as managerial. However, even if AI does not become a significant contributor to demand planning accuracy, addressing these managerial challenges can only improve a company's demand planning performance.

AI needs data

The most striking challenge when it comes to applying AI to demand planning is in the availability and accuracy of data. Internally, companies already struggle to maintain accurate data, starting with the most basic element of all, the product code. Ever-accelerating launch programs and shrinking product life cycles mean more product churn than ever. One corporate head of planning that we spoke to said: "Let's show we can correctly link product codes in substitutions before thinking about AI."

In order to build an accurate demand plan, one-off events have to be identified and accounted for, such as service issues and one-time promotions. These events would need to be fully understood and coded before an AI application could learn from them – no mean feat. External data in the form of market intelligence would also need to be acquired and leveraged, such as competitor actions, customer behaviors, and trade disruptions like price changes and sell-out data.

Yet many companies today struggle with their digital culture and level of savviness. Our conversations with executives at large multinationals that have invested heavily in demand planning tools reveal that almost all of them face the same struggle: Their planners prefer to build demand plans in Excel and upload them into the expensive, integrated tools they have to use to propagate their demand plans. The usual explanation for this resistance to using the tools is that they do not have enough of the internal and external contextual data to build pertinent statistical plans.

The survey by *Supply Chain Quarterly*[12] discussed in the introduction to this chapter revealed that Excel is by far the most common analytical tool used by supply chain planners, with advanced tools like supply chain control towers used by about 60% of companies. This matches our anecdotal observation that about half of companies use an advanced planning system (APS).

The absence of data, resistance to using the existing suite of statistical tools, and level of digital savvy represent non-negligible challenges to the deployment of AI-enabled demand planning.

AI in Sales and Operations Planning (S&OP)

Demand planning is a critical activity in the S&OP process. The objective of S&OP is to obtain alignment from all actors in the company, ideally ensuring that operations mobilizes its resources to supply what the business needs to meet its financial goals, while also ensuring that the financial goals take the current operational constraints into account.

A fundamental pillar of the S&OP process is the notion of "one set of numbers," which means that operations and finance are working off a shared understanding of the forward-planned activity for the business. The primary drivers for this goal are that no market opportunities are missed, and operations is focused on the true business needs.

By tying the financial plan to the operational plan, general managers are driven to invest themselves, along with their commercial and marketing teams, in the demand planning process in order to have the most viable demand plan possible. This involvement is critical, as it helps provide the demand planners with the valuable external market intelligence mentioned earlier. Just as importantly, from a managerial perspective, having one set of numbers means that any effort by general managers to manipulate the demand plan would also change the financial plan, which they are loath to do as it constitutes their commitment to executive leadership.

Consider the connection of S&OP to the deployment of AI for demand planning. A successful AI-generated demand plan would also have to follow the "one set of numbers" principle. If it did not, the necessary external data and market intelligence would be difficult to obtain, as general managers would return to their old reflexes of considering the demand plan outside their sphere of interest, and perhaps again adjust the numbers to their subjective tastes.

But maintaining the tie between the AI-generated demand plan and the financial plan would inevitably imply asking general managers to *allow their financial projections to be generated by the AI application*. This is a significant management hurdle for supply chains to overcome.

The introduction of AI-generated demand plans would bring with it what is termed the "explainability problem" of AI. This term describes managers' reluctance to use AI applications that seem like a "black box," where the reasoning and logic used to obtain results are difficult to explain, even if they are of high quality. The explainability problem is currently a tangible hurdle for successful AI deployments.

Research suggests[13] that very few companies have truly achieved the "one set of numbers" practice. The benefits of a more accurate AI-enabled demand plan that poses a serious obstacle to implementing S&OP because of the explainability problem does not necessarily seem like a winning trade-off. In other words, are companies better off having (perhaps) a highly accurate AI-generated demand plan that does not reflect the true business activity, or a slightly less accurate non-AI generated one that matches the company's ambitions?

This does not preclude the use of AI for demand planning, but it does suggest that it should be considered only for companies that have achieved very high S&OP maturity and integration between operational and financial planning activities.

AI as performance lever

The challenges of applying AI to demand planning should not be seen as insurmountable. Rather, AI could be an accelerator to help companies confront these data and managerial issues head-on, creating a foundation for using AI not only in demand planning but also in deploying stock to different markets, production planning and scheduling. A sound, participatory S&OP process that assembles and leverages robust and accurate internal and external data to reach a consensus number for both operations and finance should be the target for all companies.

4 THE EMERGING E-COMMERCE INFLECTION POINT

Our prediction a couple of years ago that "if people had to pay the real cost of their e-commerce, we'd have less of it"[14] seems to be gaining ground. By this we meant that since most e-commerce activities were unprofitable, eventually either consumers would have to pay more for their e-commerce purchases or they would have less choice of products and services.

A careful look at some developments in the e-commerce space paint a picture of just this sort of dynamic emerging.

Evolving e-commerce strategies at Amazon

Amazon reported record profits and revenues in 2018. This was good news for Amazon and its shareholders. However, deeper scrutiny reveals how this result indicates an approaching inflection point in e-commerce economics. To begin with, most of the profit was not from retail activities. Amazon Web Services (AWS), its cloud-hosting activity unrelated to e-commerce, generated more operating income[15] than Amazon North America's retail operations, doing so with margins over five times higher. Nevertheless, the retail division's results were a significant improvement over 2017, when North American retail operating income was completely offset by international retail losses. In fact, in 2017 all of Amazon's operating income came from AWS.[16]

In 2018, to improve the profitability of its e-commerce retail operations, Amazon took concrete steps, many of which had a direct impact on the real cost of e-commerce to consumers.

For example, early in the year, Amazon increased the cost of Prime membership[17] by 20%. This surely contributed to its improved e-commerce profitability: One estimate has the increase accounting for nearly a third[18] of Amazon North America's operating margin. However, shrinking growth[19] and even reductions in Prime membership ensued as customers at the margin chose not to bear the cost increase. The intuitive result is: Fewer customers who pay more for their top-notch e-commerce service.

Amazon wasn't done, however. Late in 2018, it approached key vendors to try to improve the margins on what it calls CRaP products,[20] which stands for cannot return a profit. These are products on which Amazon recognizes that it cannot make a profit due to a combination of small margins or logistical challenges such as product weight or size. Think of bottled water, soda and snack foods as examples. Amazon began pressuring these manufacturing companies to lower their sales costs to the online retailer so that it could earn a profit. It is unlikely that this will enjoy large-scale success – and in some regulatory environments is even not permitted. This means Amazon will either charge more for these products or delist them. For the consumer, this will mean less e-commerce choice or higher prices.

Not all of Amazon's initiatives were at the expense of the consumer, however. The company reported a 4% improvement in fulfillment costs[21] as it increased throughput in its distribution center network. This was a welcome development for Amazon, since it had seen both fulfillment and transportation costs increase as a percentage of sales each year[22] from 2010 to 2017.

It has also succeeded in increasing both third-party sellers and those who use Amazon's distribution centers as a third-party logistics provider[23] rather than as a customer, which creates both a new revenue stream for Amazon and lowers working capital for them. This is not an inherent efficiency, however; rather it offloads some expenses to manufacturers that will likely eventually be passed on to consumers in the form of higher prices. This service is a complement to Amazon's significant and growing third-party sales – now at 58% of retail sales – whereby sellers use Amazon as an e-commerce platform without either selling Amazon goods or using Amazon as a fulfillment service. This resembles the business model[24] of the Chinese e-commerce giant Alibaba.

A look at the competition

Amazon may be the biggest e-commerce player, but it is not the only one. Major rival Walmart has its own techniques for trying to drive e-commerce activities towards profitability.

In a creative cost-saving measure with shades of Amazon's CRaP initiative, Walmart simply hides unprofitable products from view.[25] It has begun removing products that are not profitable from consumer search results, instead showing them as out-of-stock and offering suggestions that are more profitable for the company.

An interesting new development is Walmart's announcement that it will pilot free next-day grocery delivery[26] from Walmart stores without the customer having to sign up as a member or buy a large minimum order. The wrinkle is that the offering is limited to a small slice of the product catalogue comprised of high-volume, higher-margin products. In both of these examples, Walmart is pruning the choices available to consumers in an effort to find a profitable e-commerce model.

We spoke to an experienced grocery retail manager and he explained that it is "impossible" to make money with such models in online grocery, but they are necessary as marketing loss leaders. He added, "Right now, online grocery is about 2% of the market, with much of the market not receptive to shopping for groceries online. This is the only reason the grocery chains can afford it, because it is so small." His thinking is supported by a Capgemini study[27] that found that online grocery orders have a *negative margin* of about 15%. It is very reminiscent of the old business joke about losing money on every sale but making it up in volume.

The pressure to compete with these players remains high, however. To understand the mindset of other retailers who are not purely online players, we can return to the insights offered by a supply chain consultant we spoke to about cost to serve (see Chapter 3 for more on cost to serve). He explained that the cost impacts are in fact eroding margins, but that offline companies are prioritizing speed of change before profitability. "With many of our clients, omnichannel is not a choice so we have to 'go' anyway, and prioritize implementing and execution. It's a logic of desperation as much as it is of strategy."

We can see the consequences of this in an interesting survey by SCM World.[28] It found that in 2017, 61% of supply chain executives reported an increase in stock-keeping unit (SKU) count due to e-commerce, up from 55% in 2013. Asked about the impacts on the distribution network, 26% of respondents noted that they are implementing smaller, more localized distribution centers because of e-commerce service expectations, up from 20% in 2013.

These increases in product portfolio and distribution footprint inevitably lead to higher costs as these companies try to compete with major players like Amazon and Walmart. Over time, these costs – at least in part – will be passed on to the consumer, as a direct result of the growing expectations of e-commerce, particularly delivery lead times.

Lead time expectations

Another factor hastening the arrival of this inflection point is the growing pressure on delivery lead times. In mid-2019, Amazon started gradually moving from free two-day shipping for Amazon Prime members to free one-day shipping.[29] Importantly, the $25 minimum spend before a customer could buy an "add-on" low value item was phased out in parallel.

The first results are as might be expected, but with a twist. In the third quarter of 2019, Amazon's revenue increased by 24%[30] on the previous year, to $70 billion. However, profit was $2.1 billion, a 28% decrease. It seems that consumers were pleased with the faster delivery time, but that the cost of fulfilling these orders not only ate into profits but proved to be simply unprofitable.

Amazon's CFO said of Prime customers, "They are buying more often, and they are buying more products."[31] The first part of that statement seems to be correct, but the second part is nuanced. According to Morgan Stanley, a two-day order from Amazon of $23.33 costs the company $5.08 to fulfill, giving a cost to serve of almost 22%.[32] However, fulfilling a one-day order costs $8.32, and the cost to serve is an astonishing 127%. This means Amazon is losing money on every order even before the cost of goods and overheads are taken into account.

So, although consumers are indeed buying more often and buying more products, they appear to be buying much less *per order*. About two-thirds less, in fact. So, while one would expect Amazon to pay more for transportation to achieve one-day shipping, the order preparation cost has surely increased as well. The costs of processing an order are fixed, so larger order sizes help keep logistics costs in check. As the consumer response to one-day shipping seems to be to order in much smaller quantities, Amazon's fulfillment costs have increased in addition to the transportation costs. Undeterred, Amazon announced that it spent $800 million in the first quarter of 2020 supporting this initiative. One element to watch moving forward is the basket size of a Prime order and the level of Prime membership. This will help explain whether this initiative has allowed Amazon to convert new users and where profitability might be heading.

Others are following Amazon's lead. Walmart countered with its own one-day shipping program, called NextDay.[33] The program seems to be less extensive and more cost conscious. Walmart limits the products available for next-day shipping as a function of where the customer lives and the stock position of the nearest Walmart store or distribution center. Items are offered in such a way as to prevent the company from having to ship from multiple locations.

The inflection point

The recent past has brought some interesting developments in the broader e-commerce market: More expensive subscription packages, higher prices, less choice from pure online players coupled with higher costs and complexity from online/offline players. These are all ways in which consumers have begun to pay more for their e-commerce experience.

Perhaps this is the beginning of an inflection point for e-commerce growth, where e-commerce offerings will be more targeted and cost conscious, with narrower selections of SKUs, geographic coverage and lead times – and perhaps even higher prices – all combining to slow the growth curve.

The next e-commerce battlefield

In addition to one-day shipping for Prime members, Amazon announced free two-hour grocery delivery in more than 20 metropolitan centers in the US[34] for them, as long as the order reached a modest $35 minimum. This will be supported by the Amazon Fresh fulfillment center infrastructure, rather than the Whole Foods Amazon grocery program. This comes hot on the heels of reports[35] that Amazon is finalizing plans to build a new grocery network, one more suited to serving both online and offline orders.

If true, the Amazon grocery landscape is becoming crowded, with Amazon Go, Whole Foods, Amazon Pantry and Amazon Fresh already on the scene. This is a complex, risky bet, particularly when the structural cost challenges to online grocery profitability[36] are considered.

Other tech giants continue to innovate in the grocery space. Alibaba's Hema shops in China[37] offer a unique blend of restaurant, shop and local online grocery fulfillment center. Hema has upped the ante by offering 30-minute free delivery within a 3-kilometer radius with an emphasis on upscale prices and freshness. By linking Hema to the Alipay app, the potential for online to offline conversion is high, and there are rich data collection possibilities.

5 RFID: YESTERDAY'S BLOCKCHAIN

Blockchain is a hot topic these days in supply chain circles. Starting with a near-apocryphal story of a Walmart executive frustrated by the company's lack of traceability, blockchain is being touted as a key to the future of supply chain.[38] The array of potential applications is dizzying, covering traceability, customs formalities, international shipping documentation, safety and sustainability data, and supply chain financing. Some of the media coverage is breathless and borders on hype.[39]

Others are more sanguine about the potential of blockchain.[40] An article in *Harvard Business Review* captured much of the current state of discourse around blockchain: "Virtually everyone has heard the claim that blockchain will revolutionize business and redefine companies and economies. Although we share the enthusiasm for its potential, we worry about the hype."[41] The authors offer an interesting point of comparison for the potential path of adoption of blockchain – the slow and incremental implementation of TCP/IP (the groundwork for the development of the internet). They suggest that blockchain is not a "disruptive" technology, but rather a foundational technology from which many innovations may flourish.

Other compelling comparisons can be made for the future of blockchain. In fact, to us much of this seems oddly familiar: *A new technology that will revolutionize supply chains through improved visibility, data reliability and productivity.* It is eerily reminiscent of the increasing popularity of radio frequency identification (RFID) in supply chain about two decades ago. A look at the influential Gartner Hype Cycle helps to illustrate the comparison. In 2003, passive RFID was at the *peak of inflated expectations*, according to Gartner.[42] In 2017's Hype Cycle, blockchain is in the same spot, among a handful of other technologies.[43]

The comparisons go further than merely excited predictions or retailers like Walmart making headlines with pilot implementations. Just as RFID was beset by competing standards for hardware, software and data management,[44] blockchain today has a variety of platforms coming online, such as Hyperledger and Ethereum, which each hope to win the battle of becoming the universal standard.

It is still early days for blockchain. Its benefits, according to proponents, derive from the power of having autonomous, extended networks bringing together information and transactions from diverse actors across the supply chain. Before exploring how RFID implementation has fared over the past 15 years, let's take a closer look at blockchain.

Blockchain in the supply chain

The benefits of blockchain in supply chain generally fall into three domains:

- *Traceability*: The ambition for blockchain in logistics is that it will provide an independent, inviolable ledger of all movements of goods along a supply chain. The blockchain could allow companies and consumers easy access to information about the provenance and legitimacy of the goods in question. Product recalls would be easier and faster, the thinking goes, and consumers could make more informed choices. The distributed nature of the blockchain ledger would overcome issues of IT interfaces and siloed information stored at each step in the chain.[45] A Walmart pilot in 2017 led to the announcement of a multi-company venture in the United States to implement blockchain in the food sector.[46] Other pilots are focusing on high value items for which transparency and sourcing are highly sensitive, such as diamonds.[47] The market is fluid, however, and most current pilots in blockchain traceability initiatives seem trapped in closed dyadic systems that are difficult to scale.[48]

  One of the most significant hurdles to implementing traceability through blockchains is the capture of transactions along the supply chain, for example a fruit harvest. These steps are difficult to record reliably and risk creating an elaborate blockchain ledger with source information of dubious reliability. Ironically, an often-suggested solution is to expand the use of RFID to help accelerate the deployment of blockchain.[49]

- *Smart contracts*: Some blockchain protocols can be configured to automatically trigger contractual commitments, through a mechanism called smart contracts.[50] For example, a bill of lading along with the International Commercial Terms (incoterms) could be coded into a smart contract on the blockchain. The receipt of goods at the destination, once confirmed on the blockchain, could trigger payment from the customer's bank to the supplier's bank provided that all conditions, such as price and quantity, were met. The hope is that administrative costs and delays could be wrung out of logistics and customs execution.

- *Supply chain finance*: The approach here would be to use blockchain to facilitate the financing of credit for small companies or those that have difficulty securing financing for their inventories.[51] The blockchain could allow receivables to be bought and sold without the intervention of banks, allowing for smoother, faster markets for factoring or reverse factoring. Although the concept is intriguing, we have not been able to find any reports of pilots in progress or completed in this area.

But the goal here is not to explore the potential and the challenges of blockchain for supply chain per se. Rather it is to look back to a time when RFID was the technology of the supply chain future, explore what really transpired and reflect on where RFID brought benefits to businesses. We believe that this analogy can teach managers many valuable lessons about finding the right applications for innovative technologies including blockchain.

RFID origins

As an emerging technology in the supply chain, RFID began attracting attention in the early 2000s. It offered the promise of significant benefits in productivity and visibility. The most intuitive appeal of RFID was as a successor to bar codes, but with much greater efficiency. *The Economist* hailed RFID as "the best thing since the bar code,"[52] while others proclaimed it "the biggest thing since Y2K."[53]

RFID tags could be read without having a line of sight on the bar code, multiple reads were possible and the information on the tags could evolve at different stages in the supply chain.[54] This would provide item-level accuracy with considerably less effort and more precision. Taken together, the reduced effort and increased precision offered significant warehousing labor efficiencies in receiving, movements, shipping and counting.[55]

Advocates of RFID also touted the visibility benefits of the new technology. With higher accuracy related to movements and almost effortless cycle counting, RFID would enable supply chain planners to base their decisions on a clearer view of actual inventory positions along the chain. These enthusiasts went on to suggest that – when looking at retail in particular – knowing when a product was moved from the storeroom to the shelf would improve demand planning and on-shelf availability.[56] The heightened visibility would dampen the bullwhip effect, and so lower inventories, lower expediting costs and reduce stockouts for all supply chain actors.[57]

The notion of visibility extended to transportation and traceability. RFID tags would allow transporters and their clients to pinpoint exactly where a specific item was in the supply chain and to whom it had been sold.[58]

RFID in retail supply chains

We will focus specifically on RFID in retail supply chains. This is where expectations were highest and most prominent, and can therefore offer valuable insights into the benefits and limitations of RFID. In 2004, as Walmart began an RFID initiative – examined in detail below – some researchers were hailing RFID as "the next revolution in the world of retailing," placing the retail sphere front and center in the excitement generated by the possibilities of RFID.[59]

Recently, the head of operations of a well-known hard luxury retailer gave us a tour of his flagship store. He had much to be proud of: The retailer was investing heavily in digitalization of operations to provide immediate visibility of all store and warehouse stock. Through a mobile app, a salesperson could ring up an order for an in-store customer or generate a home-delivery or click-and-collect order using available stock anywhere in the network. It was an impressive display of an omnichannel supply chain.

When the tour moved to the backroom, the level of sophistication changed. We observed a clerk processing the receipt of a shipment from the central warehouse. The transactions were executed by scanning a classic bar code, and even then the bar codes were a recent implementation. In light of the retailer's heavy investments in digital omnichannel capability that we had just witnessed, there was a reasonable expectation for something more cutting edge in productivity and accuracy. Something like RFID, perhaps.

The retailer explained that they had carefully considered implementing RFID for their store fulfillment process. He agreed that having RFID tags on the products would speed up store receiving. But the volume was so low that the productivity gains would be very small – certainly too small to justify investing in the hardware to scan the tags. He continued by pointing out that RFID tags are useful for quick cycle counting of store inventory, but for luxury retailers the merchandise is so valuable that great care is taken at every step to account for stock. The operations director went on to say that there are virtually no inventory errors that are not fully explained, for example by security cameras. So RFID had little to offer in terms of improving inventory accuracy.

His experience is representative of other hard luxury supply chains. If hard luxury retailers did not have the volumes to warrant investing in RFID, then it stands to reason that high volume actors like mass retail chains would find RFID attractive.

RFID in consumer mass retail

In 2003 the German grocery chain Metro announced an RFID initiative involving a "store of the future" concept.[60] Metro worked with key suppliers like Gillette, Kraft and Procter & Gamble to place item-level tags on products and track their movement all the way to the shelf.

Metro's RFID initiative quickly ran aground, however. As part of its efforts to explore potential RFID applications, Metro installed RFID chips on about 10,000 customer loyalty cards without advising its customers.[61] Under siege from privacy advocates for using "spy chips" and facing a barrage of negative publicity, Metro placed its RFID project on hold in 2004.[62]

This was not the only privacy misstep RFID would encounter in the mass channel. In 2003, both Walmart and UK retailer Tesco ran pilots with Gillette, the razor manufacturer. Razor blades are a notorious target for shoplifters due to their high price and small size. The pilot had a new approach to addressing the shrinkage problem: First, Tesco photographed every consumer taking razor blades off the shelf. Then an RFID scanner at the exit would trigger another photograph of consumers who left with razor blades. The idea was to compare the two photos and ensure that all those who left the store with razor blades had indeed paid for them.[63] Under pressure once again from privacy groups and even lawmakers, these pilots were abandoned.[64]

Despite these privacy concerns, it was in the mass channel that RFID had its most prominent splash. Walmart, the biggest mass retailer of all, garnered attention and surprise when it announced in 2003 that its top 100 suppliers would have to have all cases and pallets equipped with RFID tags by the start of 2005.[65] This was the big moment for RFID, the time when it would become a standard feature in all efficient supply chains. For Walmart, this was part of an effort to position itself as supply chain leader. Observers believed that the heft of Walmart would drive others to adopt the same initiative. "Other U.S. retailers will likely follow Walmart's lead" was a commonly held conviction at the time.[66]

Walmart justified the new initiative by emphasizing two benefits. The first was improved supply chain visibility. Walmart insisted that RFID would improve the visibility of product movements from the backroom to the shelf. It argued that the improved visibility would help suppliers improve their demand planning, be more responsive and lower inventory. Not everyone agreed with this assessment at the time. Said a principal analyst at Gartner, "We already know how much inventory is in the store and what is moving out. What's new is what is in the back and what is in the front [of the store]. But we don't know if that is really enough to justify all these RFID tags. It is not clear."[67]

The second justification was improved logistics efficiency. That this was a benefit for Walmart seemed clear enough. Having RFID readers register every pallet and case moving through the Walmart supply chain rather than scanning each bar code would provide significant productivity savings for the retailer. Walmart's own estimates put the efficiency gain at US$8 billion.[68]

It's here that things began to get tricky with the Walmart RFID edict. Walmart refused to share any of the productivity savings due to RFID with its suppliers. Nor did it offer to help defray the costs of RFID implementation or tags. It reasoned that suppliers should find benefits from RFID within their own supply chains, just as Walmart would.[69] Yet suppliers did not see a need to track case and pallet-level movements by RFID when the tags were often placed right before shipment. There were little to no logistics productivity gains to be had for suppliers, only for customers like Walmart, and they were not ready to share. Many prominent analysts, like Forrester, supported the suppliers' skepticism about the benefits.[70]

To the suppliers, Walmart's position was galling. Estimates for RFID implementation costs ranged from $13 million to $23 million per supplier.[71] Suppliers were already unconvinced of the visibility and productivity benefits and about being asked to shoulder the huge costs, and all the while not sharing in the benefits Walmart was claiming for itself.

Not surprisingly, the effort faltered and eventually petered out. Almost every supplier failed to meet the 2005 target date, and RFID faded from the supply chain conversation.[72] Ironically, Walmart did not meet its own internal RFID readiness deadlines and admitted in 2007 that not a single Walmart distribution center had operational RFID capability.[73] Despite this, a year later the Walmart-owned Sam's Club began placing RFID tags on pallets upon receipt at its distribution center and charging suppliers a $2 fine per pallet, although this initiative also did not last long.[74]

The Walmart result was not entirely unforeseeable. Some had identified the risks that unbalanced cost and benefit sharing posed for RFID and put forward just, equitable ways to address them.[75] The dynamics of the real-life experiment showed that the only retailer that might have had enough weight to bring the entire industry along with it did not have the clout to impose all the cost on the manufacturers.

The Walmart experience is instructive and revelatory. The high volumes of mass retail should have made RFID attractive. But no agreement was reached for sharing the costs and benefits. This was due in large part to Walmart refusing to contribute to the suppliers' RFID expenses. The RFID tags, approximately $0.20 each at the time, simply represented too high a share of the cost of the underlying product. This led the retailer to try to push the costs on to the manufacturers, who have less revenue but higher margins. As the suppliers would not see most of the benefits brought by RFID, they refused, and the initiative stalled.

The Walmart story shows how efforts to reap the benefits of RFID while offloading the costs created a true obstacle to RFID implementation in a low-margin context. The overall chain would enjoy higher efficiencies, but the commercial actors could not agree on a mutually beneficial cost-sharing arrangement.

RFID in consumer apparel

By just focusing on the consumer mass channel, one could be forgiven for thinking that RFID has been an abject failure. But this is not the case. There have been some notable successes in RFID implementation that have delivered the expected benefits of productivity and inventory accuracy. We will examine a few here.

Zara

Among the most prominent adopters of RFID is the Spanish fast fashion apparel manufacturer/retailer Zara. Long a darling of supply chain professionals for its highly reactive, constantly churning supply chain, Zara in 2019 was the 46th biggest brand in the world, with almost 3,000 stores in 96 countries.[76] In addition to being a leader in responsive supply chain operations, Zara is also a leading-edge retailer in exploiting the potential of RFID.

Zara applies RFID tags to all its products. As products are shipped individually to each outlet, the tags greatly speed up the receiving process in-store. The items are scanned on receipt using handheld wands, and the transactions are automatically recorded. Inventory cycle counts are done the same way, making them fast and accurate and turning a 40-hour job into a 5-hour one.[77] Zara has also placed scanners at store exits to help reduce shrinkage.[78] The tags are collected at the cash register and returned to the factories for reuse, helping keep costs under control. This practice, while clearly beneficial, would be harder to implement if Zara did not operate a verticalized supply chain, acting as both manufacturer and retailer. But Zara is pushing the use of RFID even further. In 2018, it opened two pop-up stores in the UK to act as click-and-collect points. In these stores, the fitting rooms are equipped with RFID scanners integrated into the mirrors. The customer can then browse recommendations for similar items or good matches with the clothes they are trying on.[79]

Additionally, Zara is piloting self-checkout stations using the RFID tags, making the process even more streamlined by removing the tedious search for tiny bar codes by the consumer.[80]

Decathlon

French sports equipment and apparel retailer Decathlon has over 1,000 stores, mostly in Europe but now expanding to North America, South America and Asia.[81] Decathlon is known for manufacturing and carrying its own brands alongside the best-known sports accessories brands.

Decathlon began its RFID initiative in 2013, tagging its own brands at the factory and scanning them through its 40+ distribution centers and in all stores.[82] As with Zara, Decathlon was motivated by the efficiency afforded by RFID in receiving goods, in inventory counts and at checkout. Internal surveys by the retailer revealed that the greatest cause of customer dissatisfaction was not finding products on the shelf.

This led Decathlon to explore RFID as a way to improve its inventory accuracy and, by extension, its store replenishment.[83] The company considers its RFID initiative a resounding success, claiming a five-fold improvement in inventory cycle count times, a 9% improvement in store-level accuracy and even 5% sales growth due to improved on-shelf availability enabled by RFID.[84]

One important nuance to the company's RFID approach is that non-Decathlon products are tagged by Decathlon at its warehouses, not by the supplier.[85] It is interesting to note that this approach was not adopted by Walmart or any consumer mass retailer, despite demonstrated interested in RFID.

Marks & Spencer

UK-based retailer Marks & Spencer (M&S) offers upscale selections of apparel, household items and food from over 1,400 stores, about 1,000 of them in the UK.[86] M&S was one of the pioneers of RFID, piloting the tags on its reusable food trays in 2003.[87] Satisfied with the returns, the company expanded its use of RFID to apparel, and by 2015, 100% of M&S apparel was RFID tagged and 50% of soft items like bedding.[88] The RFID tags were used at the product level, applied in the company's factories.

As with RFID implementations elsewhere, the primary motivator was to improve on-shelf availability through the increased visibility brought by RFID. In 2018, the company claimed it could attribute a 5.5% revenue increase to RFID.[89]

adidas

German sportswear and accessories manufacturer and retailer adidas began its RFID program in 2013 in Russia, with 450 stores.[90] As with the other examples, the initial goal was to improve the fundamentals of inventory accuracy and on-shelf availability. In internal interviews, the company claims that RFID has enabled it to count up to 200 different items per second. adidas also uses RFID for inventory, receipt, shelf replenishment and at checkout.

RFID was one of the fundamentals underpinning the company's success in implementing the click-and-collect and ship-from-store omnichannel models in Russia.[91] (See the case study in Chapter 4 for more details.) adidas has since expanded its use to other markets.

The examples described here illustrate the increased use of RFID in the apparel industry and are by no means the only successful implementations. A 2016 research survey by Auburn University revealed that an astonishing 96% of US apparel retailers had either deployed or had plans to deploy RFID.[92]

The RFID sweet spot

All of this points to an "RFID sweet spot": RFID should be most attractive where the *margins are higher* and *volumes lower* than in the mass market, and *margins lower* but *volumes higher* than the luxury channel. Also, if the supply chain is vertically integrated between manufacturing and retailing, as with Zara and adidas, the zero-sum gaming exhibited by Walmart would no longer be an obstacle.

Three common elements of the RFID sweet spot help to explain the context that allows for successful RFID implementation: higher margins, moderate volumes and verticalized supply chains.

Higher margins

The apparel industry enjoys much higher margins than the grocery sector. As an example, Inditex, Zara's parent company, enjoys a profit margin in the order of 13%.[93] Similarly, adidas has a profit margin approaching 9%.[94] This compares favorably with the grocery industry, which averages a profit margin of about 2%.[95]

This difference in profit margin makes the economic equation for RFID more challenging. Some of the benefits of RFID are very quantifiable, such as productivity in receiving and inventory cycle counting. Other benefits are less so, such as inventory visibility. When margins are tight, and the underlying value of the product is lower, the cost-benefit tradeoff is harder to justify.[96]

Even for issues such as preventing shrinkage or improving on-shelf availability, the lower value of products means the inventory write-down is smaller or the potential lost sale less impactful. Placing an RFID tag on these products could mean the difference between profit and loss.

Moderate volumes

Let's return to the comments of the operations director of the hard luxury retailer mentioned earlier. In this channel, the margins are very high, upwards of 20%.[97] With higher margins being a criterion for the RFID sweet spot, as outlined above, one might expect him to be an advocate of implementing RFID in his supply chain.

However, he did not see the benefit of RFID, largely because his volumes were so low. The productivity gains to be found in RFID for transactions like shipping are far less enticing when the volumes are very low. Simply put, the time saved by scanning a product with an RFID tag rather than a bar code is too small to justify the cost. The individual value of each item is so high that the retailer is quite happy to have a person ensure with their eyes that each and every unit is accounted for.

By way of comparison, Zara sells *450 million* units of clothing each year.[98] These volumes are closer to mass retail volumes. Combined with Zara's higher margins, the economic case for RFID is much easier to make: Many transactions on more expensive products with a higher margin help to justify investments to smooth the flow and track the inventory.

Verticalized supply chains

Apparel supply chains have another important difference from retail mass chains. They manage their own production through verticalized supply chains. This may be with their own factories, as is the case for much of Zara's volume, for example, or through contract manufacturers.

Having a verticalized supply chain eliminates the hurdle of sharing the benefits of RFID. The Walmart experience clearly laid bare the obstacles presented by having different actors in a supply chain sharing inequitably in both the costs of RFID and the gains in productivity and inventory visibility. When the supplier is either in-house or contracted, the costs of RFID can be more easily weighed against the benefits in a clear, dispassionate tradeoff analysis. Without the burden of commercial disputes, apparel manufacturers were free to explore RFID and have done so with great success.

Some of the elements of successful RFID implementations, such as recycled tags and circular container flows that shuttle between two points in the supply chain, are more manageable and easily coordinated when restricted to one organization as is the case in verticalized supply chains.

Testing the RFID sweet spot

As a test of the pertinence of the RFID sweet spot, it is worth asking whether private label mass retailers have moved to RFID. If the true obstacle to RFID implementation in mass retail is the inability of commercial actors to share the benefits in a satisfactory manner, then it might be expected that private labels would be candidates for RFID. Without the zero-sum tension of bearing RFID costs, mass retailers that procure private label goods from contract manufacturers could simply decide to pay for the RFID tags and readers and reap the productivity gains.

Yet a look at some prominent discounters and private label mass retailers does not reveal any wide-scale RFID implementation. Aldi and Lidl in Germany implemented RFID in their warehouses in 2011, but only to monitor access to temperature-controlled areas and limit theft by placing tags on access cards.[99] Despite gaining RFID expertise, these companies have not expanded into RFID tagging of sales products.

The Swiss chain Migros places private label goods prominently in its catalogue. It too has RFID experience through a 2011 project to use RFID tracking of reusable containers that flow between stores and warehouses carrying replenishment orders.[100] Pertinent to the discussion here, reusable containers have proved to be a successful field of application of RFID technology. The value of each container and the complexity of the movements are often high enough to warrant investment in tags and scanning equipment. The circular nature of the flows of reusable containers, often internal to one company, limits the obstacles of allocating costs to different supply chain actors.

Despite claiming that visibility and supply efficiency were at the heart of the effort, Migros has not expanded the initiative to suppliers or to sales products directly. The reason is that private label sales volume in mass retail does not satisfy all three criteria for the RFID sweet spot. Yes, the supply chain is verticalized, but the volumes are still high and the margins are still low. Without all three elements in place, the necessary conditions for RFID success for private label retailers are lacking.

There is another interesting way to demonstrate the validity of the RFID sweet spot. This would be to look at apparel, with its higher margins, verticalized supply chains and moderate volumes *in the mass retail space*.

Despite the loud, flashy failure in 2005 of RFID at Walmart, in 2010 the retail giant quietly introduced RFID tags on jeans and other apparel, this time at the item level.[101] However, Walmart paid for all the tags as the apparel was made at its contract manufacturers. Observers at the time pointed out that the verticalized apparel supply chain was the differentiating factor for Walmart after its previous disappointing efforts.[102] Walmart is not alone in this dichotomy of RFID for apparel only. In 2015 Tesco launched RFID tags for its private label clothing[103] and was sufficiently satisfied with the results to extend the program to more stores the following year.[104] M&S demonstrated the logic of this approach by having RFID first in apparel and not expanding to fast-moving mass retail items.

These examples lay out the case for the RFID sweet spot (*see* **Figure 1.2**):

- Being verticalized is not enough, as shown by the private level grocers familiar with RFID that have not adopted it for mass volume products.
- Higher margins and moderate volumes can make the RFID model attractive, as evidenced by mass retailers that abandoned RFID efforts on mass volume products but adopted it for higher margin, slower moving apparel items.

Industrial RFID

Looking beyond the world of retail to find RFID success stories only helps to reinforce the importance of the RFID sweet spot.

One of the most prominent successful implementations of RFID has been in aeronautics. The European airplane manufacturer Airbus began its RFID implementation in 2003 to track the movement of spare parts through its supply chain.[105] This came after several years of experimenting with RFID in managing its industrial tooling.

Figure 1.2: The RFID sweet spot

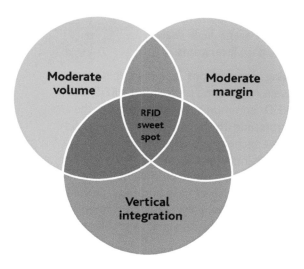

The applicability of RFID here becomes clear, particularly in light of our previous examination of RFID in retail supply chains. Aircraft spare parts are high value and high margin and of low volume. The stakes when it comes to misplaced spare parts are critical. If an airplane is grounded and needs a spare part, the inherent value of that part becomes orders of magnitude higher than the part itself due to the extremely high costs of having a plane grounded, increasing the importance of visibility at each stage in the supply chain.

Airbus was so satisfied with its RFID implementation that in 2016 it expanded the effort to include parts for its airplane assembly operations.[106]

This put pressure on its competitors. In 2009, Boeing had announced a similar program[107] for spare parts and now intends to use RFID to track component lifecycles for all parts installed on its airplanes.[108]

Comparing RFID to blockchain

In this section, we have sought to provide a lens with which to understand how RFID has become a useful part of the supply chain toolbox while not being the revolution it was once promised to be. But that is not the limit of the contribution — it can serve as a both a cautionary and a hopeful tale for blockchain. Many of the elements of the RFID experience provide keys to the future construction of a blockchain sweet spot.

Just as RFID promised visibility on physical movements, improved traceability and transparency between actors, these are the cornerstones of the potential espoused for blockchain today. *RFID did not end up replacing existing technologies like bar codes, and blockchain may not offer material improvement over existing solutions.* For example, a careful examination of the challenges in end-to-end traceability may reveal that the real challenge is in collecting the information at each stage in a usable way, not in the storage, security and accessibility of the data afterwards.

There are striking comparisons between RFID and blockchain in terms of technology as well. At the time of Walmart's RFID efforts, there were competing standards of RFID communications protocols, the technology was new to supply chain actors and there were (and still are) limits to the reliability and performance of the technology. With a complex array of vendors and platforms, blockchain is in a similar state. When we spoke to a senior supply chain executive who participated in a prominent blockchain supply chain visibility pilot, he expressed surprise at the unsteady performance of the technology, saying "That was the one thing I was not concerned about – the reliability of the underlying technology, yet it was a serious problem in the pilot."

If blockchain is going to find its place in the supply chain, it will take the participation and adoption of partners from upstream to downstream, across many industries. This echoes the challenge of the network effect and verticalization that Walmart encountered and reveals one of the keys to the RFID sweet spot.

Table 1.1 summarizes the many points of comparison between RFID and blockchain.

Blockchain may yet be a true disruptor of supply chains with impacts in traceability, smart contracts and supply chain finance. However, the more likely result is that it will find a narrower scope of applicability where the costs and complexity are compensated for by clearer, more accessible information, by facilitated shipments or supply chain financing. This last field may prove to be the most promising, as blockchain had its genesis in cryptocurrencies and is currently a driving force in financial technology innovation.

Our hope is that by looking back on RFID and examining its history in comparison to the expectations, practitioners can begin looking for the blockchain sweet spot today, and not be caught out by applying blockchain indiscriminately at the risk of souring the supply chain community on the technology. As the authors of the *HBR* article suggest, "the process of adoption will be gradual and steady, not sudden."[109] The potential for blockchain may best be served by staying focused on solid economic business cases, measured enthusiasm and incremental experimentation.

Table 1.1: Comparison points between RFID and blockchain

Element of comparison	Commonality
Track movements across the supply chain and improve traceability	RFID was seen as a replacement for bar codes in terms of capturing transactions and improving traceability. Most prominent blockchain pilots in supply chain focus on the same themes of traceability and visibility.
Barriers of new technology	Both RFID and blockchain involve a true technology barrier. RFID proposed tags to replace bar codes, using radio waves that users could not see or easily understand. Blockchain uses difficult concepts such as distributed ledgers and cryptography to replace third parties and remove the need for trust. For users, the challenge of understanding the new technology creates true obstacles to implementation.
Reliance on network effect	Blockchain only makes sense when there are several actors and trust is difficult to establish. This is particularly true for traceability, where several actors along the chain must contribute to the blockchain. The more actors use blockchain, the more other actors will feel pressure to join. Also, the validation of the transactions relies on a robust network of participants. Similarly, RFID benefits are most prevalent when all actors in a chain use it, spreading the cost of the tags and allowing for complete usage downstream.
Technology limitations	RFID has certain limitations to its use. Notably, it has issues in extreme temperatures and when in contact with liquid; it may be distorted by the presence of metal structures. Blockchain relies on continuous communication within a highly distributed network and consumes vast amounts of electricity during the proof-of-work stage of validating blocks.
Multiple standards	At the outset with RFID, there were competing standards for data storage and technology, which created friction for Walmart's RFID effort. Similarly, there are multiple competing standards for blockchain platforms, such as Ethereum and Hyperledger, all looking to emerge as the industry standard.
Supply chain resilience	Both RFID and blockchain present a genuine step into a new supply chain model, one that has few options in the event of dysfunction. For example, a failure of RFID readers can halt all transactions unless redundant bar codes are used. Similarly, if a company moves all information onto a decentralized blockchain, the risk of a network issue is expanded.
Verticalization challenge	Both RFID and blockchain become more useful and enhance productivity as one moves down the chain, yet the costs of implementation are borne by those upstream in the chain. As Walmart discovered with its RFID initiative, addressing the shared cost of implementation efforts and operations is critical to successful adoption by all actors. When a supply chain is verticalized, these constraints no longer apply.

REFERENCES

[1] Noha Tohamy. "Hype Cycle for supply chain strategy, 2019" *Gartner Research*, July 15, 2019. https://www.gartner.com/en/documents/3947438/hype-cycle-for-supply-chain-strategy-2019

[2] Zac Rogers, Lisa Harrington, Toby Gooley, Dale Rogers, Tami Kitajima and Richard Sharpe. "Big data analytics in supply chain: Tackling the tidal wave." *Supply Chain Quarterly*, Fall 2017. https://www.supplychainquarterly.com/topics/Technology/20171030-big-data-analytics-in-supply-chain-tackling-the-tidal-wave/

[3] Derek Thompson. "What in the world is causing the retail meltdown of 2017?" *The Atlantic*, April 10, 2017. https://www.theatlantic.com/business/archive/2017/04/retail-meltdown-of-2017/522384/

[4] "The top choice for 3D printed hearing aids, inner-ear devices." *Envisiontec*. https://Envisiontec.com/3d-printing-industries/medical/hearing-aid/

[5] "Stryker's spine division receives FDA clearance for 3D-printed Tritanium® C anterior cervical cage." Stryker, September 20, 2017. https://www.stryker.com/us/en/about/news/2017/stryker_s-spine-division-receives-fda-clearance-for-3d-printed-t.html

[6] Michael Mezher. "3D printing: FDA finalizes guidance for medical devices." Regulatory Affairs Professionals Society, December 4, 2017. http://raps.org/Regulatory-Focus/News/2017/12/04/28975/3D-Printing-FDA-Finalizes-Guidance-for-Medical-Devices/

[7] William Terdoslavich. "Target, L'Oréal reap benefits of good data." *DMN News*, September 28, 2017. http://www.dmnews.com/dataanalytics/target-lor%C3%A9al-reap-benefits-of-good-data/article/696480/

[8] Emma Thomasson, and Aleksandra Michalsk. "Adidas to mass-produce 3D-printed shoe with Silicon Valley start-up." *Reuters*, April 7, 2017. https://www.Reuters.com/article/us-adidas-manufacturing/adidas-to-mass-produce-3d-printed-shoe-with-silicon-valley-start-up-idUSKBN1790F6

[9] Jennifer Bissell-Linsk. "Nike's focus on robotics threatens Asia's low-cost workforce." *Financial Times*, October 22, 2017. https://www.ft.com/content/585866fc-a841-11e7-ab55-27219df83c97?mhq5j=e5

[10] Richard Markoff, and Ralf W. Seifert. "Supply chain digitalisation management challenges." *The European Business Review*, November/December 2017.

[11] Eric Wilson. "IBF survey: 70% of you say AI is future of demand planning." Institute of Business Forecasting, June 11, 2018. http://demand-planning.com/2018/06/11/ibf-survey-results-ai-demand-planning/

[12] Zac Rogers, Lisa Harrington, Toby Gooley, Dale Rogers, Tami Kitajima, and Richard Sharpe. "Big data analytics in supply chain: Tackling the tidal wave. *Supply Chain Quarterly*, Fall 2017. https://www.supplychainquarterly.com/topics/Technology/20171030-big-data-analytics-in-supply-chain-tackling-the-tidal-wave/

[13] Richard Markoff. "Who's in charge? Sales and operations planning governance and alignment in the supply chain management of multinational industrial companies." Doctoral thesis, November 2017. https://www.theses.fr/2017PA01E015

[14] Courtney Humphries. "How Amazon Prime will change the way our cities look." *Boston Globe*, December 6, 2018. https://www.bostonglobe.com/ideas/2018/12/06/how-amazon-prime-will-change-way-our-cities-look/POt25dZIWoaph01gNKkJoN/story.html#bgmp-comments

[15] Stephanie Condon. "In 2018, AWS delivered most of Amazon's operating income." *ZDnet*, January 31, 2019, https://www.zdnet.com/article/in-2018-aws-delivered-most-of-amazons-operating-income/

[16] Stephanie Condon, "In 2018, AWS delivered most of Amazon's operating income." *ZDnet*, January 31, 2019, https://www.zdnet.com/article/in-2018-aws-delivered-most-of-amazons-operating-income/

[17] Dani Deahl. "Amazon is increasing the cost of annual Prime memberships from $99 to $119." *The Verge*, April 26, 2018. https://www.theverge.com/2018/4/26/17287528/amazon-prime-annual-membership-cost-increase-price-hike

[18] Billy Duberstein. "Surprise! Amazon's North American e-commerce business is now more profitable than Walmart." The Motley Fool, October 27, 2018. https://www.fool.com/investing/2018/10/27/surprise-amazons-e-commerce-beats-walmart.aspx

[19] Karen Weise. "Amazon expanding one-day Prime shipping as sales growth slows." *New York Times*, April 25, 2019. https://www.nytimes.com/2019/04/25/technology/amazon-earnings-one-day-prime -shipping.html

[20] Dennis Green. "Amazon reportedly wants to curb selling 'CRaP' items it can't profit on, like bottled water and snacks." *Business Insider*, December 12, 2018. https://www.businessinsider.fr/us/amazon -wants-to-stop-selling-unprofitable-items-report-2018-12

[21] Karen Weise, "Amazon expanding one-day Prime shipping as sales growth slows." *New York Times*, April 25, 2019. https://www.nytimes.com/2019/04/25/technology/amazon-earnings-one-day-prime -shipping.html

[22] Felix Richter. "Amazon's ever-increasing ecommerce shipping costs." *Supplychain 24/7*, February 15, 2018. https://www.supplychain247.com/article/amazons_ever_increasing_ecommerce_shipping_costs

[23] Desjardins, J. "Breaking down how Amazon makes money." *Visual Capitalist*, December 19, 2017. https://www.visualcapitalist.com/breaking-amazon-makes-money/ (accessed February 26, 2020)

[24] Amazon's vs. Alibaba's business models: What's the difference? *Investopedia*, May 8, 2019. https:// www.investopedia.com/articles/investing/061215/difference-between-amazon-and-alibabas-business -models.asp

[25] Nassauer, S. "Why Walmart shoppers are finding more items 'out of stock'." *Wall Street Journal*, August 31, 2018. https://www.wsj.com/articles/why-walmart-shoppers-are-finding-more-items-out-of -stock-1535716801?mod=searchresults&page=1&pos=7

[26] Marc Lore. "Free next day delivery without a membership fee." Walmart, May 14, 2019. https://news .walmart.com/2019/05/14/free-nextday-delivery-without-a-membership-fee

[27] Jerome Buvat, Sumit Cherian, Kees Jacobs, Amol Khadikar, Yashwardhan Khemka, Lindsey Mazza, Marc Rietra, and Shannon Warner. "The last-mile delivery challenge.", Capgemini Research Institute, January 2019. https://www.capgemini.com/wp-content/uploads/2019/01/Report-Digital-%E2%80%93 -Last-Mile-Delivery-Challenge1.pdf

[28] Xiao Chen, and Kevin O'Mara. "Future of supply chain 2017." *SCM World*, October 2017. http://www .neeley.tcu.edu/Centers/Center_for_Supply_Chain_Innovation/PDFs/Future_of_Supply_Chain.aspx

[29] Mary Hanbury. "Amazon is now offering free Prime 1-day shipping on items that cost as little as $1 as it tries to further eliminate any reason to ever go to a store." *Business Insider* France, October 14, 2019. https://www.businessinsider.fr/us/amazon-prime-offers-free-one-day-shipping-low-cost-items -2019-10 (accessed April 22, 2020)

[30] Nick Statt. "Amazon is spending billions on shipping as it makes Prime one-day delivery a reality." *The Verge*, October 24, 2019. https://www.theverge.com/2019/10/24/20931055/amazon-prime-one -day-delivery-shipping-q3-2019-earnings-spending (accessed April 22, 2020)

[31] Karen Weise. "Amazon's profit falls sharply as company buys growth." *New York Times*, October 24, 2019. https://www.nytimes.com/2019/10/24/technology/amazon-earnings.html

[32] Ralf W. Seifert, and Richard Markoff. "Bezos' big bet – going for market share over profits." *IMD Tomorrow's Challenges*, 2019. https://www.imd.org/research-knowledge/articles/Bezos-big-bet-going -for-market-share-over-profits/

[33] Elly Cosgrove. "Best Buy follows Amazon, Walmart in next-day delivery push in time for the holidays." CNBC, October 22, 2018. https://www.cnbc.com/2019/10/22/best-buy-follows-amazon -walmart-in-next-day-delivery-push.html

[34] Karen Weise. "Amazon turns to more free grocery delivery to lift food sales." *New York Times*, October 29, 2019. https://www.nytimes.com/2019/10/29/technology/amazon-prime-fresh-whole -foods-grocery-delivery.html

[35] Karen Weise. "Amazon wants to rule the grocery aisles, and not just at Whole Foods." *New York Times*, July 28, 2019. https://www.nytimes.com/2019/07/28/technology/whole-foods-amazon-grocery .html?module=inline

[36] Richard Markoff, and Ralf W. Seifert, "Will Amazon do to the grocery industry what it did to ecommerce?" *The Conversation*, May 30, 2018, https://theconversation.com/will-amazon-do-to-the -grocery-industry-what-it-did-to-ecommerce-96874

[37] Ralf W. Seifert, and Wenshuo Max Cui. "Hema: New Retail Comes to Grocery." IMD case study, IMD-7-2144, 2019. https://www.imd.org/research-knowledge/for-educators/case-studies/Hema-new-retail-comes-to-grocery/

[38] Robert Hackett. "Walmart and 9 food giants team up on IBM blockchain plans." *Fortune*, August 22, 2017. http://fortune.com/2017/08/22/walmart-blockchain-ibm-food-nestle-unilever-tyson-dole/ (accessed April 20, 2020)

[39] James Paine. "How blockchain is disrupting supply chain management." *Inc.*, May 28, 2018. https://www.inc.com/james-paine/how-blockchain-is-disrupting-supply-chain-management.html

[40] Nouriel Roubini, and Preston Byrne. "The blockchain pipe dream." *Project Syndicate*, March 5, 2018. https://www.project-syndicate.org/commentary/blockchain-technology-limited-applications-by-nouriel-roubini-and-preston-byrne-2018-03

[41] Marco Iansiti, and Karim R. Lakhani. "The truth about blockchain." *Harvard Business Review*, January-February 2017.

[42] "Hype Cycle for emerging technologies, 2003." *Gartner*, July 2, 2003. https://www.gartner.com/doc/399359/hype-cycle-emerging-technologies-

[43] "Hype Cycle for emerging technologies, 2017." *Gartner*, July 21, 2017. https://www.gartner.com/doc/3768572/hype-cycle-emerging-technologies-

[44] Stefan Stroh, and Jürgen Ringbeck. "RFID: Thinking outside the closed loop." *Strategy+Business*, November 30, 2004. https://www.strategy-business.com/article/04411

[45] Stephen Laaper, and Joseph Fitzgerald. "Using blockchain to drive supply chain transparency." *Deloitte*, 2017. https://www2.deloitte.com/us/en/pages/operations/articles/blockchain-supply-chain-innovation.html

[46] Kim S. Nash. "Walmart-led blockchain effort seeks farm-to-grocery-aisle view of food supply chain." *Wall Street Journal*, June 25, 2018. https://blogs.wsj.com/cio/2018/06/25/walmart-led-blockchain-effort-seeks-farm-to-grocery-aisle-view-of-food-supply-chain/

[47] Ron Miller. "IBM introduces a blockchain to verify the jewelry supply chain." Tech Crunch, April 26, 2018. https://techcrunch.com/2018/04/26/ibm-introduces-trustchain-a-blockchain-to-verify-the-jewelry-supply-chain/

[48] George Smith. "French retailer joins the blockchain revolution with eggs, mince and more." *New Food*, March 7, 2018. https://www.newfoodmagazine.com/news/65254/french-retailer-joins-the-blockchain-revolution-with-eggs-mincemeat-and-more/

[49] Michael Lierow, Cornelius Herzog, and Philipp Oest. "Blockchain: The backbone of digital supply chains." *Oliver Wyman*, 2017. http://www.oliverwyman.com/our-expertise/insights/2017/jun/blockchain-the-backbone-of-digital-supply-chains.html

[50] "Smart contracts." https://blockchainhub.net/smart-contracts/

[51] Erik Hofmann, Urs Magnus Strewe, and Nicola Bosia. *Supply Chain Finance and Blockchain Technology: The Case of Reverse Securitisation*. Springer, 2018.

[52] "The best thing since the bar-code." *The Economist*, February 6, 2003. https://www.economist.com/business/2003/02/06/the-best-thing-since-the-bar-code

[53] Scott Lundstrom. "RFID will be bigger than Y2K." *CSO*, September 2, 2003. https://www.csoonline.com/article/2116536/data-protection/rfid-will-be-bigger-than-y2k.html

[54] Gary M. Gaukler, and Ralf W. Seifert. "Applications of RFID in supply chains." In *Trends in Supply Chain Design and Management*. Eds. Hosang Jung, Bongju Jeong, and F. Frank Chen. Springer, 2007.

[55] J. Banks, D. Hanny, M.A. Pachano, and L.G. Thompson. *RFID Applied*. John Wiley & Sons, Inc., 2007.

[56] Hau Lee, and Özalp Öze. "Unlocking the value of RFID." *Production and Operations Management*, January 5, 2009.

[57] S.J. Wang, S.F. Liu, and W.L. Wang. "The simulated impact of RFID-enabled supply chain on pull-based inventory replenishment in TFT-LCD Industry." *International Journal of Production Economics*, 2008.

[58] M. Tajima. "Strategic value of RFID in supply chain management." *Journal of Purchasing and Supply Management*, 2007.

[59] "RFID a retail revolution?" CNET, July 5, 2004. https://www.cnet.com/news/rfid-a-retail-revolution/

[60] Bob Violino. "Metro opens 'store of the future'." *RFID Journal*, April 28, 2003. http://www.rfidjournal.com/articles/view?399

[61] Jan Libbenga. "German revolt against RFID." *The Register*, March 1, 2004. https://www.theregister.co.uk/2004/03/01/german_revolt_against_rfid/

[62] Simson Garfinkel. "German metro retreats on RFID." *Technology Review*, March 1, 2004. https://www.technologyreview.com/s/402559/german-metro-retreats-on-rfid/

[63] Andy McCue. "Gillette shrugs off RFID-tracking fears." *CNET*, August 15, 2003. https://www.cnet.com/news/gillette-shrugs-off-rfid-tracking-fears/

[64] "Lawmakers alarmed by RFID spying." *Wired*, February 26, 2004. https://www.wired.com/2004/02/lawmakers-alarmed-by-rfid-spying/

[65] "Wal-Mart, DOD forcing RFID." *Wired*, November 11, 2003. https://www.wired.com/2003/11/Walmart-dod-forcing-rfid/

[66] M. Fitzgerald. "Wal-Mart drives RFID." *Extreme Tech*, April 1, 2004. https://www.extremetech.com/extreme/56006-walmart-drives-rfid

[67] Ephraim Schwartz. "Wal-Mart promises RFID will benefit suppliers." *Info World*, June 17, 2004. https://www.infoworld.com/article/2667832/database/Walmart-promises-rfid-will-benefit-suppliers.html

[68] M. Fitzgerald. "Wal-Mart drives RFID." *Extreme Tech*, April 1, 2004. https://www.extremetech.com/extreme/56006-walmart-drives-rfid

[69] Carol Sliwa. "Wal-Mart suppliers shoulder burden of daunting RFID effort." *Computer World*, November 10, 2003. https://www.computerworld.com/article/2573814/Walmart-suppliers-shoulder-burden-of-daunting-rfid-effort.html

[70] "Report: Most Wal-Mart suppliers won't meet RFID deadline." *Information Week*, March 30, 2004. https://www.informationweek.com/report-most-Walmart-suppliers-wont-meet-rfid-deadline/d/d-id/1024162

[71] Carol Sliwa. "Wal-Mart suppliers shoulder burden of daunting RFID effort." *Computer World*, November 10, 2003. https://www.computerworld.com/article/2573814/Walmart-suppliers-shoulder-burden-of-daunting-rfid-effort.html

[72] Mel Duvall. "Wal-Mart's faltering RFID initiative." *Baseline*, March 10, 2007. http://www.baselinemag.com/c/a/Projects-Supply-Chain/Cover-Story-WalMarts-Faltering-RFID-Initiative

[73] Marc L. Songini. "Wal-Mart shifts RFID plans." *Computer World*, February 26, 2007. https://www.computerworld.com/article/2553166/mobile-wireless/Walmart-shifts-rfid-plans.html

[74] Dave Blanchard. "Wal-Mart lays down the law on RFID." *Industry Week*, April 26, 2008. http://www.industryweek.com/companies-amp-executives/Walmart-lays-down-law-rfid

[75] Gary M. Gaukler, and Ralf W. Seifert. "Item-level RFID in the retail supply chain." *Production & Operations Management*, 2007.

[76] "The world's most valuable brands 46: Zara." *Forbes*, May 2019.

[77] Edgar Alvarez. "How RFID tags became trendy." *Engadget*, August 22, 2017. https://www.engadget.com/2017/08/22/rfid-tags-in-fashion/

[78] "Inditex deploys RFID technology in its stores." *Inditex*, July 17, 2017. https://www.inditex.com/article?articleId=150174&title=Inditex+deploys+RFID+technology+in+its+stores

[79] Nikki Gilliland. "How Zara is using in-store tech to improve its frustrating shopper experience." *Econsultancy*, April 20, 2018. https://www.econsultancy.com/blog/69960-how-zara-is-using-in-store-tech-to-improve-its-frustrating-shopper-experience

[80] "Zara turns to robots to speed online order pick-up." *Retail Info Systems*, June 3, 2018. https://risnews.com/zara-turns-robots-speed-online-order-pick

[81] https://www.decathlon.fr/

[82] "Decathlon uses Tageos RFID labels to identify millions of items worldwide." *Cisper*. https://www .cisper.nl/decathlon-uses-rfid-to-identify-millions-of-items-worldwide/

[83] Bob Violino. "Decathlon scores a big win with RFID." *RFID Journal*, June 20, 2016. www.rfidjournal .com/articles/view?1462

[84] "Decathlon's RFID project achieved remarkable results." *RFIDHY*. http://www.rfidhy.com/decathlons -rfid-project-achieved-remarkable-results/

[85] Claire Swedberg. "Decathlon sees sales rise and shrinkage drop, aided by RFID." *RFID Journal*, http:// www.rfidjournal.com/articles/view?13815/2

[86] https://corporate.marksandspencer.com/investors/key-facts

[87] Daniel Thomas. "Marks & Spencer begins the UK's largest in-store trial of RFID tagging technology." *Computer Weekly*, October 2003. https://www.computerweekly.com/feature/Marks-amp-Spencer -begins-the-UKs-largest-in-store-trial-of-RFID-tagging-technology

[88] Claire Swedberg. "Marks & Spencer expects to achieve 100 percent RFID-tagging by 2017." *RFID Journal*, May 11, 2015. http://www.rfidjournal.com/articles/view?13028

[89] Paul Skeldon. "M&S and new report show RFID increases retail sales by up to 5.5%." February 27, 2018. *Internet Retailing*. https://internetretailing.net/themes/themes/mamps-and-new-report-show -rfid-increases-retail-sales-by-up-to-55-16097

[90] Jessica Binns. "How Lululemon and Adidas use RFID to set the stage for omnichannel." *Apparel Magazine*, January 25, 2017. https://apparelmag.com/how-lululemon-and-adidas-use-rfid-set-stage -omnichannel

[91] Dale Benton. "Supply chain 4.0: Adidas and Amazon re-write the rules on supply chain management." *Supply Chain Digital*, February 10, 2017. https://www.supplychaindigital.com/scm/supply-chain-40 -adidas-and-amazon-re-write-rules-supply-chain-management

[92] "2016 state of RFID adoption among U.S. apparel retailers." *Auburn University*, July 25, 2016. https:// rfid.auburn.edu/papers/2016-state-rfid-adoption-among-u-s-apparel-retailers/

[93] https://www.inditex.com/investors/investor-relations/financial-data

[94] "adidas Profit Margin (Quarterly)." https://ycharts.com/companies/ADDYY/profit_margin

[95] Tiffany C. Wright. "What is the profit margin for a supermarket?" *AZCentral*. https://yourbusiness .azcentral.com/profit-margin-supermarket-17711.html

[96] Matthew Malone. "Did Wal-Mart love RFID to death?" *ZDNet*, February 14, 2012. https://www.zdnet .com/article/did-wal-mart-love-rfid-to-death/

[97] Simon Crompton. "Luxury profit margins." *Permanent Style*, December 27, 2014. https://www .permanentstyle.com/2014/12/luxury-profit-margins.html

[98] "How Zara sells out 450+ million items a year without wasting money on marketing." www. beeketing.com/blog/zara-growth-story/

[99] Claire Swedberg. "German supermarkets use RFID to manage warehouse access and send alerts." *RFID Journal*, August 19, 2011. http://www.rfidjournal.com/articles/view?8711

[100] La Rédaction. "La chaine de magasins suisse Migros déploie la RFID sur l'ensemble de ses 10M de RTI (returnable transport items)." *Filrfid*, November 11, 2014. http://www.filrfid.org/2014/11/la-chaine-de -magasins-suisse-migros-deploie-la-rfid-sur-l-ensemble-de-ses-10m-de-rti-returnable-transport-items .html

[101] Leslie Hand. "Walmart's RFID efforts in apparel — not what some might have you believe." *IDC Community*, August 8, 2010. https://idc-community.com/retail/retailomnichannelstrategies/ walmartsrfideffortsinapparelnotwhatsomemig

[102] SCDigest Editorial Staff. "RFID news: Will WalMart get RFID right this time?" *Supply Chain Digest*, October 28, 2010. http://www.scdigest.com/assets/On_Target/10-07-28-1.php?cid=3609

[103] Katie Smith. "Tesco rolls out RFID for F&F Clothing." *Just-Style*, April 9, 2015. https://www.just-style .com/news/tesco-rolls-out-rfid-for-ff-clothing_id124868.aspx

[104] Grace Bowden. "Tesco to roll out RFID smart labels to a further 300 stores." *Retail Week*, February 4, 2016. https://www.retail-week.com/technology/tesco-to-roll-out-rfid-smart-labels-to-a-further-300 -stores/7004491.article?authent=1

[105] "Airbus applies RFID technology to supply of aircraft spare parts." *Airbus*, September 18, 2003. http://www.airbus.com/newsroom/press-releases/en/2003/09/airbus-applies-rfid-technology-to -supply-of-aircraft-spare-parts.html

[106] "Ubisense Enterprise Location Intelligence Solution to further support Airbus in the production ramp up of its A350 XWB final assembly line in Toulouse." *Cision*, February 18, 2016. https://www.prnewswire .com/news-releases/ubisense-enterprise-location-intelligence-solution-to-further-support-airbus-in -the-production-ramp-up-of-its-a350-xwb-final-assembly-line-in-toulouse-569228111.html

[107] "Boeing tracks parts and reduces inventory with RFID tags." *Material, Handling & Logistics*, April 1, 2009. http://www.mhlnews.com/archive/boeing-tracks-parts-and-reduces-inventory-rfid-tags

[108] "Boeing ups the ante with RFID." *Connected World*, July 5, 2017. https://connectedworld.com/boeing -ups-the-ante-with-rfid/

[109] Marco Iansiti, and Karim R. Lakhani. "The truth about blockchain." *Harvard Business Review*, January-February 2017.

CHAPTER 2
PROOF BEYOND THE PROMISE

Keeping perspective about the hype surrounding Industry 4.0 and supply chain digitalization (SCD) is important in managing expectations, making the right technology decisions and building a roadmap. While a touch of healthy skepticism can be useful, it is also important to identify and explore the success stories.

Some technologies are looking promising in terms of delivering new capabilities that can add value to supply chain management. These innovations are cause for optimism, and managers can learn from them. They bring the dreams triggered by new technology into a tangible, concrete reality that can be understood, leveraged and built upon.

CHAPTER OVERVIEW

Topic 1: Predictive maintenance

We believe that one promising technology is artificial intelligence (AI). There are ways that AI can be brought to bear to address areas that many would not have considered ripe for disruption. The example explored here is the application of AI to equipment maintenance, which has created the new field of predictive maintenance (PM). PM offers a fresh way to look at a long-standing practice and offers an attractive first step, as we describe in the first section – "Predictive Maintenance: Industry 4.0's Killer App."

An exploration of the potential of PM is followed by an interesting perspective on the fields of application of PM. We borrow the sweet spot approach from Chapter 1's article on RFID and blockchain and apply it to PM. This is a useful exercise in demonstrating that even the most promising Industry 4.0 capabilities have limitations, and the sooner they are recognized, the more effective the digital transformation will be. The example of Dassault Aviation's fascinating efforts to implement PM helps illustrate the potential of advanced analytics and PM, as well as the organizational impetus required to succeed.

Topic 2: The big picture of AI in the supply chain

Taking a step back from the previous topic and coupling it with the insights from the section in Chapter 1 on "Demand for AI in Demand Planning," there are broad contours forming around the fields of application of AI in supply chain. In the second section — "Dream Small: AI's Best Path in Supply Chain" — the combination of AI's black-box explainability problem, the challenge of having accurate data to learn from, and the tangible benefits in concrete, on-the-ground areas all point to a clear path for AI in supply chain.

Topic 3: Supply chain personalization

Consumers are becoming ever more demanding. Expectations for new products and services, delivered more quickly and through more channels, are putting pressure on supply chains.

This is not just a challenge, it is also an opportunity. Rather than simply responding to market pressures as optimally as possible, supply chains can become a strategic part of the value proposition for companies. One illustrative example is the emerging trend of product personalization. In the section entitled "Have It Your Way: The Upside of Personalization of Consumer Goods," we explore how supply chains can think about product personalization as a strategic lever for positioning the supply chain within the company, as well as identifying some surprising impacts it may have on the way things have been done for years.

Topic 4: Digitalization in retail execution

Moving from manufacturing to the downstream end of the supply chain, the supply link from warehouse to store is one of the knottiest supply chain execution problems. Often the greatest source of on-shelf availability problems, it can also mean significant waste of perishable food items.

The section "Digitalization: A Fresh Idea for the Fruit and Vegetable Supply Chain" provides a look, with hard data, at the causes of food waste in a leading Swiss grocery chain and shows how readily available digital supply chain tools can lead to significant improvements.

Topic 5: Omnichannel supply chains

The advent of e-commerce and now omnichannel is transforming how people shop and how brands interact with their customers, literally changing the retail landscape. Amazon is one of the largest companies in the world, and one of the markets it is looking at as a next field of conquest is online grocery delivery, as discussed in Chapter 1.

Online grocery provides a useful lens through which to see how omnichannel supply chains are integrating the supply chain into the most fundamental strategic decisions a company faces. Comparing Ocado, a purely online grocery player in the UK, with its competitor Tesco, a classic grocer that also sells through the online channel, leads to a reflection on how supply chain is moving from a cost/service/working capital dynamic to become a key element that defines what a company's value proposition is.

In this section, we share a business case study that compares these two UK online grocers — "Tesco and Ocado: Competing Online Models." We then analyze the advantages of each, how they reflect fundamentally different supply chain approaches and the competitive advantages of each company. The result is a thought-provoking look at an articulation of business and supply chain strategy in the age of supply chain digitalization.

1 PREDICTIVE MAINTENANCE: INDUSTRY 4.0'S KILLER APP

Predictive maintenance (PM) brings together and represents the potential of Industry 4.0. By combining sensors, connectivity and machine learning, PM helps anticipate equipment failures before they happen. This prevents over-maintenance and unnecessary stoppages, resulting in better equipment uptimes, improved quality and lower maintenance costs as a result of fewer and shorter downtimes, lower technician time and fewer spare parts in stock. Assets that can be repaired before they fail are also safer for people and the environment. The appeal of PM as the "killer app" of Industry 4.0 lies in its broad applicability in almost any sector, its intuitive benefits and lastly in its significant, measurable results. One estimate[1] found that PM had the potential to improve asset availability by up to 15% and reduce maintenance costs by up to 25%. These sorts of improvements get noticed.

Be smart, not big

Predictive maintenance is an illustrative example of how success in exploiting Industry 4.0 technologies is about going smart, not going big, especially when it comes to data.

Among the most appealing targets for PM are windmill turbines. A McKinsey study[2] found that superior maintenance management could improve the internal rate of return on a windfarm investment by up to 19%, and new projects have a lifetime expectancy of 30 years,[3] double the longevity in the 1990s.

With such compelling stakes, we spoke about the challenges of successfully implementing a windfarm PM program with Yvan Jacquat, CEO of Optimized Systems Technologies (OST), a firm specialized in providing turnkey PM solutions — from sensors to analytics, including windmills for utilities customers — about the challenges of successfully implementing a windfarm PM program. He pointed out some aspects of windfarms that make them particularly attractive candidates for PM:

> *"Windfarms are usually in remote locations. This creates a challenge for availability of spare parts and personnel, as well as cranes for lifting spare parts. Weather can be a factor also, making smart and proactive maintenance planning critical."*

Yvan also explained that windfarms are not like, say, production equipment in their capacity usage:

"A production line must run to produce to demand. Any downtime will likely be made up through overtime. But windfarms can and should run every hour of every day. An hour lost to downtime is an hour that can never be recouped."

According to Yvan, the first step is to be smart about the data used for the PM analysis:

"Customers often do not yet have a clear vision of what problems they are looking to address and imagine PM as a solution for everything. It's easy to get lost in the weeds and try to solve every single maintenance or downtime issue. The key is not trying to capture and process every variable and solve every issue. We have to be smart about what are the critical failure modes to be detected proactively, what data is needed to support detection, what is the gap between the available and the required data and how to fill the gap at the lowest cost."

OST has found that a smart combination of a handful of data points delivers much better PM than a pure analytics approach processing large sets of data. For example, production power data, processed with a few temperature readings through unsupervised machine learning, are able to predict fairly accurately power converter overheating that leads to failures. This is important for offshore wind farms, where data accessibility and connectivity are challenging dimensions.

This approach keeps data capture costs limited while still harvesting important PM returns quickly. This simplicity and turnaround time offer other benefits as well. "There is a mindset in tension among managers when it comes to machine learning and analytics," noted Yvan. "At the same time, they feel that it can solve all of their problems and also that it cannot reveal insights that they do not already possess. There is an apprehension of 'black-box' solutions." If the customer does not understand how an underlying problem has been uncovered and addressed, there can be resistance. By keeping projects targeted, the solutions are clear enough that the customer can accept them, integrate them and leverage them.

Going beyond predictive maintenance

If the PM program has smartly chosen the data that will enable maintenance anticipation, the "signal in the noise" can offer other benefits. For windmills, one of these benefits was efficiency in power conversion. Yvan described:

"During the course of our projects, we found underlying issues that had impacts beyond PM and were affecting the operational efficiency of the windmills in generating electricity. Issues on the pitch, yaw or generator can

easily affect the power output by 3%. Our AI tool helps to detect such issues at the right time and quantify their impact on the power efficiency."

By bringing these sorts of tangible benefits and return on investment, PM can be a way to leverage data, connectivity and AI to address real-world problems, alleviate managerial reluctance, and change the conversation from big data to smart data.

Putting advanced analytics to work

Leveraging the ongoing huge investments[4] in Industry 4.0 technologies like machine learning and the internet of things (IoT), companies are developing the capability to collect vast data sets of conditions from connected assets, ranging from environmental variables like ambient temperature to process variables like pressure, vibrations and product flow. Tetra Pak,[5] for example, invested in sensors to monitor every step in the manufacture of its packaging materials to fully capture all of the potential areas of production disruption. The amount of data being collected is staggering. Per Dmitry Smolin, director of the Smart and Connected Factory Program, noted: "We record, on a daily basis, one billion data points from all of our machines. For example, a laminator has 400 sensors which are constantly recording information."

The predictive maintenance sweet spot

Although PM seems like the perfect real-world opportunity for Industry 4.0, closer consideration leads to the realization that there is a set of circumstances that must come together for PM to be effective – a sweet spot of conditions that will enable it to be a true game-changer. Should one of the key elements be missing, PM will either be difficult to implement or will not fully harvest the benefits.

The first element of the PM sweet spot is that *the necessary data be collectable and connectable*. Data sources can include IoT connected sensors, soft data like repair logs and local root cause analysis trees. In almost any sort of data collection there is a challenge of standardization of data (some may be in local units, handwritten or in a different language!). Data availability is far more likely when an organization already has a culture of discipline in lean or *kaizen* to push for continuous improvement. From there, cloud capability and data lakes are needed to store the data, so the asset must have opportunities for connectivity.

The second element of the PM sweet spot is that there must be a *moderate volume of data and root causes of failures*. As with other machine learning applications, PM will have a difficult time developing reliable, actionable predictions if there are too many variables or too many potential sources of failures. The system will be too complex to develop algorithms economically and each discrete failure cause will lack a sufficient training dataset. Yet if there are very few variables or root causes, the asset may not warrant inclusion in a PM program, since failure predictions could likely be done by traditional statistical methods without turning to more expensive machine learning.

The final element of the PM sweet spot is that *the economic stakes must be sufficiently high to warrant the investment of time and capital.* Designing and implementing a PM program requires mapping out a strategy, investing in sensors and connectivity, recruiting and training to develop expertise in machine learning and managing a transformation initiative. The benefits of PM – whether in the form of preventable equipment downtime, increased efficiency, lower labor requirements, or diminished safety or environmental risks – must be worth the investment. For this to be the case, the targeted asset must either be highly strategic, such as a critical production line, or there must be multiple very similar assets that can benefit as a whole from a single PM program, such as turbines in a windfarm.

The predictive maintenance sweet spot in action

Fabrice Lebeau, head of Big Data Analytics at Dassault Aviation, explained the sweet spot of PM in action in the aviation industry:

> *"PM emerged five years ago, along with big data technologies and machine learning algorithms, on the new planes equipped with powerful onboard recorders; it all started with the Airbus A380. Manufacturers like Airbus and airlines like Air France KLM are paving the way with maintenance of commercial aircraft. The private aviation market is ramping up and closing the gap but there are fewer business jets in service, which means less breakdowns, which means less data available to feed the machine learning algorithms that power PM. This stretches out not only the learning curve and the ramp-up time, but also emphasizes the importance of simulations that are fed by and supplement real data for training PM algorithms. This is called a 'Digital Twin' and at Dassault Aviation, we are pioneers in this field."*

The objective for Dassault and other plane manufacturers in their PM program is not to eliminate routine, scheduled maintenance. As Fabrice put it:

> *"Our goal is to increase the availability of the plane while waiting for repair and parts by avoiding unscheduled maintenance. All this data also helps us optimize scheduled maintenance and product robustness through better knowledge of its condition and environment."*

For commercial aviation, the economic consequences of having a plane grounded due to an unplanned breakdown can run to several hundred thousand US dollars per day, as airlines scramble to find alternative transportation for passengers and allocate technicians to diagnose the problem and send urgent, often expensive, parts to the grounded aircraft. For private aviation, unscheduled maintenance is mostly associated with reputational cost in a market where the clients are business executives or public officials with high service expectations.

Fabrice laid out the staggering amount of data available to feed Dassault's PM program:

> *"There are thousands of discrete pieces of equipment on each airplane, generating tens of thousands of continuous data streams recorded by onboard computers. In fact, the newest business jets can easily generate 20GB of data for every hour of operation."*

The connectivity opportunity to load this data occurs when the plane lands and finds either a 4G (soon 5G) signal.

With all of this data, it would be too complex to build PM algorithms for all systems, and choices must be made for prioritization. Fabrice explained that the priority is to look for non-redundant equipment that would cause a plane to be grounded in case of breakdown. He cited the engine, air, fuel, braking and hydraulic systems as prime targets for PM. These systems offer the most compelling savings if their repair needs can be sufficiently anticipated as to integrate them into routine maintenance. In terms of elements that are poor fits for the PM program, Fabrice mentioned structural issues such as corrosion and cracks: "To date, there's simply no way to capture and collect data. We need to inspect planes visually by highly trained technicians during scheduled stops."

Interestingly, when asked about challenges to implementation and attaining this goal, Fabrice explained that some people lack confidence in the reliability of the PM algorithms, particularly in the case of false positives. This can create a perception of unnecessary costs, should the technician replace a part that is not yet broken. Some are skeptical that the repair was warranted and the PM risks eroding trust.

The example of Dassault illustrates the PM sweet spot in action. Not all maintenance requirements on a plane can be modeled with capturable data. But for those that can, the complexity and volume of data has led Dassault to prioritize where to target its PM efforts, which it does by analyzing the high economic stakes and likeliest causes of a breakdown using its engineering expertise.

Predictive maintenance takeaways

Predictive maintenance is a powerful use case that brings together some of the key elements of Industry 4.0: machine learning, IoT and cloud computing. The example of Dassault shows how there is a sweet spot where the combination of data availability, manageable prediction variables and economic stakes creates an opportunity for PM to add real value for operations in any vertical with physical assets to manage, be it in factories or elsewhere.

As much as the technology itself, identifying and leveraging these sweet spots will help advance adoption and industry satisfaction with Industry 4.0 and supply chain digitalization solutions.

2 DREAM SMALL: AI'S BEST PATH IN SUPPLY CHAIN

Artificial intelligence (AI) remains a controversial topic in the supply chain community. It is fueled by enormous aspirations and hindered by data availability, employee capabilities and proven use cases. We have written in Chapter 1 about the potential of AI in the supply chain,[6] specifically with regard to demand planning. Our thesis is that there are serious challenges to the widespread adoption of AI in demand planning, but the challenges are not intrinsically related to the performance of AI in improving demand planning accuracy.

There are two pillars to this conclusion: The first is about the availability of important market intelligence. Information that shapes demand, such as promotion sizing and timing, media campaigns, competitor actions and customer behaviors, are often known by the sales or marketing departments, but organizations have trouble marshaling the collective information together in order to build effective demand plans. Although sales data might be available, possibly even across different sales channels, the contextual data — if not missing entirely — would typically require tedious manual extraction to feed an AI tool for demand planning.

The other pillar concerns the explainability problem. In mature sales and operations planning (S&OP) processes, the general manager (GM) is required to link their demand plan to their financial plan in order both to secure the necessary cross-functional collaboration and to avoid post hoc manipulation of the demand plan by the GM. It is understandable that a GM would not feel comfortable ceding this key role in part to AI-produced demand plans that are difficult for planners to explain and defend.

If we take a step back, this example provides broader insight into the areas of supply chain where AI might be well suited to making rapid inroads and the areas where adoption will be more challenging.

In the case of demand planning, the explainability challenge of AI is amplified due to the strategic nature of financial planning to GMs. The GM's commitment to a projection of financial performance is a key accountability, one that will drive decisions with wide-ranging impacts.

On-the-ground operations

There are two on-the-ground areas where AI can most easily be applied:

- **Logistics**: The areas of supply chain often mentioned as promising for AI applications in the shorter term are those that are very "on the ground," i.e.

transportation and logistics. This includes using AI for more efficient freight tendering and delivery routing along with warehouse optimization and automation.[7] An analysis by McKinsey identifies transport and logistics as having the second highest potential for incremental improvement from AI.[8] A major e-commerce player we spoke to uses AI to estimate fulfillment lead times within Europe.

Beyond the size of the prize, logistics has several attributes that make it attractive for AI in a way that demand planning is not. In Logistics there is a wealth of available, unambiguous data regarding costs, distances and weights. There is a lot for AI to "chew on" to look for underlying patterns and identify opportunities. Also, logistics has long been fertile ground for quantified research and trials to improve performance. Thanks to the continued rapid expansion of transportation management systems (TMS)[9] and the sophisticated efforts of delivery companies like UPS, there are fewer managerial barriers as the key decision makers are likely already open to AI solutions they – understandably – may not fully grasp. In fact, the growth of cloud-based TMS provides a natural channel for low-friction deployment of AI routing optimizations.

- **Maintenance**: Another "on-the-ground" area where AI, in the form of machine learning, comes into play is in predictive maintenance, which we discussed in more detail in the previous section. The adopters of predictive maintenance are often manufacturing or maintenance engineers, who are more apt to embrace a new technique that continues in the spirit of lean or other optimization efforts, and in fact usually play a central role in defining the scope of the program.

As important as logistics and asset maintenance are to the financial success of a company, they are more *operational* than *strategic* in the wider scope of things. They carry fewer long-term implications for senior managers, particularly those outside of supply chain. In other words, the more critical the decision, the more it leaves the realm of supply chain and enters into broader business decisions, and so the greater the managerial barrier. The explainability issue of AI in supply chain grows more prominent as the decisions become more strategic and spill beyond the supply chain.

The handful of use cases for AI that we have seen in supply chain planning have not been at the level of demand or production planning. The use cases usually involve the deployment of inventory[10] between distribution centers, or perhaps the sequencing of a production plan on a line, all based on AI-derived projections of short-term demand. These are exciting demonstrations of the optimization potential of AI, but they are also squarely in the operational horizon, as opposed to decisions such as assigning production to manufacturing sites or medium-term production.

AI takeaway

All of this points to a near-term role for AI in supply chains that stays firmly rooted in the "here and now" operational level. This is where the explainability problem can be mitigated through both avoiding the strategic levels and the managers less likely to embrace the AI-generated solutions. Perhaps this will offer a route for managers to grow trustful of AI and erode the explainability problem from within.

3 HAVE IT YOUR WAY: THE UPSIDE OF PERSONALIZATION OF CONSUMER GOODS

Personalization of consumer goods, sometimes referred to as mass customization, has been on the margins of the mainstream for several years. Often associated with footwear, thanks to efforts like NikeID[11] and Converse, personalization's track record of offering the consumer individual discretion to choose certain product attributes is mixed. P&G ended its personalization initiative called Reflect.com[12] in 2005, after six years, and adidas shut down its program[13] early in 2019 (following a first shutdown in 2005), only to relaunch it.

The business drivers seem clear enough. The customized product not only sells at a higher price and margin but also delivers a strong customer experience[14] and consumer intimacy.

In 2019 personalization was one of the key consumer trends.[15] A good example of this is L'Oréal, which unveiled in Paris a concept called My Little Factory,[16] which proposed blending custom Lancôme foundations in 22,000 variations according to customer orders. The name "My Little Factory" is telling and provides a useful lens through which to examine the potential impacts of personalization in operations.

Personalization starts with the customer

We spoke to Amir Andskog, e-commerce supply chain director at L'Oréal Luxe, to understand the challenges of initiatives like My Little Factory. He started by pointing out the need to rethink data management structures:

> "We certainly can't create 22,000 new product codes and work as we did in the past. New, imaginative ways of tracking and storing products will be needed, ones that can manage master data in a much more flexible and adaptable way than today."

There is also reactivity to consider. "The customer will expect lead times approaching those of the current standard products," Amir explained. "Our factories must rethink their manufacturing processes in order to produce and ship within one day." For a factory, this could mean redesigning not just scheduling cycles but also other fundamental aspects, like quality processes, to be faster and leaner. Another likely implication is that the finished product will ship to the consumer directly from the factory. If manufacturing has been outsourced, as is the case for companies like Nike or adidas, the role of the supplier fundamentally changes too.

All of these challenges imply that a manufacturing mindset geared towards the customer is part of the personalization journey. Amir agreed, "Capabilities that bring the customer order deep into manufacturing processes will be critical to success."

Challenging the manufacturing mindset

Increased customer proximity in the factory may also push for changes of other engrained mindsets. Manufacturing in many companies has undergone years of consolidation and "massification." Fewer production centers and larger batches have driven economies of scale in order to lower the cost of goods. This approach extended to the sourcing of materials as well, all with an emphasis on removing production inefficiencies.

The result has often been global manufacturing footprints, with large production runs. For personalization to succeed at scale, this model must evolve. Most obviously, personalization means a run size of one. But with the customer proximity and lead time expectations of personalization, global footprints may become more local or, at the very least, regional.

"Personalization will oblige the organization to be mature enough to look at the total cost of the product including obsolescence, not just the manufacturing or sourcing cost," explained Eric Lefranc, an experienced operations expert with three different luxury companies. "This new model will encourage shared profit and loss statements (P&Ls) across functions."

Eric echoed Amir's thoughts about the challenge customer proximity presents for manufacturing. "The data management and reactivity requirements will foster semi-automatic processes combined with empowered staff at the shop floor level who are highly motivated to be closer to the consumer."

A boost for lean

Small runs, customer-driven manufacturing and empowered staff are all hallmarks of lean manufacturing.

According to Florian Magnani, operations professor and co-author of the book *540° to Lean*:

> *"Lean is a dynamic system that frames and stimulates the activities of employees aiming at flow improvement and people development. It enables employees to foster and leverage organizational learning in order to always better satisfy customers."*

Florian agreed that personalization could spur companies to embrace lean in its purest sense, which indeed may be a prerequisite for success. He pointed out that even Toyota, whose production system inspired lean, continues looking to shorten its production lines and give more responsibility and autonomy to its staff in order to better respond to personalization.

Outlook for personalization

If personalization is to truly succeed at scale, companies will have to rethink fundamental pillars of their manufacturing policy.

It goes deeper than technology. Indeed, it is not apparent whether L'Oréal's My Little Factory will involve any Industry 4.0 elements. Total cost of ownership, quality processes, manufacturing footprint, supplier relationships, upstream/downstream silos, IT and data management are all elements that must be rethought in addition to channel placement. The result may be that what is old becomes new, and smaller, regional factories embrace lean as a lever for commercial success through personalization.

4 DIGITALIZATION: A FRESH IDEA FOR THE FRUIT AND VEGETABLE SUPPLY CHAIN

Finding a digital solution to the food waste problem

The cost of global food waste and loss was estimated to be $990 billion a year in 2019.[17] For businesses, this represents a significant proportion of the shrinkage in retail supply chains and it has a direct impact on companies' triple bottom lines. Tackling this problem could provide a great opportunity for cost savings and reducing environmental and social footprints, but making it happen remains a complicated problem, requiring solutions at all levels of the supply chain.

Fresh fruit and vegetables are a challenging retail category because of the extremely short product lifetime. To identify drivers of spoilage, we examined the supply chain of Migros, Switzerland's largest grocery retailer with CHF 27.4 billion in sales and a market share above 20%. Its fruit and vegetable sales account for more than 10% of total supermarket sales in the country. This is a highly competitive product group that generates store flow and requires high availability and specialized infrastructure. Plus, its portfolio must change with the seasons.

In terms of sales, best-practice retailers have spoilage levels of between 3% and 5%.[18] Migros is among these best-practice retailers, but for such a large operator, even these small spoilage levels have a significant impact on the company's annual profit in the fresh fruit and vegetable category.

Our in-depth analysis was based on roughly half a million data points of 100 fresh products on a day and store basis. It revealed three major drivers of spoilage:

1. Excess inventory
2. Order cycles and variation
3. Longer delivery lead times

The best way to reduce spoilage is to reduce the inventory in stores (see **Figure 2.1**). A half-day reduction would reduce overall spoilage costs by 40%. Smoothing both store and distribution center (DC) orders by 50% would improve spoilage costs by 30%. Increasing the order frequency to daily would reduce spoilage costs by 17%. And reducing delivery times by one day in 10% of deliveries could reduce spoilage by 8%.

How can businesses achieve these reductions in spoilage costs?

Employee training and incentive schemes can go some way to reducing order cycles and making other improvements in freshness and shrinkage performance.

Figure 2.1 The impact of lower inventory on spoilage

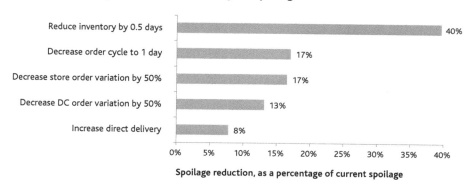

Spoilage reduction, as a percentage of current spoilage

The greatest potential, however, comes from supply chain digitalization to match demand with supply.

We recommend three main areas for digital development to address the major drivers of spoilage we identified in our study: data management; integrated collaborative forecasting; and product tracking.

Data management

This is essential for better ordering, establishing adequate inventory levels and enabling transparency within firms. The longer it takes to get hold of information, the harder it is to create accurate demand forecasts. Here are three steps for digitalizing supply chain data:

- **Obtain accurate historical data**. High-quality demand forecasting depends on this, plus it helps to reduce excessive ordering or unmet demand. This historical data can then be integrated into ordering tools to make ordering easier and to increase transparency.
- **Use live point-of-sale (POS) data** (but only if the accuracy of the data is assured). Accurate, live POS information can help decrease information lead time, so the supply chain can become more responsive to fluctuations in demand.
- **Automate orders.** Historical data coupled with live POS data create an opportunity to automate orders in real time. This allows companies to overcome issues related to order batching, which often causes excess inventory and spoilage in perishable product supply chains. Automation has substantial potential here because ordering activities often take up considerable time and resources.

Integrated collaborative forecasting

This addresses high order variation caused by rationing and shortage gaming and long transportation lead times. Integrating data systems for collaborative forecasting increases visibility and reduces the risk of overstock or stockouts along the supply chain. The benefits of visibility of supply chain partners' forecasts can further extend to the physical chain, allowing for shorter delivery lead times because deliveries do not need to be as flexible.

Product tracking

This means having digital records for the entry and exit of products at each stage of the supply chain. It can help ensure a "first in, first out" policy for fresh products, which will decrease inventory age — and therefore reduce shrinkage due to spoilage. Shrinkage rates represent up to 15% of sales in major retailers.

Putting it all together

Digital supply chain solutions therefore provide enormous potential for accurate demand forecasting and better inventory management. However, the improvements come at a price in this high-paced category. Product yields, volatile prices, fragmented suppliers, specific supply chain configurations, as well as perishability and quality issues, all mean that the value drivers are diverse and category-specific.

Before implementing new digital solutions, it is vital to interview individuals along the entire supply chain and analyze existing data to work out what business impact these solutions might have.

5 CASE STUDY | TESCO AND OCADO: COMPETING ONLINE MODELS

Richard Markoff and Ralf W. Seifert

In 2017, the world of retailing was changing rapidly. Each year, increasing numbers of consumers were making purchases online, preferring to do their shopping via e-commerce rather than visiting bricks-and-mortar stores. Nowhere in Europe was this more true than in the United Kingdom: In 2017, online sales represented more than 17% of retail sales, making the British the leading adopters of e-commerce.[19]

This embrace of e-commerce extended to the grocery segment, where the UK had a market share of 7.3% in 2017.[20] This was considerably higher than France, the second biggest market in Europe at 5.3%. The number of Britons who shopped for groceries online with some regularity grew from 28% in 2016 to 35% in 2017.[21] Fully 14% of UK consumers bought groceries exclusively online, up from 7% in 2014. IGD, the UK grocery industry group, projected that by 2021 the online segment would account for about 9% of the market, growing faster than any other segment, including discounters. As a whole, IGD predicted the UK grocery market would grow by 10% in 2021, from £179 billion to £196 billion.[22]

The online grocery channel presented challenges that other online retail segments did not. Grocery margins were much thinner, with a typical grocery store in 2017 earning only about 2% profit margin.[23] The tight margins did not allow much room to add services such as home delivery and still remain profitable. Another element unique to groceries was the need to respect the chilled or frozen chains, which added cost and complexity to the delivery logistics and equipment.

There was also the question of consumer preferences. A 2017 survey indicated that the overwhelming reason – at 84% – shoppers were reluctant to try online grocery delivery was that they preferred to physically see and choose their own items.[24] Worryingly considering the margin pressures, the second most cited reason – at 34% – was that consumers felt online groceries were more expensive than those in the store. With this heightened sensitivity to price, grocery chains had to find a profitable positioning for their online grocery offering through operational efficiencies.

These issues led some analysts to be bearish on grocery home delivery. One investment bank went so far as to proclaim, "We remain unconvinced of long-term viability of home deliveries for grocery."[25]

The UK grocery landscape

The UK market had many players competing in the online grocery space. The e-commerce giant Amazon made headlines when it announced in 2016 that it was expanding its operations in the UK with the launch of Amazon Fresh,[26] going head to head with many established players. The UK already had a high level of retail supply chain sophistication, with major chains like Tesco, Sainsbury's and Asda — the top three in terms of market share — competing not just in bricks-and-mortar but also online.

The UK grocery landscape had evolved in recent years. In 2017, two discounters were among the top ten grocers: Aldi was the fifth largest and Lidl the eighth.[27] Both offered a limited product range, even tighter margins, a no-frills shopping experience and had decided not to enter the online grocery sweepstakes. This approach was proving successful, with Aldi growing by 14% year-on-year in 2017 and Lidl by 19%, putting even more pressure on the traditional retailers.

The largest retailer in the UK was Tesco, with 28% of the total grocery market in 2017.[28] It had a footprint of 3,739 stores in the UK.[29] Tesco's dominance extended to online, where it was the channel leader with 39% market share. This represented an estimated 7% of Tesco's revenue in 2014.[30]

Far down the list of UK grocers, with only 1.3% of the total UK grocery market, was Ocado. With such a small market share, it would be easy not to recognize it as an influential actor in the sphere. But Ocado was very different from the top retailers like Tesco or Asda. It did not have any stores, it only sold groceries online. Furthermore, the way that it went about competing in the online grocery space was completely different.

Tesco: A closer look

Background

Tesco was founded in London in 1919 as a grocery stall; ten years later the first store opened its doors. It was not until 1956 that the first self-service supermarket saw the light of day. The company enjoyed steady growth, becoming the largest food retailer in the UK in 1995.[31] A year later Tesco opened its first store outside the UK. From 1995 to 2012, Tesco grew from 12% to 33% UK market share, from 1 country to 14 countries, and from £50 million to £4 billion profit.[32] Revenue peaked at £72 billion in 2012 and then followed a steady decline. Since then, the company had struggled; Dave Lewis was brought in as the new CEO in 2014 amid increased competition from the discounters and an accounting scandal.[33] In fact, Tesco reported seven straight years of shrinking UK sales until it recorded growth in 2017.

By 2017, Tesco was the largest retailer in the UK and the ninth largest in the world.[34] It had an earnings before interest, taxes, depreciation and amortization (EBITDA) margin of 2.6% on revenue of £56 billion.[35] The company employed 460,000 people and had 6,809 stores in 13 countries around the world.

Online business model

Tesco set up Tesco.com in 2006. Initially, the company fulfilled orders through its network of grocery stores. Employees traveled along the aisles with shopping carts much like a consumer, picked the items for an online order off the shelf and took the order to rear of the store. Then it was packed and dispatched to online customers. Digital tools guided order pickers through the store, informing them of the items and quantities to pick. This approach was simple, did not require any capital investment and allowed Tesco to scale up quickly and enter the online grocery market.

In 2009 Tesco complemented this network by opening up "dark stores."[36] Initially, dark stores were similar to regular grocery stores, but they were dedicated to online orders and not open to the public.[37] Employees in the dark store prepared multiple orders at the same time, loading them into oversize carts. Over time dark stores at Tesco evolved into "dotcom centers":[38] small distribution centers equipped with automation to assist in order preparation.[39] By 2013 Tesco had six dotcom centers in operation serving the greater London area,[40] while the rest of the country was served through the retail store network.[41] Overall, Tesco had 23 distribution centers supplying products to both the dotcom centers and the store network.[42]

Delivery fees for online shopping were fairly complex. They ranged from £3 for two- to five-day delivery and up to £5.95 for next day delivery. Tesco also launched a membership package, whereby a monthly fee of £7.99 allowed unlimited deliveries; the minimum order was raised in 2015 from £25 to £40 per order for members.[43]

In 2011, Tesco launched a click-and-collect online model, available in about 300 stores. Customers ordered online and collected their groceries at the store, packed and ready to load into their car.[44] The service was free or up to £2 for next day pick-up, and up to £4 for same day pick-up, with a three-hour delay between placing the order and collection.

Tesco did not show online sales separately in its annual reports, but it said it made a profit of £127 million in 2013.[45] Tesco's primary retail chain competitors — Sainsbury's, Asda and Morrisons — did not release figures, and some analysts believed that online grocery lost £5 to £7 per order.[46] The prices of products for home delivery and click-and-collect were generally the same as in the stores, but Tesco explicitly did not guarantee this to be the case at all times for all products.[47]

Ocado: A closer look

Background

Ocado was a UK-only grocer with no stores. It offered home delivery of online grocery orders. The company was founded by three former Goldman Sachs investment bankers and began operations in 2001. It went public in 2010 and reached £1 billion in annual sales in 2015.[48] Ocado claimed only about 1% of the total UK grocery market, but it was the largest purely online player competing in the space and claimed over 13% of the online market in 2014.[49] It had 580,000 active customers and 12,000 employees in 2016.

Although Ocado focused primarily on groceries, it also offered pet supplies through its Fetch subsidiary, and kitchen and dining supplies through Sizzle. In 2015 it entered the beauty segment in partnership with the magazine *Marie Claire*, with which it opened its first physical store. Since Tesco's 2017 announcement that it would cut its range of products by 30% to 60,000,[50] Ocado was catching up in terms of product variety, with a steadily growing count of 50,000 SKUs.

Online business model

Ocado serviced its delivery market through a hub-and-spoke distribution model. Orders were picked at three customer fulfillment centers (CFCs), with a fourth due to be completed in 2018. About a third of the orders were shipped to local customers directly from the CFCs. Orders for outlying areas were shipped in full trucks to one of 17 spokes across England and delivered by vans from that point. In 2017, Ocado covered only 70% of the UK market.[51]

As the CFCs were dedicated to customer delivery, Ocado invested heavily in automation, in terms of both software and equipment. The automated systems in the CFCs, as well as the software packages that drove the supply chain — from customer interaction through to last-mile delivery — were developed in-house by Ocado. In fact, Ocado generated revenues by leveraging its technology to provide online fulfillment solutions for other retailers. Ocado provided a turnkey service for the online segment of bricks-and-mortar grocer Morrisons, handling order-to-cash, customer-facing solutions and order fulfillment using the Ocado distribution network. This arrangement accounted for 8% of Ocado's revenue (*refer to* **Exhibit 1**).[52] In late 2017, the company announced a similar agreement with Groupe Casino in France for both software and the installation of material handling equipment in Casino facilities.[53] And in early 2018, Ocado entered into a deal allowing Sobeys, Canada's second largest supermarket group, to use its e-commerce platform.[54]

Ocado showed its first positive EBITDA in 2013 and registered an EBITDA margin of 2.3% in 2016.[55]

As with Tesco, the pricing model was complex. Orders had to be for a minimum of £40, with delivery charges ranging from £2.99 to £6.99; delivery for orders over £75 could be free. Similarly, for an annual fee of over £100, deliveries were free. Deliveries were generally next day, but it could take two days for customers served from a spoke.

Exhibit 1: Ocado Financials 2016 and 2015

	FY 2016 £ million	FY 2015 £ million	Variance %
Revenue[1]	1,271.0	1,107.6	14.8
Gross profit	435.3	375.1	16.0
EBITDA before exceptional items	84.3	81.5	3.3
Operating profit before share of result from JV and exceptional items	21.9	19.1	14.7
Share of result from JV	2.1	2.3	-8.7
Profit before tax and exceptional items	14.5	11.9	21.8
Exceptional items	-2.4		
Profit before tax	12.1	11.9	1.3

[1] Revenue is sales (net of returns) generated at Ocado.com, and the other retail banners – Fetch, Sizzle and Fabled, including charges for delivery but excluding relevant vouchers/offers and value added tax. The recharge of costs to Morrisons and fees charged to Morrisons are also included in revenue.
[2] Morrison MHE JVCo impact includes the income arising from the leasing arrangements with Morrisons for MHE assets and share of results from joint venture.

Revenue

	FY 2016 £ million	FY 2015 £ million	Variance %
Retail	1,171.6	1,033.7	13.3
Morrisons recharges	79.9	55.1	44.9
Morrisons fees	19.5	18.8	3.7
Total revenue	1,271.0	1,107.6	14.8

Source: Ocado annual report and accounts 2016

Insights from the case: Two fundamentally different approaches

Ocado and Tesco approach the challenge of online grocery delivery from very different angles.

Tesco is looking to leverage its existing store network as a ship-from-store fulfillment model. Its substantial store network is, in effect, its distribution network. Ocado does not have any stores and has chosen to invest substantially in state-of-the-art distribution that leverages Industry 4.0 and supply chain digitalization (SCD) to the fullest through a ship-from-warehouse model.

Each model has its advantages and disadvantages. **Table 2.1** shows some of the key differences.

Some broad themes emerge from this comparative list of each model. The first is that Ocado's model is less expensive overall. The DC picking using Industry 4.0 technologies[56] is faster than the pick-to-cart manual methods Tesco employs. And crucially, there is an entire link in the chain that Ocado manages to eliminate. It does not have to pick, pack and ship products to stores, which are then unloaded and placed on shelves. Eliminating this step provides labor savings and also leads to less damage, less residence time in the chain for a given product, and so a fresher supply chain overall with less waste.

But it is also clear that Tesco's approach offers faster delivery to customers. This is directly because there are hundreds of Tesco stores acting as distribution centers, and these stores are invariably closer to customers ordering online. Ocado is obliged to compensate for the much higher transportation costs of trying to service all of England from a handful of DCs by using overnight hubs. These hubs serve as way stations to receive full trucks of consolidated orders picked at Ocado DCs. The individual orders are shipped to customers the next morning, as much as 24 hours later than Tesco.

So which model is better? From a supply chain perspective, this is very much up for debate. Overall, Ocado would seem to have a lower cost structure, while Tesco would seem to offer better perceived service.

We would argue that the supply chain configuration is such an integral part of the business strategy that the proper framing of the question is to ask which company is "better." One way to consider "better," then, is to think about the shareholders. Even here there is no consensus, with one prominent investment bank considering Ocado's ship-from-warehouse model a competitive advantage[57] while another argues the exact opposite.[58]

Table 2.1 Advantages and disadvantages of two order fulfillment models

Ship-from-warehouse model	
Advantages	**Disadvantages**
• Cost of picking and packing orders is optimized, as a dedicated facility processing a high number of orders can justify investing in automation.	• There is a supply chain risk, as an incident at one DC will affect a large part of the customer base.
• Eliminating the step of shipping products from a DC to a store means products are generally fresher when they reach the customer.	• The DCs, with heavy automation to leverage their advantage, require considerable upfront capital investment.
• Lower handling costs, since the steps of unloading products at a store and placing them on a shelf are eliminated.	• This investment and lead time make the network inflexible.
• Inventory accuracy is easier to maintain in a DC setting than in a store network.	• The last delivery step, to the customer's door, is done from very few origin points. This means higher transportation costs and, for the customer, longer lead times.
• Product catalogues are more homogenous and so easier to link to a given customer while browsing.	

Ship-from-store model	
Advantages	**Disadvantages**
• From the customer's perspective the order arrives very quickly, as the store network offers a large physical footprint with deep reach.	• Catalogues can vary from store to store, making it difficult to have a clear product offering for the website or app for a given customer.
• The store network allows the customer to develop trust in the grocer's quality for fresh products like meat and vegetables.	• It is notoriously difficult to ascertain accurate store inventories and on-shelf availability, creating a higher risk of promising products for online orders that are not physically in-store.
• Online grocery allows the store to defray fixed costs that are already incurred to run the brick-and-mortar operation.	• Physical shoppers may be bothered by order pickers competing for the same products in the same aisles.
• The network is flexible, with low capital costs for expansion thanks to the existing network.	• There is a limit to the number of orders per store due to the space on the shelf.
• With higher demand for the shelf inventory, the overall freshness of the products sold by a given store will improve.	• Products are generally arranged to maximize the experience and basket of the physical shopper, further hindering the efficiency of order picking, which is already a purely manual process.

Digitalization as part of the company DNA

We would argue that wrestling with the question of which model is better is not the proper lens through which to look at online grocery in the context of supply chain digitalization.

Instead, we can look at how British consumers view the performance of the different online grocery companies (*see* **Figure 2.2**).

Figure 2.2 Online grocers compared

Webiste and sample size	Ease of finding products on website	Choice of substitute items	Availability of delivery slots	Value for money	Customer score
Ocado (825)	✳	✳✳✳	✳✳✳✳✳	✳✳✳	82%
Waitrose (507)	✳✳✳✳	✳✳✳✳	✳✳✳✳	✳✳✳	79%
Tesco (815)	✳✳✳✳	✳✳✳	✳✳✳	✳✳✳	72%
Sainsbury's (772)	✳✳✳	✳✳	✳✳✳✳	✳✳	71%
Morrisons (177)	✳✳✳	✳✳✳	✳✳✳	✳✳✳	71%
Iceland (84)	✳✳✳	✳✳	✳✳✳✳✳	✳✳✳✳	70%
Asda (191)	✳✳✳	✳✳	✳✳✳	✳✳✳	65%

Source: Reproduced with permission from Which?. © Which? 2020
https://www.which.co.uk/news/2020/02/which-reveals-best-supermarket-of-2020/

Ocado is clearly the preferred online grocer in the UK, with a significantly higher score than Tesco, the largest player.

In particular, Ocado scores highest on its website experience. This does not appear to be an accident. The company has fostered a digital culture whereby the website, and the intelligence that drives it, are positioned as a competitive advantage.[59] Because Ocado is an online-only retailer, it can focus its resources, attention and value proposition around the omnichannel experience in a way that a traditional retailer likely cannot.

Ocado's innate digital savvy has allowed it to drive Industry 4.0 and SCD innovations, deploy them at scale and create a new business model. It offers proof beyond the promise that it is possible for companies to fully embrace digitalization, bring supply chain into the essential fabric of the company's strategy and show a path for others to follow.

REFERENCES

1 Steve Bradbury et al. "Digitally enabled reliability: Beyond predictive maintenance." *McKinsey & Company*, October 2018. https://www.mckinsey.com/business-functions/operations/our-insights/ digitally-enabled-reliability-beyond-predictive-maintenance (accessed April 30, 2020)

2 Carlos Marin, Filippo Rossi, and Nuno Santos. "McKinsey on electric power and natural gas." *McKinsey & Company*, Winter 2018. https://www.mckinsey.com/~/media/mckinsey/dotcom/client_service/epng/ pdfs/mck%20on%20epng/wind_assets.ashx

3 Arnout de Pee, Florian Küster, and Andreas Schlosser. "Winds of change: Why offshore winds might be the next big thing." *McKinsey & Company*, May 18, 2017. https://www.mckinsey.com/business-functions /sustainability/our-insights/winds-of-change-why-offshore-wind-might-be-the-next-big-thing

4 Sara Castellanos. "IT execs see promise in IoT, reinforcing Microsoft's $5B Investment." *Wall Street Journal*, April 5, 2018. https://blogs.wsj.com/cio/2018/04/05/it-execs-see-promise-in-iot-reinforcing -microsofts-5b-investment/

5 Ralf W. Seifert, and Richard Markoff. "Tetra Pak: A digitally enabled supply chain as a competitive advantage." IMD case number IMD-7-2033, 2018 https://www.imd.org/research-knowledge/for -educators/case-studies/tetra-pak-a-digitally-enabled-supply-chain-as-a-competitive-advantage/

6 Ralf W. Seifert, and Richard Markoff. "Demand for AI in demand planning." IMD, January 2019. https:// www.imd.org/research-knowledge/articles/demand-for-ai-in-demand-planning/

7 Kritika Pndey. "How AI is revolutionizing global logistics and supply chain management." *Readwrite*, April 15, 2019. https://readwrite.com/2019/04/15/how-ai-is-revolutionizing-global-logistics-and-supply -chain-management/

8 Michael Chiu, James Manyika, Mehdi Miremadi, Nicolaus Henke, Rita Chung, Pieter Nel, and Sankalp Malhotra. "Notes from the AI frontier." McKinsey Global Institute, April 2018. https://www.mckinsey .com/~/media/mckinsey/featured%20insights/artificial%20intelligence/notes%20from%20the%20 ai%20frontier%20applications%20and%20value%20of%20deep%20learning/notes-from-the-ai -frontier-insights-from-hundreds-of-use-cases-discussion-paper.ashx

9 "Global transportation management system (TMS) market: Growth, trends & forecasts (2019-2024)." *Business Wire*, November 13, 2019. https://www.businesswire.com/news/home/20191113005613/en/ Global-Transportation-Management-System-TMS-Market-Growth

10 https://www.aeratechnology.com/

11 https://www.nike.com/ch/en/nike-by-you

12 Mark Brohan. "Why P&G shut down Reflect.com." *Digital Commerce 360*, September 7, 2005. https:// www.digitalcommerce360.com/2005/09/07/why-p-g-shut-down-reflect-com/

13 Mike Destefano. "Why Adidas discontinued the miAdidas customization program." *Sole Collector*, February 1, 2019. https://solecollector.com/news/2019/02/here-is-why-adidas-discontinued-the -miadidas-customization-program

14 Katie Sweet. "Personalization trends: 2019 survey results." Business 2 Community. May 7, 2019. https://www.business2community.com/online-marketing/personalization-trends-2019-survey-results -02197432

15 "2019 trends in personalization." Demandgen Report, May 10, 2019. https://www.demandgenreport .com/resources/infographics/2019-trends-in-personalization

16 Sara Ahssen. "L'Oréal presents system for large scale personalisation of cosmetics products." Fashion Network, May 13, 2019. https://us.fashionnetwork.com/news/L-Oreal-presents-system-for-large-scale -personalisation-of-cosmetics-products,1098448.html

17 Usaid Siddiqi. "World Food Day: The fight against food waste." Al Jazeera News, October 16, 2019. https://www.aljazeera.com/news/2019/10/world-food-day-fight-food-waste-191016120808684.html

18 Raphael Buck, and Arnaud Minvielle. "A fresh take on food retailing." *McKinsey & Company*, Winter 2013. http://www.mckinsey.com/~/media/mckinsey/dotcom/client_service/retail/articles/ perspectives%20-%20winter%202013/3_fresh_take_on_food_retailing_vf.ashx

[19] Dave Chaffey. "Forecast growth in percentage of online retail/ecommerce sales." Smart Insights, December 21, 2017. https://www.smartinsights.com/digital-marketing-strategy/online-retail-sales -growth/

[20] "UK online grocery sales reach 7.3% market share." Kantar, June 2, 2017. https://www .kantarworldpanel.com/en/PR/UK-online-grocery-sales-reach-73-market-share-

[21] "The UK online grocery market: sales & growth statistics." HIM, September 7, 2017. http://www.him .uk.com/latest-thoughts/article/uk-online-grocery-market-sales-growth-statistics/

[22] Fiona Briggs. "UK food and grocery forecast to grow by 10% over next five years, IGD reports." Retail Times, June 16, 2016. http://www.retailtimes.co.uk/uk-food-grocery-forecast-grow-10-next-five-years -igd-reports/

[23] "Grocery store industry profitability." CSI Market, https://csimarket.com/Industry/industry_ Profitability_Ratios.php?ind=1305

[24] Alison Griswold. "There's still one big reason why people aren't buying their groceries online." Quartz, September 14, 2017. https://qz.com/1077743/people-dont-buy-groceries-online-because-they-prefer -to-pick-things-out-in-stores/

[25] Jim Edwards. "HSBC makes a huge, counterintuitive call: Online grocery delivery is 'the emperor's new clothes.'" Business Insider, March 8, 2016. http://www.businessinsider.fr/us/hsbc-we-remain -unconvinced-of-long-term-viability-of-home-deliveries-for-grocery-2016-3/

[26] Sarah Butler. "Amazon starts UK fresh food delivery." Guardian, June 9, 2016. https://www .theguardian.com/technology/2016/jun/09/amazon-starts-uk-fresh-food-delivery

[27] Elias Jahshan. "Almost 2/3 of Brits now shop at Aldi or Lidl." Retail Gazette, September 19, 2017. https://www.retailgazette.co.uk/blog/2017/09/grocery-market-share-two-thirds-brits-shop-aldi-lidl/

[28] "Great Britain grocery market share." Kantar. https://www.kantarworldpanel.com/global/grocery -market-share/great-britain

[29] "Number of Tesco stores in the United Kingdom (UK) and the Republic of Ireland from financial year 2012 to 2019." Statista. https://www.statista.com/statistics/490947/tesco-group-stores-united -kingdom-uk/

[30] "DEEP DIVE: Online grocery series: The UK — a battle for profitability." Fung Global Retail and Technology, 2017. https://www.fungglobalretailtech.com/research/deep-dive-online-grocery-series-uk -battle-profitability/ (At the time of writing, the latest year for which figures were available.)

[31] Tim Clark, and Szu Ping Chan. "A history of Tesco: The rise of Britain's biggest supermarket." Telegraph, October 4, 2014. http://www.telegraph.co.uk/finance/markets/2788089/A-history-of-Tesco -The-rise-of-Britains-biggest-supermarket.html

[32] Seán Meehan, and Christopher Zintel. "The Winner's Tornado." insights@IMD, 2015. https://www.imd .org/research/insightsimd/the-winners-tornado/

[33] Thomas Colson. "Ex-Tesco executives 'connived and manipulated figures' to cover up £250 million accounting black hole, court told." Business Insider, October 3, 2017. http://www.businessinsider.fr/uk/ tesco-fraud-trial-executives-connived-manipulated-figures-2017-10/

[34] Ray Gaul, "Top 50 Global Retailers." National Retail Federation, 2017. https://nrf.com/2017-global -250-chart

[35] "Global 2000 Food Retail." Forbes.2020 https://www.forbes.com/global2000/list /#industry:Food%20Retail

[36] "Tesco to open customer-free 'dark stores.'" Telegraph, December 6, 2009. http://www.telegraph.co .uk/finance/newsbysector/epic/tsco/6743329/Tesco-to-open-customer-free-dark-stores.html

[37] Tim Muffett, "Online food shopping: What is a 'dark' supermarket?" BBC, January 17, 2014. http:// www.bbc.com/news/av/business-25774679/online-food-shopping-what-is-a-dark-supermarket

[38] Mark Wulfraat. "E-grocery success story: The Tesco dotcom UK business model and lessons learned." MWPVL International [blog entry], October 3, 2014. http://www.mwpvl.com/html/tesco_dotcom_uk_ business_model_.html

[39] "Building a multichannel Tesco." YouTube video, December 3, 2013. https://www.youtube.com/watch ?v=QONyKR0KdYs

[40] "Tesco opens sixth dotcom centre in Erith." *Retail Gazette*, November 29, 2013. https://www.retailgazette.co.uk/blog/2013/11/42203-tesco-opens-sixth-dotcom-centre-in-erith/

[41] Mark Wulfraat. "E-grocery success story: The Tesco dotcom UK business model and lessons learned." MWPVL International [blog entry], October 3, 2014. http://www.mwpvl.com/html/tesco_dotcom_uk_business_model_.html

[42] "Tesco simplifies distribution operations." News release, January 9, 2017. https://www.tescoplc.com/news/news-releases/2017/tesco-simplifies-distribution-operations/

[43] Chloe Rigby. "Online grocery growth slows at Tesco but overall sales rise." Internet Retailing, June 24, 2016. http://internetretailing.net/2016/06/online-sales-growth-slows-tesco/

[44] https://www.tesco.com/collect/

[45] Simon Neville. "Tesco: Who says it's hard to make home delivery profits?" *Independent*, February 26, 2014. https://www.independent.co.uk/news/business/news/tesco-who-says-its-hard-to-make-home-delivery-profits-9153185.html

[46] Neil Craven. "Big Four supermarkets lose £5 to £7 on every online order." This is Money, October 10, 2016. http://www.thisismoney.co.uk/money/news/article-3828648/Deliveries-hit-Big-Four-supermarkets-500m-lose-5-7-online-order.html

[47] https://www.tesco.com/direct/faq/are-online-prices-the-same-as-store-prices/551.faq

[48] http://www.ocadogroup.com/who-we-are/our-story-so-far.aspx

[49] "DEEP DIVE: Online grocery series: The UK – a battle for profitability." Fung Global Retail and Technology, 2017. https://www.fungglobalretailtech.com/research/deep-dive-online-grocery-series-uk-battle-profitability/

[50] "Tesco's cull of 30% of SKUs highlights importance to be range review-ready." Bridgethorne, February 12, 2015. https://www.bridgethorne.com/tescos-cull-of-30-of-skus-highlights-importance-to-be-range-review-ready/

[51] Ocado Group plc annual report and accounts, 2016. http://www.ocadogroup.com/~/media/Files/O/Ocado-Group/reports-and-presentations/2017/ocado-annual-report-2016.pdf

[52] Ocado Group plc annual report and accounts, 2016. http://www.ocadogroup.com/~/media/Files/O/Ocado-Group/reports-and-presentations/2017/ocado-annual-report-2016.pdf

[53] http://www.ocadogroup.com/~/media/Files/O/Ocado-Group/reports-and-presentations/2017/annoucement-of-international-partnershi-between-ocado-solutions-and-groupe-casino.pdf

[54] Nichola Saminather, and Kate Holton. "Ocado shares rise following deal with Canada's second largest supermarket." *Independent*, January 23, 2018. http://www.independent.co.uk/news/business/news/ocado-shares-rise-latest-sobeys-canada-supermarket-deal-a8173741.html

[55] https://www.marketwatch.com/investing/stock/ocdgf/financials

[56] "Inside a warehouse where thousands of robots pack groceries." YouTube Video. May 9, 2018. https://www.youtube.com/watch?v=4DKrcpa8Z_E

[57] "Ocado still structural winner in online grocery: Analyst." CNBC, September 13, 2016. https://www.cnbc.com/video/2016/09/13/ocado-still-structural-winner-in-online-grocery-analyst.html

[58] Ashley Armstrong. "Ocado business model faces fresh scrutiny from Amazon." *Telegraph*, September 1, 2017. https://www.telegraph.co.uk/business/2017/09/01/ocado-business-model-faces-fresh-scrutiny-amazon/

[59] "Luke Jensen, CEO, Ocado Solutions." YouTube Video. November 18, 2018. https://www.youtube.com/watch?v=hdyHnak61Ol

CHAPTER 3
SUCCESSFUL EXECUTION
OF THE BASICS

Chosen with care and implemented properly, Industry 4.0 capabilities can truly be revolutionary for a supply chain. The potential improvements in visibility, working capital, cost, reactivity, new business models and products are exciting and unprecedented.

But to be durable and lasting, the transformation must be built on a solid foundation. Industry 4.0 will not paper over weaknesses in supply chain governance, management or skills. It *can* allow companies to leapfrog over some steps along the way, but only if the starting point has been rendered simple and harmonized.

This chapter shines a light on some of the fundamental aspects of segmentation, service, cost control, core competencies and governance that will create a solid starting platform and enable organizations to move into the future with Industry 4.0.

CHAPTER OVERVIEW

Topic 1: Product segmentation

Any supply chain effort must be targeted for maximum effect. If every product is a priority, then no product is a priority. The standard go-to method for deciding which products should be protected in terms of stock, capacity and service has always been ABC classification. The first section – "Getting ABC Classifications Right' – shows how this is easier said than done and may, in fact, reveal some underlying truths about how the company is structured.

Topic 2: Winning conditions for omnichannel

The underlying premise of omnichannel is that the supply chain can deliver products from multiple locations to fulfill orders received from many different platforms. This section – "Omnichannel Launching Pad" – shows how the real starting point is not found in Industry 4.0 or supply chain digitalization (SCD) technologies, but in the eternally bedeviling problem of on-shelf availability (OSA) and the continued difficulties in getting reliable, actionable measures of the problem.

Topic 3: Service measures

As fundamental as ABC classification, the idea that service is a key measure of supply chain performance is now part of supply chain DNA. But even though service is universally accepted as a supply chain yardstick, it is still hard to demystify and accurately capture, as shown in this section – "Service Measures in an Integrated Supply Chain." Using this key performance indicator (KPI) as a lever for improved cross-company collaboration can expose quick wins for everyone and create winning conditions for SCD initiatives.

Topic 4: Capturing cost to serve

Even if the supply chain has a strong grasp of the service level it offers its downstream partners, it is rare to find one that truly understands the cost required to deliver that service. In the section "The Hidden Cost of Cost to Serve," we explore why it is so difficult for companies to reach this understanding and highlight the implications for omnichannel retailing.

Topic 5: Reconsidering core competencies

The supply chain already has a challenge in being the rare function that operationally spans the entire end-to-end scope of a company. From its inception in the world of logistics, supply chain now includes demand and supply planning, customer care and sometimes more. This demand for versatility is being tested with the new capabilities brought by Industry 4.0 and digital supply chain management (DSCM). In the section "Is Fulfillment Still an FMCG Core Competency?" we explore an interesting dynamic playing out in the fast-moving consumer goods sector, where the rise of third-party logistics providers (3PLs) is challenging the idea of what a supply chain core competency is today.

Topic 6: S&OP governance benchmarking

Many SCD capabilities are centered on supply chain control towers, improved visibility of upstream and downstream activity, and planning algorithms. The objective is always to fluidify the flow of information in order to make better real-time decisions on what the demand signals are saying and how to respond.

But all of this assumes that the sales and operations planning (S&OP) process has the wherewithal to process and exploit all of this information and these tools. Based on an in-depth, innovative benchmark, the section "Who's in Charge? The Role of S&OP Governance" explains the different S&OP governance models in use today and puts forward an argument as to which is better. The result is four golden rules of S&OP governance that every company should consider before investing in SCD.

Topic 7: IT and purchasing organizations in the Industry 4.0 world

Continuing to explore the implications of managerial governance, we suggest in the section "Supply Chain Digitalization: IT Management Challenges" that long-standing managerial expectations when it comes to IT and IT purchasing have proved to be barriers to implementing Industry 4.0 and DSCM transformations. After years of structuring IT around large players, the consequences of bringing Industry 4.0 niche players on board is a challenge that must be recognized.

Topic 8: Industry 4.0 roadmaps: Where to start?

The final section in this chapter offers something different – a workshop, based on a real case, that challenges readers to consider not only what Industry 4.0 technologies might be the best fit for their situation but also what would be the right roadmap. It demonstrates the different dimensions to consider when sequencing technology implementations and helps show that, once again, Industry 4.0 transformation is about much more than simply buying and installing a new technology into an old paradigm.

1 GETTING ABC CLASSIFICATIONS RIGHT

ABC classification is one of the oldest, most reliable methods of catalogue or customer segmentation. It relies on the properties of the Pareto distribution and states that about 20% of a population will account for about 80% of the volume. ABC classification has entered popular language and is often referred to as the "80-20 rule." A quick Google search yields many real – and not-so-real – examples of the 80-20 rule, explaining distributions in fields ranging from the natural to the sociological.

For supply chains, the 80-20 rule has demonstrated its merits. In most contexts, about 80% of the sales volume is indeed from about 20% of the product catalogue. This gave rise to the ABC classification, which has been a staple of supply chain inventory management for over 30 years in applying segmentation strategies.

If a company is going to perform an ABC classification, the first, most basic, question is *why*? This may be harder to answer than one might think. We asked supply chain planners in the same company how they manage their stock-keeping units (SKUs), i.e. whether an "A-SKU" should have more inventory or less inventory than the "B-" and "C-SKUs." About half said that A-SKUs should have *less inventory* because they have such a great impact on stock levels. The other half felt that A-SKUs should have *more inventory* than the other SKUs, since they are most vital to revenue.

The right answer, we would argue, is that the A-SKUs return the highest value in finding the right balance between service level, required inventory and supply chain agility. Getting that message out to and respected by a broad, extended community of planners is in itself a managerial challenge. In multinational organizations it is not even evident which product catalogue should be used for the classification. Should it be done for each market, for each factory, or for both? In addition, different functional managers have different perspectives on what should constitute "the volume" basis. Should it be revenue, units, profit or something else altogether?

With these questions in mind, it is worth returning to the foundational principles of something as basic as ABC classification, especially now that the idea of supply chain digitalization tends to get everyone excited about big data, artificial intelligence and predictive analytics. They can serve as a reminder of how even the most apparently simple concepts entail real implementation challenges, which can be categorized as *data* challenges and *managerial* challenges.

Data challenges

In order to calculate an ABC classification, only two pieces of data are needed – the product catalogue and the volume of each SKU. However, for each of these there are nuances that must be addressed. Starting with the product catalogue, many companies prefer not to include SKUs that have just been launched or that are being discontinued. Including recently launched SKUs could overstate their weighting as the volume likely includes pipeline build, and incorporating products close to discontinuation would needlessly dilute the importance of ongoing SKUs and quickly render the ABC classification obsolete when those products drop out of the offering.

The method for swiftly identifying and excluding these SKUs is by means of a product lifecycle status indicator. We live in an age where consumers have ever-increasing expectations of customization and product renewal, and this drives increased product churn. Maintaining accurate product lifecycle status is critical, as well as being a real data management challenge. Planners are often understaffed and have many operational responsibilities. It can be tough to convince them to maintain this additional data field that has no apparent immediate benefits for them, when they already know in their heads which products are launching or being dropped.

Once the right SKUs have been identified, the volume used to classify them can be the subject of much internal debate. Finance managers may prefer to use gross or net margin, arguing that the most critical element is not revenue, but margin. Another approach is to use direct product costs rather the cost of goods, with the reasoning that fixed costs would be spent in any case. This may sound trivial, but we have seen large, mature companies reject automated, APS-embedded ABC classification tools in favor of Excel for this reason.

In some industries, such as luxury goods, the promotional products supply chain plays a critical role in the distributional channel presence and customer expectations. It could be argued that these SKUs should be included as well. But since these products do not generate revenue or margin, this further clouds the picture of which dataset to use.

Managerial challenges

Today, supply chains usually have multinational footprints, with a many-to-many supply chain configuration. A factory could service many markets, which in turn are serviced by many factories. This reality leads companies to ask where the attention to A-SKUs should be paid: upstream or downstream? This is critical for deciding which population of SKUs to use for the classification.

If one of the goals of ABC classification is to identify upstream bottlenecks, it could be argued that the classification should be done for the production catalogue of each factory. In other words, each individual factory would perform an ABC classification for its specific catalogue. The downside to this approach is that the ABC classification no longer reflects revenue importance. It can be difficult for the supply chain to justify additional flexibility (often in the form of component inventory) for SKUs not seen by the business actors as critical.

The temptation then is to look downstream and perform the ABC classification for the population of products sold in the markets. This, too, has its downsides. If the ABC classification is performed in each market, the difference in product catalogues in each market means that far more than 20% of the total company catalogue could potentially be identified as A-class. It is also possible that some factories may find the majority (or almost none) of their products are A-class.

Simply complicated

The net effect of these considerations is that companies face a challenge in obtaining end-to-end alignment on what constitutes a critical product that warrants investment in resources for greater reactivity time spent in demand planning and defining service expectations. Even if ABC classifications are properly calculated, companies often have several competing versions.

The ever-increasing catalogue turnover and promotional intensity for products also means that, even if companies succeed in finding the right managerial level for the ABC classification, it is quickly obsolete and must be redone to maintain relevance. As we have discussed, the wide range of potential catalogues makes it challenging for the ABC "refresh" to be an automatic process.

Some supply chains also look at identifying a second dimension of product segmentation, often referred to as the XYZ classification. The objective is to identify the references that are more variable and thus more difficult to forecast. If an SKU is both A-class and highly variable, the logic of this approach would be that it warrants more effort in demand planning and upstream agility. The XYZ classification can be a powerful tool for secondary segmentation, but only as a complement to the ABC classification with its inherent complexities.

Getting it right

So, how do practitioners enact ABC classifications? We spoke to Jeremy Basckin, who has held senior supply chain positions at three major FMCG companies. Jeremy described the approach he has refined over time – one that addresses the issues we describe and may constitute a best practice. He explained that his strategy is to develop a collaborative ABC classification for each region, bringing together the supply chain, commercial and marketing teams along with general management. Jeremy formalizes the process around four criteria: volume in units, service/lead time, strategic importance and margin. The exercise is done at the market level, so when tallied up for each region, this usually leads to far more than 20% of the catalogue being A-class. The regional general management then arbitrates to lower the A-class to 20% of the catalogue. Jeremy admits that the process is a bit heavy and manual, but with discipline and training, the classification can be updated twice yearly.

For companies facing the array of choices and opportunities that supply chain digitalization has to offer, this is a reminder that it is vital to pay attention to the underlying foundation of data rigor, discipline and aligned cross-functional priorities.

2 OMNICHANNEL LAUNCHING PAD

The term "omnichannel" is omnipresent in retail supply chain circles these days. It promises an exciting array of consumer choices but also presents unique challenges to supply chain execution. One of these challenges is surprisingly fundamental and predates e-commerce. It is the ability of the supply chain to know the on-shelf availability (OSA) of the products on offer. That is to say, how much there is of a given product on the shelf in the store.

Omnichannel is the term used to describe seamless interaction with consumers between online and offline settings that offers them multiple ways to obtain their purchases.[1] It covers online orders from a computer or mobile app, home delivery, click-and-collect in the store and shipping from store locations and is often encapsulated by the ethos of the consumer being able to find the product "anytime, anyplace, anywhere."[2]

Connecting the physical and digital spaces

In order for omnichannel to succeed, the retailer must have the capability to identify inventory levels in both the warehouse and the retail network and determine the best compromise between order fulfillment cost and proximity to the consumer to satisfy the order, all without causing stockouts for other consumers. To be able to do this properly, one of the key factors is reliable on-shelf availability data. An omnichannel network that relies on using stores as localized distribution centers needs both the product reliably on the shelf and accurate information about inventory levels.

This most basic requirement has proved elusive to retailers. The organization Efficient Consumer Response[3] (ECR) estimates that on-shelf stockouts in Europe range from 7% to 10%. With omnichannel demand now pulling from the shelf stock, this number will likely rise. The consequences of poor on-shelf availability can be dramatic. In 2014 Walmart estimated that it was losing US$3 billion[4] in sales due to empty shelves, driving incoming CEO Doug McMillon to put OSA improvement among the retail giant's priorities.[5]

The reason for empty shelves is often that the store inventory count is incorrect (although this is not much consolation for the customer). The retailer does not know the shelf is empty, so they are likely not taking rapid steps to resolve the problem. And, more crucially, they are promising the omnichannel consumer rapid deliveries they cannot honor, often based on using stores as satellite distribution centers.

In its e-commerce battle with Amazon, Walmart is trying to leverage its expansive US network[6] of over 4,000 stores for click-and-collect and order fulfillment. Amazon bought Whole Foods in 2017,[7] in part to use its networks of stores to complement warehouse-based order fulfillment. Having an unreliable store inventory poses significant risks to the consumer lead time commitment. Store inventory inaccuracy has even driven one large UK retailer to prepare all of its click-and-collect orders centrally and ship them to the stores for pickup by customers, thus undermining one of the key potential benefits of the store network.

Another UK retailer admitted to us that they have so much difficulty identifying shelf stockouts that they use their omnichannel activities to perform zero-stock checks. This retailer fulfills online home-delivery orders directly from store shelves. When an order preparer arrives at a shelf and finds that there is no stock, they correct the inventory information in the system and pick the defined substitute for the customer. This is helpful for inventory accuracy, but at the expense of disappointing an omnichannel customer who will not receive the product they were promised when they placed the order.

Growing consumer expectations for accurate information is exposing this weakness in the retail supply chain. Many retailers provide details of store inventory on their website, as a service and to steer consumers to the right store. However, this information might not only be inaccurate but it is also usually updated just once per day,[8] leaving plenty of time for inaccuracies to mount as the day goes on. What was intended as a value-add for consumers ends up being a source of frustration when they arrive at the store, do not find the products and realize they have been misled.

The root causes of store stockouts

If omnichannel success hinges so critically on on-shelf availability, it is worth looking at the root causes. It is not hard to imagine reasons why the store inventory might be wrong – theft, lost inventory and misplaced products are always going to be part of the retail challenge. But, according to ECR, the most common reasons are wholly within the scope of execution of the retail supply chain – an inefficient store ordering process due to a combination of poor demand plans and suboptimal order planning cycles. Even if the orders were planned correctly, the products might remain stuck in the back room and not be used to replenish the shelves in a timely manner, often because understaffed stores seeking to keep costs down leave products on the receiving docks overnight.

Clearly, the success of omnichannel is linked to having correct information about on-shelf availability and adjusting store inventory counts accordingly. Yet capturing the availability of stock on the shelves accurately has proved elusive. The most common method is to measure the sell-out point-of-sale (POS) scans, using the logic that an unusual dip in sales could be due to a lack of products on the shelf. This approach is appealing for those who would use this information for big data analysis. But there are limits to its usefulness if the product does not have a high sales velocity.

A more expensive approach is to hire auditors to physically check the store shelves. Major retailers in both the US and UK have embarked on collaborative pilots with suppliers with the goal of at least trying to develop an accurate baseline of on-shelf availability. We spoke to one hardware retailer who has staffed key stores with employees dedicated to checking the hundreds of thousands of SKUs in the aisles to identify zero-stock locations.

Using managerial incentives to drive focus on on-shelf availability has led to unexpected consequences. One retailer told of the implementation of a bonus program for store managers who maintained high on-shelf availability — at least according to the retailer's IT system. Store managers then began walking the aisles looking for products with only one unit remaining. They would take this last unit from the shelf and hide it. This would improve on-shelf availability, but at the cost of losing the sale of the last unit — certainly an unintended outcome for the retailer.

The impacts on omnichannel extend beyond overly long lead times or higher costs into poorer consumer choice online.[9] As we saw in Chapter 1 with the example of Walmart, some e-commerce retailers will prevent a product from appearing in search results of they know it is not available. The root causes of poor online availability are more focused upstream with suppliers. The problem is starting to draw the attention of suppliers and is increasing pressure for collaborative solutions.

Looking ahead

These solutions seem strikingly low-tech in this age of big data and artificial intelligence. In the same vein as the self-checkout concept of Amazon Go[10] and Alibaba's Tao Café,[11] new technology approaches may finally provide a way for retailers to measure on-shelf availability and target their efforts to address the root causes. One promising avenue is to use robotics[12] or store cameras,[13] along with recognition software, to report an empty shelf space.

Vertical supply chains may help show the way towards managing on-shelf availability. Zara[14] and adidas[15] are two prominent examples of companies that have implemented radio frequency identification (RFID) tags on all their products. This speeds up inventory counts, reduces shrinkage and can help identify whether the products have made it all the way to the shelf. Since they have vertical supply chains, these companies have not encountered the obstacles that other retailers have come up against in the past when looking to implement RFID – the question of who will pay for the tags. As we saw in Chapter 1, Walmart, despite its enormous influence, famously did not succeed in convincing its supplier base to move to RFID over cost issues.

The advent of omnichannel may change the dynamic. Having accurate data will help the supply chain develop action plans and measure their impacts. One of the hidden benefits of the rise of omnichannel is that it will help exert pressure on all the actors to work together to find enduring solutions to this most fundamental of problems. This will help build the business case for investing in durable, lasting solutions to on-shelf availability.

3 SERVICE MEASURES IN AN INTEGRATED SUPPLY CHAIN

In any supply chain, service level should be the clearest and most impactful key performance indicator (KPI), capturing the ability of a company's supply chain to satisfy its customers' expectations. For many companies, service level is considered the ultimate performance measure, and every other KPI – such as cost, inventory level or forecast accuracy – is either derivative, secondary or simply a means to an end to achieve high service levels.

A closer look at this KPI reveals that calculating it and managing around it come with challenges but, nonetheless, it can be a lever to improve customer orientation in a supply chain organization.

More than meets the eye

The notion of service level has evolved over time for many companies. At their most basic, service level measures try to answer the question, "Did we ship the order on time?" In this respect, the debates within companies tend to revolve around details such as whether the measure should be by order line item or by order header.

Some companies go further and look at the non-serviced volume in the order, in an effort to appreciate the extent of the service disruption. But the curious dynamics of service measures can lead to complications. Imagine a customer that orders 10 units three times a week, using the common "fill-or-kill" policy of cancelling orders that cannot be serviced in their entirety. If the customer's order of 10 units on Monday is not fulfilled, the order they place on Wednesday will not be for 10 units, but for 20 units – the 10 units for Wednesday plus the 10 units that were ordered on Monday and not shipped. If the stockout persists until Friday, the customer will not order 10 units as usual, but 30 units – the 10 units for Friday plus the 10 units not shipped on both Monday and Wednesday. A weeklong stockout that should have impacted service levels by 30 units has in fact resulted in an impact of 60 units of unfilled orders. The service level impact has been artificially doubled!

One supply chain executive in a global consumer goods company shared how a C-class stock-keeping unit (SKU), a slow mover, was out of stock for three weeks, and this dynamic of cumulative ordering in the face of non-serviced volume dragged down his service level and raised alarm bells across the company. The service performance as expressed by the measure was so severe that he even had to explain to the highest management levels that the service KPI they were seeing did not represent a serious problem.

There can be operational impacts as well. "I began to push for us to implement VMI [vendor managed inventory] with our key accounts," he explained, "but not out of a noble desire to move our supply chain forward with best practices. It was because I wanted to exert some control on the order behavior when products were out of stock."

The supply chain executive noted that some supply chain managers responded to these misleading results by removing orders for SKUs that were out of stock after the first order. In other words, after the customer has ordered the SKU once and not been satisfied, the SKU no longer affected the service level KPI. The practice became so pervasive that it began to hide serious service issues, and the company's CEO accused the entire supply chain management of bad faith and of attempting to hide its poor performance.

Another major consumer goods company attempted to resolve such issues by not integrating the escalating customer orders, and instead asked the commercial teams to enter "phantom orders" in the company's enterprise resource planning (ERP) system that represented typical customer ordering patterns. Not surprisingly, this effort was not successful, since asking commercial teams to invest effort in keying in data to arrive at a robust KPI for a situation they find fundamentally frustrating is not a firm foundation to rely on for accurate service measures.

One company told us how commercial teams would be reluctant to inform customers of product discontinuations in order to delay product returns as long as possible. The result was that a customer, unaware that the product was no longer available, would continue ordering it and not be served, and the service level KPI became deeply corrupted as a consequence.

The result of all of these dynamics is a KPI that does not drive behavior towards satisfying customers, but rather creates counterproductive internal friction and misunderstandings. But it can also set the stage for a company to resolve these issues by focusing more on customer expectations.

Service level as a business lever

The advent of electronic data interchange (EDI) and then transportation management systems (TMS) has allowed companies to think about service in more expansive terms. Rather than limiting service measure to the notion of whether an order respected its ship date and volume, companies can now more easily measure when the order arrived at the customer, which is, of course, more meaningful for the perception of service. This step towards a more customer-centric approach has led to the notion of the perfect order – the idea that an order that contains everything that was ordered, arrives on time and has no damages is a more enlightened service measure. Indeed, it is the KPI often used by the supply chain advisory firm Gartner[16] when discussing service level.

In the previous section we discussed on-shelf availability (OSA), the difficulty of capturing it accurately and its importance in successful omnichannel implementation. On-shelf availability is itself an effort to overcome the limitations of a service level KPI that narrowly attempts to capture the performance of just one link in the supply chain.

The idea that both a manufacturer and a retailer would collaborate on a shared KPI is far from universally accepted. For those companies that have embraced a shared vision of the service goals of a supply chain, the natural evolution is a spirit of collaboration for the benefit of all supply chain actors. Rather than being a point of contention, the service KPI becomes a lever for an integrated supply chain and deeper best practices for mutual benefit.

An illustrative example is one consumer goods company that began collaborating with a key retail customer by using point-of-sale (POS) scan data to measure on-shelf availability. This led the manufacturer to expand the use of POS data to examine the supply chain performance for key product launches. The manufacturer discovered that there could be a gap of as much as 30 days between the *first store* selling at least one unit of the new product and *all stores* reporting at least one unit sold. This was despite the retailer insisting that each store, at least according to its IT system, had the launch product in stock at the same time. Because of the constructive, collaborative notion of service that had been fostered, the retailer was open to digging into the problem and discovered that many stores were not getting the launch products out of the backroom and on to the shelves in a timely manner. The last 10 meters were undermining months of effort by all parties to execute a successful product launch, and the key to identifying the problem was a collaborative spirit around service. The willingness of both supply chain partners to work together and move past siloed notions of service level led directly to higher turnover and more successful launches and, in fact, deepened the commercial relationship.

Next-stage service

As companies move deeper into the "Age of the Consumer," the role and objective of KPIs like service could benefit from a rethink. Deepening mutual collaboration around service objectives can help create a context for leveraging cost-to-serve analyses, a topic we cover in more detail in the next section. Cost-to-serve techniques can help both supplier and customer understand all the aspects of supply chain service, such as order parameters and lead time, and make informed tradeoffs between cost and service.

These tradeoffs are valid for all supply chain configurations, not only in retail distribution. In e-commerce, each company must make choices about lead time and transportation charges. And for project supply chains,[17] which provide products for a unique customer and must be specially configured or even designed from scratch, a more holistic view of service would include setting objectives or expectations of customer order lead time and incorporating them into the company's differentiation strategy.

Looking at service measure as a key element in the business strategy of market positioning, segmentation and cost structure can turn a potential point of contention into a lever for the supply chain to contribute to success.

A modern supply chain evolution may turn out to be the catalyst for resolving a classic supply chain challenge. Progress indeed!

4 THE HIDDEN COST OF COST TO SERVE

Every supply chain executive has had the frustrating experience of witnessing inefficient practices in their fulfillment operations. One of ours was during a tour of a consumer product manufacturers' distribution center. Workers were carefully taking products that were shrink-wrapped by three, cutting off the plastic film, putting two units in a box and returning the third to storage. The distribution center manager, when asked about this seemingly slightly dangerous and low-added-value task, explained that their biggest customer had requested an order minimum of two for this product, even though it arrived from the factory shrink-wrapped by three. Later, when we arrived in the order preparation area, the floor was filled with pallets with only a few boxes on each. Here the manager sheepishly explained that another big customer had requested mono-SKU pallets, despite the wasteful effort and space it required. He was having to fulfill promises made by the sales force without consulting him, and his operating costs were spiraling as a result.

Simple, intuitive and hard

This story is a common one. In an effort to please customers, price rebates are replaced by supply chain services that offer non-monetary benefits in operations. These often take the form of high delivery frequencies, small order multiples, direct-to-store deliveries and customized shipping conditions. Another manifestation may be allowing a customer to engage in inefficient operations practices such as manual ordering rather than electronic data interchange (EDI), suboptimal delivery slotting, excessive claims or tailored product offerings.

The best-known approach to trying to understand and address this dynamic is cost to serve. At its core, cost to serve is an application of activity-based costing. A company looks at its fulfillment processes, including reception, put-away, storage, order treatment, order picking, shipping and possible returns. Activity keys are selected for each step – for example, orders and order lines for order treatment, or pallets and weights for shipping – as a means of breaking down each step into granular activities and their associated costs. Each customer can then be evaluated by tallying up the activities executed on their behalf and the costs this generates. The total is the cost to serve for that customer.

Cost to serve is one of those supply chain ideas that is so intuitive and the benefits so clear, yet our conversations with supply chain executives have revealed that, in fact, it is rarely applied in a sustainable, repeatable way.

The first hurdle with cost to serve – as is the case with many analytical approaches – is securing reliable, clean data from which to start the analysis. The basic required data of number of orders, order lines, units per line, type of picking, and shipment type and cost seem reasonable enough. Yet one partner at a major supply chain consulting company told us that even in mature, large companies that have invested extensively in enterprise resource planning (ERP), obtaining satisfactory data sets is difficult, and almost impossible to do repeatedly. One key reason is the multitude of sources required for the base data: warehouse management system (WMS), customer relationship management (CRM) and transportation management system (TMS), to name a few. These are often discrete applications in a larger ERP footprint.

From there, managerial questions can bog down a cost-to-serve initiative. Disagreements can arise about what data to include as part of supply chain costs, for example the value of returned goods, or what activity key truly drives the cost of a given task. Some companies use the notion of a "logistics rebate" to capture the difference in fulfillment costs for different consumers. Its utility is that the more the cost to serve a customer is optimized, the higher the rebate they are offered. We spoke to one consumer goods market leader that adds the logistics rebate to its internal supply chain costs, reasoning that lost revenue due to the rebate is the equivalent of logistics avoided. However, our impression is that this company's sophistication in implementing the logistics rebate is an exception, and that most companies have allowed the logistics rebate to be polluted by other commercial variables so that it no longer reflects the true cost to serve.

There is a temptation to try to capture cost to serve by implementing dedicated cost-to-serve tools, but that does not address these issues or the need for buy-in from senior management to change underlying behaviors. However, when cost to serve is part of a larger effort to capture the full cost of doing business with a customer, including other expenses like trade and merchandising, these friction points can be avoided.[18]

In one example that emphasizes the need for senior management sponsorship, we spoke to a company that was incurring elevated handling and transportation costs to deliver promotional displays to large retail accounts direct-to-store rather than through the usual customer distribution center. After much investigation, the supply chain manager discovered that it was the marketing team that insisted on the direct deliveries. The later shipping dates allowed marketing more time to define the promotional materials, and they were not concerned with the associated supplemental supply chain costs. Senior management intervention is often needed to resolve cross-functional situations like this that are exposed by cost-to-serve analyses.

Folding cost to serve into a broader managerial analysis can help overcome other potential obstacles. As we have seen, many supply chain cost drivers can be explained by the sales force promising services without bearing accountability for the costs they generate. Once these services are in place, it is a sensitive negotiation to return to the customer and claw them back. A full customer profit and loss approach, of which cost to serve is just one element, can help mobilize management to address the root causes of supply chain inefficiencies. The supply chain consulting partner we spoke to echoes this view:

"The tradeoffs between distribution efficiency and commercial costs are difficult to quantify. On top of that, the impacts of changes are hard to simulate in terms of changes to the distribution center footprint, transportation costs or, in the case of omnichannel, the amount of returns."

These challenges were confirmed by the head of the cost-to-serve initiative at another consumer goods company. This company is experiencing difficulty rolling out a sustained Europe-wide program:

"We've only had success where there was a passionate champion for the project. But there is too much turnover in the supply chain and on the business side to maintain the analytics, much less get to root causes and remedies."

Omnichannel impacts

However, he offered the insight that omnichannel risks becoming an inflection point for cost to serve:

"The rise of omnichannel changes the order portfolio, driving up costs and complexity. We are being challenged to explain the increased costs just as senior management is trying to determine the true profitability of our omnichannel business."

Perhaps the advent of omnichannel will drive a willingness to push cost-to-serve efforts forward.

Even the champions are feeling the pressure of execution costs. Amazon announced in 2018 that the cost of Amazon Prime would increase by 20%.[19] In fact, in the first quarter, Amazon's shipping costs as a percentage of sales increased 260 basis points,[20] helping to explain its first-ever increase in Prime membership rates. Yamato, the Japanese logistics company supporting Amazon in Japan, also announced its first shipping rate increase in 27 years, in large part due to the complexities brought on by the rapid rise of omnichannel sales.[21]

The essentials of cost to serve

The basics can be hard to do, and cost to serve would seem to be a fundamental, essential practice. But the realities of extracting data, complex ERP, and management commitment can impede even the most foundational analysis. "Going digital" with Industry 4.0 tools will not help this old-school problem. The solution lies in disciplined application of data management along with clear sponsorship from senior management to address the identified root causes of supply chain inefficiencies.

The increasing cost pressures being brought to bear by the desire to meet the expectations of omnichannel may force companies to look at their operations differently and stimulate a readiness to call into question these business drivers. If the supply chain is to play a meaningful role in the formation and implementation of business strategy, then only analyses conducted through the lens of business practices can lead to a real understanding of the cost drivers and paths to improvement.

5 IS FULFILLMENT STILL AN FMCG CORE COMPETENCY?

Over the past several years, consumer packaged goods (CPG) companies have looked more and more to third-party logistics providers (3PLs) to manage their order fulfillment processes. The reasons for and impacts of this trend may point to the future of distribution in the e-commerce age. CPG companies are considered among the leaders in supply chain trends in manufacturing. Names like Procter & Gamble and Unilever are perennially among the leaders in Gartner's Supply Chain Top 25 – included in the "Masters" category of sustained leadership over the last 10 years – and CPGs represented 7 of the Top 25 in 2019. Looking at these companies can be instructive for understanding the future direction of supply chain management for manufacturers.

As manufacturers are increasingly rethinking what constitutes a core competency in supply chain, we spoke to supply chain distribution leaders at a major CPG manufacturer, a global 3PL and a major online retailer to understand the drivers of this trend of outsourcing order fulfillment and what it means for supply chains moving forward.

Why move to third-party logistics providers?

The first key takeaway from our conversation is that the primary motivation is not always cost. Moving to a 3PL will not necessarily be cheaper. This is especially the case for detail picking – the preparation of less-than-full-case orders. 3PLs are more price-competitive for simpler full-case or full-pallet orders. In fact, the most immediate benefit is flexibility.

A 3PL has more ability to absorb volume increases or fluctuations in volume than an in-house operation. The ability to share facilities and labor allows a 3PL to move resources around and respond in ways the manufacturer cannot. This has strong appeal for CPG companies that have intense launch and promotional cycles, which can create distortions in regular flows.

It is not only CPG companies that can benefit from the flexibility offered by working with 3PLs. Supply chain managers at a major online retailer explained that even the global e-commerce giants have a growing 3PL activity. When this retailer is looking to penetrate more deeply into a market, working with a 3PL is a flexible, agile way to establish a presence.

"Building an in-house facility can take 15 months, but starting up with a 3PL can be done in 3 months," they explained. One might think a giant online retailer would be present everywhere in Europe. Although this is largely true, not every product category is available in each market, nor is every service offer — for example, same day shipping. For large, bulky items like major appliances, working with a 3PL makes sense for online retailers in these new markets. These items are not ideal candidates for the efficiencies of automation, and the volume is relatively low. This means that there is a limited cost impact to foregoing this industry's well-known efforts in warehouse automation and robotics.

There are challenges for online retailers in working with 3PLs, however: "It would be fair to say that most 3PLs do not live in the same IT world as us," they confessed. This position is supported by some recent survey data that points to gaps between customer expectations in digitalization and the ability of 3PLs to respond: Only 35% of 3PL customers feel that the 3PL can support their big data initiatives, for example, and only 65% of 3PL customers are satisfied with their 3PL's IT capabilities. This places a strain on the interfaces between the online retailer and the 3PL, especially if the latter is to maintain its service standards.

Detail picking for retail chains comes with classic, well-understood expectations of accuracy and reactivity. But e-commerce has its own set of unique challenges. In order to succeed at e-commerce fulfillment, there needs to be seamless integration from the customer's front end to execution at the back end. This requires live information on stock availability, order processing status and secure customer credit data. Despite this, CPG companies have a different perspective. Since online sales are not their core business, they perceive that working with 3PLs in this area reduces complexity.

A senior executive at a major global 3PL player we spoke with provided an interesting perspective on this expectation of simplicity. She observed that when CPG companies turn to 3PLs to manage an entire e-commerce operation, including front end and payment processing, as well as classic retail fulfillment, the result is what she calls "extensive mediocrity." The execution is mediocre across the board, neither excellent nor poor. She believes the optimal configuration is partnerships between traditional 3PLs and experts in e-commerce front-end solutions. This would maintain the simplicity for the CPG manufacturer while allowing it to benefit from the expertise of each actor.

But this isn't to say that order fulfillment has become purely a commodity, and that 3PLs do not offer expertise. Most big 3PL players have their own version of continuous excellence to push for cost and efficiency gains, but CPG manufacturers have demanding retail customers and consumers that they have to answer to. This means finding 3PL partners that can innovate in sustainability and service quality as well. This alignment along social values and sustainability has created a competitive space for 3PLs to distinguish themselves, by investing in carbon-neutral distribution facilities and strong labor standards, for example.

What it means for CPG companies

One potentially counterintuitive consequence of the shift to outsourced order fulfillment has been improved business practices that impact the supply chain. When distribution is in-house, much commercial inefficiency that negatively impacts logistics costs falls — fairly or not — on the shoulders of supply chain managers, who are strongly encouraged to lower their per order costs and their share of revenue costs. Yet, often, the cost drivers are behaviors that are outside the scope of a logistics manager. The nature of the order profile can strongly influence logistics costs. Order frequency, order minimums, preparation specifications and paperwork requirements are examples of how commercial teams can negotiate terms with a customer that have outsized impacts on fulfillment costs.

The transition to a 3PL exposes the different practices around order management, laying bare the real drivers of logistics inefficiencies. If this sounds familiar, it may be because it is the foundation of assessing cost to serve, the method of looking at order treatment costs at the customer level, from order reception through fulfillment to returns and cash collection. The transparency of working with a 3PL is a vector for giving cost to serve a big boost. (For more on cost to serve, see the previous section — "The Hidden Cost of Cost to Serve.")

In fact, because the 3PL works with other CPG companies, it may well be more in tune with the best practices in logistics arrangements between CPG manufacturers and retailers, helping make the case and identify even more productivity opportunities. So, there is indeed a cost opportunity of working with 3PLs, just in an unexpected, indirect way. The 3PLs understand the value that they add in this respect and are increasing their analytics in order to gently push and challenge their CPG customers, a bit like a personal trainer helping a client who has shown they want to improve.

Returning to the 3PL executive, she believes that CPG companies may be falling into a trap of their own making: By considering fulfillment as a non-core competency and outsourcing it, the manufacturers are beginning to conflate fulfillment with a commodity, for which the quality is constant across the spectrum of service providers. She has observed that many large players seem to be ever more focused squarely on cost and less on service differentiation.

What it means for third-party logistics providers

The 3PL space is not quite at the same level of maturity as its CPG manufacturer customer base. The market is still predominantly made up of what can be termed "local heroes" — 3PLs that are strong in one particular market and have a deep connection with the retailers, transporters and regulatory bodies there. Even large 3PLs like DHL and Kuehne+Nagel have had challenges in standardizing the level of performance across markets, and it is still very much a function of the local personnel, perhaps even down to site level. This can be at odds with CPG manufacturers, who have powerful brands and a global presence. They would rather have a limited set of preferred partnerships, not a patchwork of contracts with local players.

3PLs will have to look to automation, robotics and learning algorithms to be even more efficient in their operations in order to justify their role. Indeed, the idea of warehousing on-demand could emerge as a real threat unless 3PLs continue to improve productivity and support cost-to-serve initiatives as added-value offerings. It will be a challenge for 3PLs to avoid a race to the bottom when over three-quarters of their customers consider cost the most important vendor selection criterion.

Takeaways

Most CPG companies started outsourcing logistics operations to 3PLs before supply chain digitalization with all its facets and opportunities took off, be it e-commerce, omnichannel or big data. Most do not seem to have called this choice into question but consumer expectations seem to be evolving fast and 3PLs will need to upgrade their service offering in turn.

Should the trend in CPGs of outsourcing order fulfillment continue, it could fundamentally alter what is considered part of the supply chain's core competency in operations. The emphasis may shift towards a deeper focus on the business drivers of logistics costs, rather than on logistics per se. This would support the positioning of sales and operations planning (S&OP) by nudging supply chain to be included as a core activity along with marketing, sales and finance.

6 WHO'S IN CHARGE?
THE ROLE OF S&OP GOVERNANCE[i]

In the past few years, the term "sales and operations planning" (S&OP) has become quite universal in supply chain circles. It is common to encounter arguments that there needs to be agreement between sales, marketing, finance and the supply chain on what the demand plan should be every month or every week. However, there does not appear to be consensus among multinational companies on how to structure the planning process. The key questions revolve around how to secure the buy-in and engagement of all the actors needed to reach agreement on the different types of plans in a company and how to obtain senior management sponsorship.

These debates often come up in the context of how to set up the communication flows when factories are not dedicated to a single market. Multinational companies seem to be at various stages of specializing production and moving away from the concept of having a factory dedicated to producing for a single market or having a market supplied by dedicated factories. Overall, however, they are looking for guidance on how to build their S&OP governance structure. And this applies especially to multinationals with their own internal production networks of factories serving more than one market.

The S&OP governance challenge

S&OP seems to face a dilemma in these multinationals. How can the S&OP process be close enough to both the factories and the markets? Proximity is needed to understand and influence the capacity and agility of the factories, on the one hand, and market intelligence such as launches and promotions, on the other. Both are needed to properly align supply and demand, but if there is too much influence in either area, the visibility and engagement of the actors breaks down and the end-to-end integration is lost. Not enough influence in either area results in silos, and the ability to drive alignment from end to end disappears.

This dilemma is a direct result of specializing production and having factories and marketing in a complex many-to-many relationship – a multi-nodal supply chain. The factories and the markets either have their own independent senior managers or the common authority is too high to encourage collaboration effectively. When the relationship is one-to-one, these questions can be addressed quickly because the country general manager is accountable for overall performance.

---

[i] This article is a summary of academic research by Richard Markoff. For more detailed information regarding the methodology, definitions, research design and findings, please consult the full doctoral thesis at https://www.theses.fr/fr/2017PA01E015.

We attempted to address this question by conducting a series of interviews with senior supply chain staff at major multinationals to try to understand and chart the S&OP governances of their companies.

In all, executives from 27 companies were interviewed. Every respondent was able to speak about their organization's S&OP capability and process, with roles including head of S&OP at the center of excellence; operational head of S&OP globally or regionally; and head of operations for the company, with S&OP as part of their broader responsibilities. The participating companies were of significant size, with average 2014 sales of about US$32 million, and nearly half ranked in the Fortune Global 500. Seven industry sectors were represented: consumer goods, life sciences, apparel, electronics, chemicals, automotive, and industrial.

To interpret the results of our interviews and create a benchmark, we developed an S&OP governance typology – a simple matrix that classifies S&OP governance models into four easily recognizable types. Production planning was used to reflect S&OP authority over upstream planning activities, while demand planning reflected S&OP authority over downstream activities. Production planning is the activity where key manufacturing constraints are identified, captured and weighed against the supply needs identified in the demand consolidation. Here, it is understood to mean the moment of decision about what production the factory will produce or is projected to produce. Demand planning is part of the forecasting process and involves coordinating multi-functional actors to bring together different views, market intelligence and financial targets.

To help understand which model is best, we then looked at alignment. A successful S&OP process achieves alignment along two axes: the *horizontal axis*, from the demand plan through to the factories and the corresponding supply generated to meet this demand; and the *multi-functional axis* where alignment is sought between sales, marketing, finance and supply chain, as shown in **Figure 3.1**.

Building an S&OP governance benchmark

Each supply chain manager we interviewed provided insights into whether their company demonstrates non-alignment behaviors, such as willfully increasing the demand plan to generate buffer inventory or knowingly overproducing to achieve a lower cost of goods. The S&OP types differ in their ability to inhibit these non-alignment behaviors.

One of the hallmarks of S&OP is alignment between the demand plans and the forward financial plans of a company, i.e. the idea that sales, marketing, finance and general management are so fully aligned around the demand plan, which is

Figure 3.1: The two axes of sales and operations planning alignment

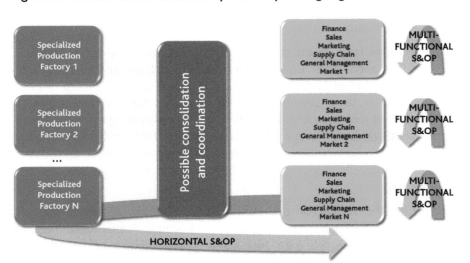

the same as – or very close to – the projected financial performance. This notion of demand and financial alignment implies that the general manager is encouraged to fully engage in the demand planning process, since it is entwined with the financial planning process. This only serves to underscore the importance of the multinational nature of S&OP governance. The demand planning process now directly influences an accountability that is core to the role of the general manager – the financial commitment of the market. This raises the stakes even higher when it comes to maintaining local proximity in the demand planning part of the S&OP process.

The hierarchical structure companies implement to permit the supply chain management to span the upstream and downstream ends of multi-nodal supply chains is crucial to describing how companies attempt to achieve S&OP alignment. Achieving horizontal alignment in multi-nodal supply chain management requires *at least* coordination and *at most* control over S&OP activities occurring in several markets and several factories. The usual performance measures of S&OP for inventory, service and cost tradeoffs are dictated by constraints and decisions occurring at opposite ends of the S&OP horizontal dimension. Companies have taken different approaches to dealing with the competing management dimensions.

Taking service as an example, there are many reasons a service issue may arise – at any point in the company. Poor service might be due to poor demand plans, poor production planning, quality issues or material supply issues at a vendor.

These typical supply chain causes occur across the horizontal dimension. Looking at the multi-functional dimension, service issues may arise because of an uncommunicated pricing change or promotional plan, or failure to coordinate media plans with new product planning. Each company has its own suite of performance measures – with associated accountabilities – to try to capture all the questions around the root causes and drivers of service performance.

Potential governance configurations include multiple reporting lines to different authorities. To accommodate this possibility, we included two types of reporting authority:

- *Solid line* reporting authority is the principal accountable authority providing day-to-day direction, prioritization and counsel, covering all tactical decisions to resolve issues and drive performance. It is also the primary source of determining performance evaluations of employees.
- *Dotted line* reporting authority is a secondary provider of orientation and priorities. The focus here is on accountability for process standards and techniques, strategic orientations and a lesser determination of performance evaluation.

The next benchmarking step was to identify measures that capture the extent of S&OP alignment on both the horizontal and multi-functional axes. There is no universal quantified, normalized measure available to capture this alignment and every company has different internal measures of the success of the S&OP process.

We used a behavioral approach to identify the success or failure of alignment. In practice, alignment is not possible if there is a willful intent on the part of operational actors to distort or skew information and reduce transparency. These distortions ensure that the supply chain is not aligned, since they demonstrate a willingness to drive decisions in the supply chain that otherwise would not have been taken.

With this notion of intent and collaboration in mind, in order to capture horizontal misalignment, we used the notion of *willful supply/demand imbalance*. This misalignment occurs when upstream factories intentionally supply products that are not required to meet the demand signals provided. In other words, a misalignment between supply and demand is knowingly created. Examples of this are a factory producing in order to cover fixed costs and not to respond to expressed demand. Factory managers are often more strongly incentivized for their site's economic performance than for inventory generated and housed downstream. Along these lines, a factory may increase the batch size to levels incompatible with the expressed demand in order to improve manufacturing costs or it may anticipate production to an exaggerated degree to prevent equipment setup costs.

Turning to multi-functional alignment, we used a similar approach, focusing on the notion of *willful demand manipulation*. As the start of the operational S&OP process, the demand plan is the expression of the downstream alignment of multiple actors in the forecasting process. It cannot be aligned if operational actors have intentionally altered the demand plan. The most common example of willful demand manipulation is to overstate the planned demand in order to generate inventory that the supply chain would not otherwise plan to provide. This is done in an effort to ensure service continuity if there is a lack of confidence in the supply chain's ability to meet the demand. Early work into the bullwhip effect recognized this sort of behavior. Experience has shown that if sales personnel are responsible for the demand plan, willful manipulation may occur in the opposite direction, i.e. the demand plan is lowered to manage expectations of the sales targets they are evaluated with.

Having defined two measures of alignment for our benchmark, we needed a third measure to capture the company's ability to align the demand plan with its overall financial planning activities. This was measured in a straightforward way by asking the binary question of whether the company actively compares and aligns the demand plan with the financial plan as a matter of policy.

The different S&OP governance models

Using the two core S&OP activities of accountability for demand planning and accountability for production planning, S&OP governance can be captured in a three by three matrix as shown in **Figure 3.2**. It summarizes the number and percentage of multi-nodal companies in which the supply chain function has strong (solid line), weak (dotted line) or no authority over upstream S&OP or downstream S&OP. Four S&OP models emerge: strong bidirectional S&OP owners, weak bidirectional S&OP owners, partial S&OP owners and connectors.

Strong or weak bidirectional S&OP owners

Some companies have authority – strong or weak – over both the upstream and the downstream core S&OP activities at the same time. There are 17 companies in this category, or nearly two-thirds of the companies interviewed. In these companies, supply chain managers lead S&OP governance across multiple markets and multiple factories in a multi-nodal supply chain configuration. Of these 17 companies, 5 have supply chain managers exerting solid line authority over both extremes of the S&OP process. These managers do more than simply move information along to disparate internal actors; they exert influence and authority over the dual constraints of the S&OP process that need aligning – supply and demand. They are truly the owners of horizontal S&OP alignment. The 5 companies that have solid line, or strong, authority over both upstream and downstream activities can be termed *strong bidirectional S&OP owners*; the 12

Figure 3.2: Sales and operations planning (S&OP) governance typology matrix

Accountability for Demand Planning Process

		Strong downstream	Weak downstream	No downstream
		17	7	3
	27	63%	26%	11%
Strong upstream	11	5	4	2
	41%	19%	15%	7%
Weak upstream	8	5	3	0
	30%	19%	11%	0%
No upstream	8	7	0	1
	30%	26%	0%	4%

Accountability for Production Planning

- Strong bidirectional S&OP owners
- Partial S&OP owners
- Weak bidirectional S&OP owners
- Connectors

companies that have at least one of the upstream or downstream authorities in dotted line, or weak, authority can be labeled *weak bidirectional S&OP owners*.

Partial S&OP owners

There are nine companies with solid or dotted line authority over one of the two ends of the S&OP alignment process, but no authority over the other. The supply chains of these companies cannot exert influence over the whole S&OP process, at least not in a formal way. It is difficult to frame the supply chain managers in these companies as owners and orchestrators of the entire S&OP process. These companies are labeled *partial S&OP owners*.

Connectors

Lastly, in one company, the supply chain managers were in the unique position of possessing no solid or dotted line authority over either end of the S&OP process. This type of governance is simply as a *connector*. It would be difficult for this company to argue that the supply chain managers influence and orchestrate the generation of a true demand plan, or a production plan to meet it, when they have no influence over either the process or the result.

This result is a bit startling. Over one-third of the companies interviewed – 10 in all – are *partial S&OP owners or connectors*. Planning *what* a company should and will produce and *when* it produces it are the key operational deliverables of the S&OP process. For 10 of the 27 companies we interviewed, a significant part of the S&OP process – the *raison d'être* of supply chain management – is not under the authority of the broader supply chain organization.

The next step is to explore to what extent these four governance models – *strong bidirectional S&OP owners, weak bidirectional S&OP owners, partial S&OP owners and connectors* – succeed or fail in achieving the two S&OP alignment objectives in the horizontal and multi-functional dimensions.

S&OP governance: Which model is best?

Having defined the four S&OP governance models, we can compare the extent of their S&OP alignment. For each model, **Table 3.1** shows the percentage of companies achieving horizontal alignment of supply and demand and the vertical alignment of demand using the definitions described earlier. It reveals that the type of S&OP governance clearly influences the ability of the S&OP process to obtain horizontal and vertical alignment.

Table 3.1: S&OP alignment by governance typology

		Achieve supply alignment		Achieve demand alignment		Achieve finance alignment	
Strong bidirectional S&OP owners	5	4	80%	2	40%	0	0%
Weak bidirectional S&OP owners	12	10	83%	5	42%	3	25%
Partial S&OP owners	9	5	56%	1	11%	2	22%
Connectors	1	0	0%	0	0%	0	0%
Achieve finance alignment	5	4	80%	3	60%	1	100%

The horizontal alignment of supply shows a marked difference between the two governance types that exert bidirectional authority over the S&OP process and the others. Both *strong bidirectional S&OP owners* and *weak bidirectional S&OP owners* have four out of five companies reporting no willful manipulation of the production plan. This is in contrast with five out of nine companies for *partial S&OP owners*, and the lone connector governance type did not succeed in obtaining alignment. This result should not be surprising. Most of the companies interviewed had the supply chain management group as part of a wider operations group including production, quality and other technical activities. As a result, managers in production and supply chain, even if separate groups, usually have to move up only one level in the company hierarchy to find a common accountable manager. With this proximity of management, it is understandable that there is little difference between *strong* and *weak bidirectional S&OP owners*.

Looking at the multi-functional downstream demand alignment, the result is very similar, at least in terms of trend. The *strong* and *weak bidirectional S&OP owner* governance typologies are much more successful than the *partial S&OP owner* governance type in exerting authority over the S&OP process. However, the scale is much different. S&OP demand alignment is only about half as successful as upstream supply alignment, and even less than half for the *partial S&OP owners*.

One implication of this is that companies are less experienced and advanced in implementing the downstream S&OP process and so less proficient at it. Here governance may play a particularly critical role, since the downstream alignment for multi-nodal supply chains often occurs in many markets in parallel. Even with S&OP governance that enables a central supply chain management group to influence the process, the effects of distance take their toll. Many companies described the downstream part of their S&OP process as something novel or recently implemented. They reported difficulty in wresting the remnants of previous demand planning processes from their owners who were still in place and might resist the change. This combination of a less mature process replacing an archaic method and battling entrenched lines of ownership over greater distances helps explain the relative lack of downstream multi-functional alignment.

It is worth looking at the results of companies that achieve financial alignment. These are companies that have a set policy of aligning their demand plan resulting from the S&OP process with the company's financial planning activities. Only five companies reported that this policy was in place. These five companies had markedly better success in achieving both horizontal supply alignment (4) and multi-functional alignment (3). These results almost match those of a simpler linear supply chain configuration. It clearly suggests that a distinct policy of aligning financial and demand planning is at least as critical as governance in achieving both axes of S&OP alignment.

There appears to be a link between the governance type and the implementation of this policy. Of the five companies with demand and financial plan alignment, four have either *strong* or *weak bidirectional S&OP owner* typologies. The companies interviewed seem to implicitly recognize this. In addition to the 5 companies that have this policy in place, an additional 11 companies stated that they *intend* to implement a policy of aligning demand and financial plans.

Risks of excessive financial involvement in S&OP

Aligning the S&OP process and the demand plan with the finance plan is highly important, as we have seen, but you can have too much of a good thing. We received valuable testimony in our interviews of the pitfalls of having too much financial control over the S&OP process.

The first point to be clear about is that the managerial objectives are not always the same. Financial plans sometimes represent aspirations — even unreasonable aspirations that serve as "north stars" for the company — used to express orientations and priorities, but not really founded in concrete reality. Forcing alignment between the demand plan and the financial plan of a company that does not see the financial plan as a true representation of forward performance will inevitably cause friction. Either the demand plan will be willfully distorted to match the unrealistic financial plan or the financial plan will no longer serve the same historical purpose and will be transformed into a more grounded financial forecast. This is not necessarily undesirable, but if senior management and the financial community are not in agreement, they will invariably put pressure on the demand plan to conform to the financial plan, thus undermining the S&OP alignment.

Another risk is that finance may not fully appreciate the many tradeoffs occurring in the S&OP process and may see it as a way to reach an inventory target, making working capital the immovable goal of S&OP, not the alignment of supply and demand. This can lead to having too little inventory at the end of a financial period or not anticipating capacity crunches down the line.

Respondents frequently mentioned the challenges of translating a unit volume demand plan into a monetized financial plan. The S&OP process is vulnerable to getting bogged down in discussions about using average costs or per product costs to transform the units into value.

This highlights the difficulty of keeping master data clean and actionable. Even a figure as fundamentally important as price may change rapidly, particularly in a developing market, making the task of monetization challenging.

Another challenge may be temporary price reductions, or volumes of products given away for promotional purposes. These must be accounted for in the S&OP demand planning process, but not in quite the same way as for the financial plan. In many companies, the top line financial plan is the gross revenue less expenses such as returns and volume rebates. Since these variables are both unknown and have no impact on the S&OP process, it is difficult for demand planners to integrate them.

Perhaps most importantly, several companies testified that the financial process simply is not credible. The budgets and trends reported back to corporate entities for consolidation are often unrealistic, general managers know this is the case and this is how the financial game is played in their company. This seemed to be more common in emerging markets. Here the financial plan does not act as a managerial aspiration, but rather as a "nod and a wink" to corporate headquarters in respect of the goal that has been set, with the mutual understanding that these volumes will not be met and the financial plan will slowly drift downwards as the year progresses. In other words, the financial planning process may not be a credible corporate actor and it would be counterproductive to use it as a source of input and alignment for the S&OP process.

Turning to more concrete – even technical – considerations, there are sometimes real differences in the plans themselves. Finance may not be as concerned with the forward months if they fall into the next year, or may only want quarterly buckets, whereas supply chain managers needs weeks or months.

In the same way, S&OP may need planning for each product at the SKU level, while finance may only need the product family. If finance begins running the S&OP process, these supply chain management considerations may not be taken into account and the demand plan will not be fully exploitable for the rest of the end-to-end S&OP process.

Lastly, some actors in Finance follow a strong logic of local profit and loss (P&L) and balance sheet ownership, and they push for solutions where each inventory actor should be optimizing their link in the chain. This goes against the idea of end-to-end, integrated supply chain management, where the inventory is placed at the best spot to service the whole chain, and decisions about supply or demand constraints are taken with the whole chain in mind.

Golden rules of S&OP governance

There are four key takeaways from this benchmarking exercise, four golden rules of S&OP governance to help guide supply chain managers when implementing S&OP.

Rule 1: Build an S&OP structure that spans from end to end

Multi-nodal companies with bidirectional S&OP ownership have demonstrated a greater ability to achieve S&OP alignment in both supply and demand than companies with S&OP governance that does not span both directions. In order to construct governance that fosters successful S&OP alignment, the company must recognize that S&OP activities occur from many factories to many markets. Broad bidirectional governance tamps down willful manipulations and bias, yielding alignment. The bidirectional authority does not appear to have to be in the form of a solid line. Dotted line authority on the part of supply chain managers appears to bring as much alignment as solid line authority.

This structure calls for a centralized supply chain management organization that shares authority and accountability from demand planning to production planning. With this governance in place, supply chain managers can credibly be held accountable for the service and working capital performance of the company.

Rule 2: Implement formal alignment with financial plans

Having a formal policy of aligning the demand plan and the financial plan has more impact than S&OP governance structure on promoting transparency, limiting bias and achieving alignment between supply and demand. After putting in place a bidirectional S&OP governance structure, a financial plan that is in line with and reflects the demand plan is the most powerful combination for successful S&OP. The importance of financial planning and intricate relationships to the authority and territory of the general manager can be conferred onto the S&OP process, bringing credibility and collaboration.

Rule 3: Be mindful of the maturity of the financial planning process

Although the importance of linking the demand plan and the financial plan to achieve successful S&OP has been established, it is vital not to go faster than the music of the financial planning. The foundation of the S&OP process will be built on sand if the financial planning process is *immature* or *not credible*.

It was shown that only a handful of companies have a firm, stated policy of aligning the demand and financial plans. This is critical, but not sufficient. There is still the possibility that the demand plan is *forced to match* the financial plan rather than the financial plan being *derived from* the demand plan.

Even if a company's financial maturity is high and the financial plan is derived through the S&OP process, this does not mean the two plans should be completely identical. One can imagine situations where a company does not feel that a potential development warrants inclusion in financial plans but would like supply chain managers to be fully prepared for the eventuality.

An example from personal experience serves to illustrate this. A few years ago, after much commercial effort, we were optimistic that one of our young product lines would be placed in a major American retailer, but the deal was far from certain. This would represent a significant breakthrough for the brand and an opportunity not to be missed or put at risk. Yet the prospect of this occurring was not high enough for it to be included in the company's financial projections. This was the decision of the general manager and, as a team, we were fully aligned with his direction. In order to take the right decision, in the

S&OP process all functions agreed and aligned on the potential volumes, and the supply chain managers performed a scenario analysis on the risks to working capital should the opportunity not pan out. Armed with this information, we all agreed that the working capital risk was small compared with the risk of being unable to react if the new client retailer placed an order in a short time frame. This is an example of a high financial maturity environment in which the S&OP process drives the financial planning through scenario analysis.

In order to measure and close the gaps between the demand and financial plans, the S&OP process requires some data sophistication. Monetization of demand plans may seem anodyne, but there are plenty of pitfalls to avoid in order to get it right. Starting with averages is fine, but it is necessary to move to real costs, ideally integrated in the demand planning tools, to allow real-time demand to shape decisions.

The final objective is to have the capability to predict not just top line but also bottom line impacts for a true cost-to-serve vision. At this point, the goal of alignment is to have not just one set of numbers but also the ability to evaluate different scenarios on working capital and company profitability. This is coherent with the next ambition of the S&OP process as expressed by the more mature companies, a process often referred to as total cost of ownership.

Rule 4: Do demand planning where the business decisions are made

The value of aligning the S&OP with the financial plan is that it has the mediating effect of having all actors working on the process in a transparent, collaborative way. The understanding is that all are bound by the authority and territory of the general manager, who will arbitrate and drive towards achieving the best solution, since it binds him to a credible financial plan. The implication is the actors have the necessary information required to build a complete demand plan and have the decision-making authority to shape the demand as a result of constraints and opportunities. If marketing plans and sales plans are built locally, and general management accountabilities are at a local market level, then that is "where the action is" and where the demand planning should be conducted.

This insight argues against demand planning conducted in part or in whole at a centralized level unless tactical or short-range strategic decisions are made centrally as well. Many companies we spoke to see the appeal of centralizing demand planning. Centralization allows companies to implement better, more sophisticated statistical analysis tools. They can recruit more talented people to get the most out these tools. Also, the center of excellence can more easily implement demand planning procedures and check that they are respected. But these understandable, rational benefits are overshadowed by the importance of proximity and shared authority to the business owner of the decision-making P&L and his functional team.

There are more tactical, tangible reasons as well. Many companies are looking to develop shared demand plans with key accounts, through a process called collaborative planning, forecasting and replenishment (CPFR). The value of CPFR is not limited to having improved demand plans. It also contributes to a stronger, more collaborative commercial relationship with the account. This strong relationship can then be leveraged by supply chain managers to implement initiatives such as vendor managed inventory (VMI), which on its own can smooth out flows, limit downstream inventory build-up and so inherently improve demand planning.

Lastly, companies are looking to leverage the potential of demand shaping, the practice of using supply information on opportunities and constraints to help shape demand. One example of demand shaping may be to propose or modify a promotional program based on product availability or excess inventory positions. With the ongoing prominence of e-commerce permitting a more direct link between manufacturer and consumer, the potential of demand shaping is growing. In order to fully exploit demand shaping, supply chain management teams must be in close proximity to sales and e-commerce management teams. This allows the fluid exchanges of information needed to take advantage of opportunities for demand shaping, which often occur at very short notice with small windows.

It is up to each company to examine the structural authority constructed by the business and implement S&OP governance accordingly. The two must be compatible for the S&OP process to succeed in its alignment objectives. This last rule is critical to leveraging a credible, mature financial planning process into a credible, mature S&OP process.

7 SUPPLY CHAIN DIGITALIZATION: IT MANAGEMENT CHALLENGES

The digitalization of supply chains is happening quickly. Much of the attention is centered on innovations like cloud computing, software as a service (SaaS) and advanced analytics. But there is another aspect to this rapidly changing landscape: Companies must rethink their IT management approaches, from their purchasing strategy to the interaction between IT and business processes.

The expanding vendor ecosystem

Just a few years ago, most IT purchasing functions relied on a handful of large vendors to manage their supply chain IT solutions. The most prominent example would be SAP, of course, which offers a complete suite of functionalities, even to large and diverse companies. Depending on a company's priorities and its competitive advantage, SAP would usually be complemented by a management execution system (MES) or warehouse management solution (WMS) supplied by a niche IT vendor with an attractive product.

There are many advantages to consolidating vendors. First, focusing spend increases penetration into the vendors' customer base and creates leverage for price negotiations. Second, companies can influence the development priorities of vendors. For example, instead of modifying the core vendor product to suit their needs, they can have their needs integrated into the next version of the vendor's core package. There are also significant technical considerations. Having fewer vendors and solution packages is conducive to fewer servers, interfaces and data incompatibility issues. This leads to lighter IT infrastructure, which lowers the cost of maintaining, deploying and enhancing a suite of supply chain solutions.

Not everyone is fully satisfied with this model, however. Users – the business functions that use the solutions operationally – must inevitably compromise. A minimalist approach to IT, and using SAP for most functions, usually means foregoing specialized, niche applications that are tailor-made for specific functions. For example, production functions typically prefer smaller vendors that offer packages that are uniquely designed for MES. They would argue it better suits their specific needs – improved material flow on the shop floor or improved tracking of equipment efficiency. Distribution teams may feel the same way. Quality service teams, too, may agree, as they seek superior traceability.

But digitalization is changing this dynamic rapidly. The functionalities associated with digitalization are coming online too quickly for the large one-stop-shops like SAP. The expectations of omnichannel have brought order management systems and distribution solutions to market that are designed to manage the complexity and demands of working with e-commerce fulfillment specialists and front-end systems, as well as the data needed to power customer relationship management (CRM). Other examples include end-to-end supply chain visibility and data/demand integration capabilities, both of which provide optimization and traceability. Even if the large enterprise resource planning (ERP) vendors are offering services in these areas, the speed of evolution is such that they are skeleton solutions compared with those of innovators. Companies are under pressure to expand their vendor base, and this pressure is coming not just from internal users but also from the fact that companies must adapt their business models to meet new customer expectations.

Companies with functions like IT management, purchasing and business process are adopting a range of practices as they try to adapt. One vertically integrated energy company we spoke to is taking an interesting approach. It understands that it must adapt and move away from trying to limit the IT vendor ecosystem. To manage the transition, the leaders of the business functions have agreed on a core of 15-20% of business functions that the company considers to be its competitive advantage. These are the functions that warrant the increased complexity and cost to support smaller, specialized digitalization vendors.

The remaining functions are not necessarily condemned to settling for the pre-packaged ERP options. These processes are transitioning to what the company considers the "industry standard" solution – the most common, readily available, reasonable tradeoff between niche player and price/complexity. The company works with influencers like Gartner and industry groups to determine the industry standard solution for each business function. This combination of industry standard and targeted, niche leaders is forming the company's roadmap for the future. The IT purchasing function is now rethinking its sourcing approach. Rather than looking at the raw spend they used to have with large ERP players, they may now use the fact that they are a large customer for a smaller vendor (albeit with less raw spend) to try to influence the vendor's development roadmap.

There was understandable resistance at first. No one likes to think that the function they work in is not a competitive advantage for the company. One of the keys to success in an approach like this is full engagement and support from senior management. A disciplined, consistent message and adherence to the policy are essential.

Rethinking the role of IT

One large multinational consumer goods company realized that adopting digitalization solutions from new vendors required rethinking the way the company's support center was organized. It wasn't enough for the requirements and expectations to be set by the business process owners and an IT function that was accountable for solution delivery, training and improvement. The company found that the IT teams lacked the business expertise to appreciate the potential benefits offered by new vendor solutions, and the business process owners were often too consumed by other responsibilities and not sufficiently exposed to supply chain digitalization. To address this, it created a new function – the Supply Chain Digitalization Director – to help bring IT and the business process owners together to discover the possibility of new innovations and explore their impact on both business practices and IT management.

Another major consumer goods company is also embracing the IT management changes brought on by digitalization. The rapid expansion of powerful niche tools led the company to realize it had placed too much emphasis on process automation, and not enough on the user. In response, the company is not only actively deploying best-in-breed digital solutions but also building central cockpits so that users have the best of both worlds – niche tools that allow them to benefit from exciting new IT solutions, but with a central portal so they can move freely between tools. For example, a customer care representative can use the cockpit to move from the order management B2B portal to the CRM tool to chat with a customer, then to the ERP to see the orders being processed, and finally to the TMS to check order delivery status. A demand planner can have the most powerful, collaborative planning platform to work with customers, and move easily to the integrated data management tool to change a planning parameter. Indeed, this company has embraced the digital future to such an extent that it uses crowdsourcing and social media to allow its community to propose solution enhancements and vote for their favorites.

However, both companies said that tension still exists between users' desire for specialized vendor offerings for their function and the IT imperatives for managing complexity of data, plus interfaces and maintenance.

IT management takeaways

The possibilities opened up by supply chain digitalization are dizzying. It is an exciting time to be working in the field and participating in a real revolution in the way companies plan, source, make and deliver their goods. But companies must rethink much of their internal IT management:

- The vendor ecosystem and cost management expectations of support solutions
- Which business processes merit attention — new frontiers cannot be pushed everywhere at once
- How new IT vendors are identified and selected, with buy-in from all functions
- How to bring it all together to limit complexity for the user.

8 CASE STUDY WORKSHOP | BUILDING AN INDUSTRY 4.0 TRANSFORMATION ROADMAP

We have stressed throughout the book just how complex the Industry 4.0 landscape can seem, even to those with some familiarity with the different technologies and capabilities.

In Chapter 1, we stressed the importance of three key questions that supply chain managers must ask themselves before embarking on an Industry 4.0 transformation journey. The key questions are how to identify the business drivers that the selected capabilities should address, how to build the business case and how to overcome barriers to lead the implementation.

In order to illustrate just how complicated the interplay of these three elements is, we designed an interactive workshop targeting experienced supply chain managers.[ii] The objective of the workshop is to help participants connect the technologies and managerial challenges of Industry 4.0 through a collaborative group exercise.

Participants are presented with a fictionalized version of an actual consumer goods factory. They are given information about the current state of the factory and provided with 33 cards describing potential capabilities the factory could choose to adopt. Working in groups, they are asked to select up to 10 technologies to apply, in a sequence of their choosing.

This exercise helps foster an appreciation of several aspects of an Industry 4.0 implementation program:

- Insight into a representative starting point for a factory looking to adopt a strategic Industry 4.0 transformation roadmap.
- The basic considerations that must be taken into account when constructing an Industry 4.0 roadmap.
- More detail about several key Industry 4.0 applications and their potential.
- The importance of selecting the best mix of technologies from a complex array of possibilities, weighing up cost, quality, productivity and perception of value.
- The challenge of sequencing implementation to gain buy-in of personnel and harvest the benefits of an Industry 4.0 implementation.

[ii] The workshop, presented in the form of a case study, was designed in conjunction with SmarterChains. The case won the Supply Chain Management category in the 2019 EFMD case writing competition.

The situation

Participants are positioned as consultants with a mandate with an important client. The client is a global leader in personal care who has hired the consultants to build an Industry 4.0 roadmap for its pilot factory, which is in Germany and produces fragrances. The client's objective is to transform the pilot factory into a center of excellence (CoE) that will serve as an example to inspire the company's seven other factories.

Some key information is provided about the factory, including the top 10 manufacturing losses (see below and **Figure 3.3**), which will fuel the decisions made by the groups during the exercise:

1. Downtime due to machine stops — *losses due to short unplanned machine stoppages such as line parameter adjustments or packaging availability*
2. Product recipe inconsistencies — *losses due to errors in following the recipe for manufacturing the bulk*
3. Material utilization losses — *losses due to high scrap levels of packaging materials*
4. Palletizing — manual labor — *losses due to manually assembling pallets of finished goods at the end of the line*
5. Pick and place — manual labor — *losses due to manually picking finished products from the line and placing into cases*
6. Primary and secondary packaging — *losses due to quality issues with primary and secondary packaging*
7. Downtime due to equipment failure — *losses due to long unplanned machine stoppages as a result of equipment failure*
8. Repetitive maintenance tasks — *losses due to repetitive maintenance tasks such as machine calibration, verifying parts that wear out, lubricating, etc.*
9. Planned downtime for resource activities — *line stoppages due to resource activities such as team meetings or training*
10. Production order management — *losses due to suboptimal sequencing of product orders*

We invite the participants to work together in small groups for about an hour to develop their proposed Industry 4.0 roadmap. The roadmap should focus on **loss improvement** and **waste elimination**. The groups should be prepared to present their roadmap to the others in a plenary session and explain the reasoning behind it.

Figure 3.3: Top 10 losses in plant as a percentage of total

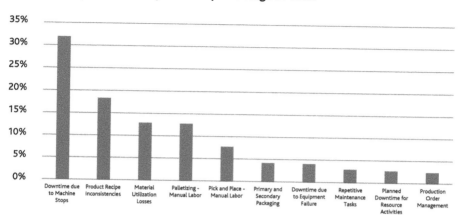

To prepare their roadmap, the groups must choose from 33 different technology or organizational constructs summarized in **Tables 3.2** to **3.7**. Each group's proposed roadmap should be limited to 10 technology or organizational constructs so that they focus on prioritization.

As **Tables 3.2** to **3.7** show, it is a daunting list of capabilities to sift through. There are so many, in fact, that there is no shame if one is not familiar with all of them. Indeed, with these workshops, each group always asks for clarification or more information to understand some of the capabilities listed. This is understandable. Every supply chain manager has day-to-day operational responsibilities and cannot possibly find the bandwidth to be up to speed on all the technologies and innovations coming online in an ever-evolving landscape.

Table 3.2: Data collection and management

Name and short description	Benefits	Losses affected
Process historian Collects, stores & analyzes high volumes of data from all processes in real time.	Less time spent on reporting Increased data storage capacity Improved process reporting and production visibility	Data collection processes
Data integration platform Combines data from all the different systems into a single platform.	Less time spent mitigating data across systems Faster access to data Increased visibility across the plant	Data collection Data reporting
Data lake Analyze and get insights from big data.	Raw data can be a gold mine for data scientists seeking to establish a robust advanced-analytics program In general, data lakes cost less to operate than enterprise data warehouses Less complexity in the data architecture management	Time of analysis Cost & complexity of data storage IT budget spent on data architecture management
IIoT analytics platform Build the capability to collect real-time data from all your sources into a central platform with advanced analyzing capabilities.	End-to-end visibility Continuous process improvement Less time spent on data collection, analysis & reporting Optimal production planning Data-driven decision making Reduced scrap	Material waste Quality defects Planned equipment maintenance Material utilization losses Downtime due to changeover Data gathering and reporting
Smart sensors Perform inline quality control measurements with wireless IoT sensors.	Increased visibility across the plant Improved health and safety Reduced energy costs	Data collection process

Table 3.3: Digital management

Name and short description	Benefits	Losses affected
Design IT/OT organization Organization structure design to reflect new capabilities, eliminating silos and enabling a chief information officer.	IT/OT organization will drive the system strategy for: Operational excellence and compliance Increasing innovation and productivity with launch or re-use of existing applications and scale of new applications across sites for automating workflows, data analysis, creating new data, data security, data connectivity and mobility Driving innovation through integration – analytics, modeling/simulation, data flows with no human touch Driving digital skills and mindset in the organization	
Define an Industry 4.0 company vision & strategy Design a site-specific strategy for supply chain digitalization.	Drive productivity through organizational innovation Operational excellence and compliance Drive productivity	
Industry 4.0 performance measurement Captures progression and benchmarking across all levels.	Gain an independent perspective about how well you perform compared to others Drill down into performance gaps to identify areas for improvement Develop a standardized set of processes and metrics Enable a mindset and culture of continuous improvement Set performance expectations	
Industry 4.0 masterplan Create an Industry 4.0 digitization & automation masterplan.	Drive productivity through organizational innovation Operational excellence and compliance Drive productivity	
Industry 4.0 leadership behaviors Define and manage as projects all the leadership behaviors the plant will need to have moving towards the Factory of the Future.	Build the leadership qualities to sustain digitization automation Enable exponential productivity by building the attributes that will continuously improve operations using new technologies	

Table 3.4: Digital skills

Name and short description	Benefits	Losses affected
Virtual reality training Interactive 3D models to train production line employees.	Increased efficiency of employee time Creates a safer work environment Reduces downtime due to training Easily re-applicable to similar lines Fewer human errors in production lines	Training activities
Train and build digital skills Train end users in data value, integrity, modeling and analytics.	Drive productivity Create new operational insights Empower the shop floor to use technology to automate workflows Enable shop floor people to conduct data analysis, create new data, support data security	
Data analytics skill set Hire and develop data experts to build modeling and simulation capabilities, using data mining, probabilities, statistics, machine learning and predictive analytics.	Create new operational insights and drive continuous innovation Build manufacturing data analytics workflows and capability Develop the site expertise to use & analyze data to identify & solve losses	
Data value workshop Develop an understanding of existing data type, volume, sources and tasks.	Real-time monitoring Adaptation to current trends Data quality Interface management Resiliency: failover & recovery Knowledge management	
Build a digital cultural mindset across the organization Invest in building the digital & automation mindset of site leaders to drive the transformation.	Make new technologies an exponential growth opportunity for the organization Develop the mindset to drive autonomous, bottom-up innovation from the shop floor and unleash organizational innovation Drive productivity through organizational innovation	
Digital work assistance Build a digital knowledge base with easy-to-follow, step-by-step instructions for every process across the shop floor to assist workers in their tasks.	Improved employee morale Safer work environment Fewer defective products Less onboarding training required Increases SOPs compliance among employees	Downtime due to machine stops Downtime due to equipment failure Quality defects due to human error

Table 3.5: Operations execution

Name and short description	Benefits	Losses affected
Predictive maintenance Makes complex correlations from historical data to identify patterns that indicate failure probabilities.	Reduced machine downtime due to poor maintenance Lower maintenance operations costs Increased efficiency of employee time Reduced spare parts inventory Increased equipment life expectancy	Downtime due to machine stops and equipment failure Planned equipment maintenance and unavailability of spare parts during maintenance
Digital quality A unique quality management system across the plant combines quality data from automatic inspection systems, lab equipment and suppliers into a single source.	Less time spent on manual inspection & reporting Lower indirect quality assurance costs Fewer quality defects Faster time-to-market End-to-end quality visibility	In-line defects detection Quality reporting Quality inspection data analysis Quality incidents investigation Post-production quality control Material utilization losses
Condition-based maintenance Data-driven maintenance strategy that aims to detect machine failures at an early stage and react in a timely manner.	Increased uptime, asset life Lower spare parts consumption Improved equipment performance Safer work environment Fewer defective products	Downtime due to machine stops and equipment failure Planned equipment maintenance Downtime due to maintenance activities and unavailability of spare parts
Recipe management system Streamline the process of managing product formulations and machine setup specifications.	Increases operational efficiency Accelerates changeover process Enforces product quality Real-time insights into batch genealogy for product traceability & root cause analysis	Changeover speed Defective products due to human error Material utilization
Vision picking systems Visual detail order picking aids such as pick-to-light, pick-by-voice, RFID, handheld scanners and screens.	More organized orders/items Less stressed workers Fast order completion More accurate orders Higher customer satisfaction	Production speed Production cost Picking accuracy
Forklift sensory systems Forklift sensors to capture speed, position, weight and other data to improve safety and efficiency.	Safer workplace Accurate and fast transportation Accelerated loading, unloading & palletizing Reduced risk of inventory damage during transportation Fewer returns because of damaged goods	Material movement speed Safety incidents Fewer defects

Table 3.6: Operations management

Name and short description	Benefits	Losses affected
Manufacturing execution system Software system that manages and monitors all activities that take place on the production pipeline.	Simplicity that enables productivity Company-wide visibility of production execution View KPIs & manage operations through mobile devices Advanced, customized dashboards & KPI tracking M2M communication & IIOT approach Scalable with growing operational needs Infrastructure for advanced process control & analytics Improves root cause analysis for machine stops & quality defects	Downtime due to product changeover Material utilization losses Less time transferring data between production systems Less time spent reporting machine stops
Product lifecycle management system (PLM) Implement a plant-wide PLM system to effectively manage product performance and accelerate time to market.	Faster & cheaper new product initiatives Less scrap on prototyping Faster adapting to changing demand Better understanding of consumer behavior for each specific product	Material waste Quality defects
Condition monitoring systems Give visibility on equipment wear, measure key metrics (MTTF, MTTR, MTBF, MTBT etc.).	Less time spent on manual inspection & reporting Optimized usage of consumables, durables and materials Reduced waste Faster issue identification & troubleshooting Increased shop floor visibility across the plant	Downtime due to machine stops Downtime due to equipment failure Maintenance data collection & reporting
Advanced process control Automatically adjust production process parameters using dynamic models to optimize production & reduce material waste.	Reduced material waste Less time spent on manual inspection & reporting Ensures production continuity Ensures product uniformity Does not require operator expertise Reduced energy consumption	Material utilization Defects due to human errors Manual adjustments of process equipment Operator training Utility consumption
Industrial cybersecurity platform Manage application and security data in real time and at scale. Automate threat detection & management and streamline security.	Protect plant assets from harm Fewer manhours on monitoring, upgrading & troubleshooting systems Reduced likelihood of users gaining access to unauthorized systems	Data breach risks Data security personnel cost Threat management speed

Table 3.7: Robotics

Name and short description	Benefits	Material handling activities
Autonomous mobile robots Robots capable of navigating in an uncontrolled environment without the need for physical or electro-mechanical guidance devices.	Move & feed material from the shop floor to production lines or between lines Easy workflow modification Short on-site installation Can become a shared resource, units can be shared across multiple facilities Personnel can safely & collaboratively interact with them	Machine feeding Pick and place products into cases
Soft robotics Robots that leverage blind-to-shape grippers to pick practically any object regardless of shape without dropping or crushing it.	Great flexibility among different SKUs and objects Can be used to grab oddly shaped or slender objects Work alongside humans safely	Data manipulation processes
Digital robots Automate data-intensive tasks that are currently performed by humans.	Error free processes Allows humans to concentrate on more complex processes Scale up or down as per requirements Reduction in process costs Reduction in average cycling time	Palletizing speed Changeover speed Maintenance spend
Integrated end-of-line A range of diverse products with speed and agility.	Great flexibility regarding the diversity of products to be palletized High reliability and robustness	Pick and place products into cases Changeover speed
Integrated robot for pick & place Implement robotics to handle the manual & repetitive tasks of item placing and orientation adjustment.	Increased throughput Automated production Streamlined processes	Operator productivity Equipment usage efficiency Maintenance & consumables costs
Automated dispensing systems Simplify management and distribution of critical tools and parts.	Fewer manhours spent on locating & acquiring critical assets	Fewer warehouse administration tasks

Key insights for managers

When the group work is complete, we usually ask one or two groups to share their recommended roadmap with the others. This is always a rich, interactive exercise for all involved, including the facilitators.

It must be stressed that there is no "correct" solution to this exercise, nor a prescribed methodological approach that groups should use to arrive at their proposed roadmap. This is what makes this workshop so illuminating. That so many talented and experienced supply chain managers adopt different postures and propose different roadmaps speaks to the complexity of developing an Industry 4.0 roadmap.

This workshop helps illustrate how many different ways there are to approach constructing an Industry 4.0 roadmap. No two groups select the same 10 capabilities, which in and of itself is not surprising. However, what is insightful is *the criteria used to make the selections*.

Some managers will use return on investment (ROI) as their overriding factor. The faster a project can pay for itself, the more inherently attractive it is. Others will focus on product quality, deeming that to be the most important variable. Interestingly, some groups take more of a change management approach and either place the emphasis on capabilities that will have a quick win — thus demonstrating the viability of the Industry 4.0 transformation — or choose to develop organizational capabilities rather than technologies.

A separate but related question is the sequence of the capabilities. In an Industry 4.0 roadmap, the order in which the capabilities are implemented is critical. At a minimum, this is to ensure that the foundational technology is in place if it will be required for a different technology, for example a data lake if the company is looking to push advanced analytics capabilities. But there is also a managerial perspective to consider. We have observed managers argue that a roadmap must start with quick wins in order to gain credibility, or that high ROI projects should take priority to maintain senior manager sponsorship. Still others argue for beginning with the simplest capability, so that there is a low risk of failure.

At the end of a successful session, participants come away with an appreciation of the spectrum of Industry 4.0 technologies and the ways in which they can benefit industrial companies. At the same time, they have developed an understanding of the scope of the complexity involved.

REFERENCES

1 http://omnichannel.me/what-is-omnichannel/

2 Carsten Thoma. "The omnichannel shopper: Anytime, anyplace, anywhere." *Total Retail*, December 23, 2010. http://www.mytotalretail.com/article/the-omnichannel-shopper-anytime-anyplace-anywhere/all/

3 "ECR — Efficient Consumer Response." GS1. https://www.gs1.ch/en/home/topics/ecr---efficient -consumer-response

4 Renee Dudley. "Wal-Mart sees $3 billion opportunity refilling empty shelves." *Bloomberg*, March 28, 2014. https://www.bloomberg.com/news/articles/2014-03-28/wal-mart-says-refilling-empty-shelves -is-3-billion-opportunity

5 Renee Dudley. "Wal-Mart's new U.S. chief faces bare shelves, surly shoppers." *Bloomberg*, July 25, 2014. https://www.bloomberg.com/news/articles/2014-07-24/wal-mart-s-new-u-s-chief-facing-empty -shelves-grumpy-shoppers

6 Erin Moloney. "What retailers can learn from Walmart's incredible e-commerce growth in 2017." *Forbes*, October 16, 2017. https://www.forbes.com/sites/forbescommunicationscouncil/2017/10/16/ what-retailers-can-learn-from-walmarts-incredible-e-commerce-growth-in-2017/#7dfa41045c57

7 Ralf W. Seifert, Richard Markoff. "Amazon Fresh and the disruption of the supply chain." *IMD*, June 2017. https://www.imd.org/publications/articles/amazon-fresh-and-the-disruption-of-the-supply-chain/

8 Patrick Allen. "Why 'in-store availability' is very seldom accurate." *Lifehacker*, March 28, 2017. https:// lifehacker.com/in-store-availability-is-never-accurate-1793728577

9 Declan Carolan, Daniel Corsten, Danny Silverman. "The future of online category management." Efficient Consumer Response. September 5, 2017. http://ecr.pl/wp-content/uploads/2017/09/The -Future-of-Online-Category-Management-Sept-5th-20179031.pdf

10 "Introducing Amazon Go and the world's most advanced shopping technology." *Amazon*. December 5, 2016. https://www.youtube.com/watch?v=NrmMk1Myrxc

11 "Alibaba's Tao Café develops an unstaffed concept store." Breakfast Television Toronto. July 13, 2017. https://www.youtube.com/watch?v=P9e1DJpLsJI

12 www.shelfieretail.com/

13 https://traxretail.com/technology/

14 Christopher Bjork. "Zara builds its business around RFID." *Wall Street Journal*, September 16, 2017. https://www.wsj.com/articles/at-zara-fast-fashion-meets-smarter-inventory-1410884519

15 "adidas | !D Top | RFID-based EAS." *Nedap Retail*, August 30, 2016. https://www.youtube.com/watch ?v=U0-xl3F-Vuc

16 Debra Hofman. "How to measure the perfect order." *Gartner*, February 9, 2017. https://www.gartner .com/doc/3602917/measure-perfect-order

17 Ralf W. Seifert, Richard Markoff. "Project supply chains: A different world." *IMD*, July 2017. https:// www.imd.org/research-knowledge/articles/project-supply-chains-a-different-world/

18 Blair Freeman, Steve Haasz, Stefano Lizzola, Nicholas Seiersen. "Managing your cost-to-serve." *Supply Chain Forum: An International Journal*, Vol. 1. No. 1, Taylor & Francis, 2000.

19 Dani Deahl. "Amazon is increasing the cost of annual prime memberships from $99 to $119." *The Verge*, April 26, 2018. https://www.theverge.com/2018/4/26/17287528/amazon-prime-annual -membership-cost-increase-price-hike

20 "How shipping costs have put Amazon in a bind: Dealbook briefing." *New York Times*, April 27, 2017. https://www.nytimes.com/2018/04/27/business/dealbook/angela-merkel-trump.html?rref=col-lection%2Fsectioncollection%2Fbusiness-

21 Makoto Nakanishi. "Logistics giant emerges as unexpected savior for Central Bank." *Nikkei Asian Review*, March 16, 2017. https://asia.nikkei.com/Economy/Logistics-giant-emerges-as-unexpected -savior-for-central-bank

CHAPTER 4
LEADING A DIGITAL SUPPLY CHAIN TRANSFORMATION

This final chapter is a place for looking forward with optimism. We share four case studies, each based on a real company.

The cases illustrate the real-world challenges that companies face. For readers who have begun digital supply chain transformations in their own companies, these cases will sound very familiar in terms of trying to find and select the right capabilities, build the case for change and then overcome the resistance within the organization. Each case offers insights into how a company faced these challenges and broke through to success. Although no two contexts are identical, we hope that readers will find inspiration here, as well as useful strategic and tactical elements.

CHAPTER OVERVIEW

Topic 1: The three questions revisited

In Chapter 1, we explored the three essential questions to be addressed in order to form an effective digital supply chain transformation strategy:

1. How to identify the business drivers and pair them with the optimal solutions to ensure the right Industry 4.0 fit?
2. How to build the business case?
3. How to identify organizational inertia, scalability and resistance to change in order to overcome barriers to implementation?

The first case, HungryPet, is the true story – with identities disguised – of an executive who decided that a digital supply chain software as a service (SaaS) tool was the right path for his company.

This brief case is followed by a detailed examination of how the three questions can be used to identify the challenges and key success factors faced by an initiative. This demonstrates how every supply chain manager could benefit from using the same framework to analyze their digital transformation ambitions.

Topic 2: Lessons from a successful digital transformation

The second case explores the successful digital supply chain transformation of the global packaging giant Tetra Pak. The company made a strategic decision to bring digitalization into the core of its strategy. This case takes the reader through the key steps of how Tetra Pak came to this decision, built its organization, made strategic technology choices and succeeded in its implementation.

Topic 3: Digital transformation as a turnaround vector

Like Tetra Pak, the automobile parts supplier Faurecia provides a real-world example of a company greeting the challenge of transforming its supply chain to embrace digitalization. This three-part case series, based on actual events, focuses on a Faurecia factory in Abrera, Spain, outlining the choices the company faced and describing the decisions made before giving some insights from its experience. For Faurecia, there was more of a sense of a "burning platform" that created urgency to resolve the pressing situation of a money-losing factory. By positioning digital transformation as the key to a turnaround plan that fit the company's and its client's strategic priorities, the Faurecia case offers a powerful example of the potential of Industry 4.0 and supply chain digitalization (SCD).

Topic 4: Supply chain at the heart of omnichannel implementation

adidas Russia/CIS had had some success in leading IT transformation and experimenting with omnichannel capabilities. But with the country in economic turmoil, it was confronted with difficult choices. This two-part case series, based on extensive interviews, explores how, with the confidence of senior leadership, the supply chain can lead a digital transformation in the world of omnichannel retail, by placing itself at the heart of the business strategy, showing a willingness to lead and take risks in a moment of crisis.

Topic 5: Future supply chain careers

Here, we offer some perspectives for supply chain executives on the dynamics and forces impacting the profession. The capabilities enabled by digitalization are playing an outsized role in changing and accelerating long-term trends in the skill sets required and opportunities offered by a career in supply chain.

1 CASE STUDY | HUNGRYPET: CHALLENGES TO DIGITAL SUPPLY CHAIN INNOVATION

Richard Markoff and Ralf W. Seifert

You have recently been appointed as VP materials supply chain for "HungryPet." The company has dozens of factories, each making 200 different pet foods and treats. Each factory has about 100 vendors who provide 600 different packaging materials and food ingredients. HungryPet is investing €30 million in implementing an end-to-end-planning system, with understandably high expectations of improved supply chain performance. However, with your deep understanding of the company's supply chain, you realize that the key to reactivity lies in the information flow with the vendors, especially with the market's ever-increasing promotions and launches. This task is currently very time-consuming for the factory planners and the vendors, with requirements shared and plans agreed upon via spreadsheets, e-mail and endless phone calls to clear up confusion and reach decisions. In fact, this job is so tedious, it is often left to "lower-potential" planning staff to manage, both at HungryPet and at the vendors. But if this part of the supply chain is not addressed, the expected benefits in terms of agility and working capital will not be achieved.

After much reflection, you believe this is a unique opportunity for HungryPet to innovate by adopting a digital supply chain solution: Use a cloud SaaS (software as a service) vendor, interfaced with the new planning system, to make all requirements available to the vendors online. The vendors and HungryPet could use the SaaS as a collaborative platform to share requirements and confirmations electronically, eliminating confusion and back-and-forth, and facilitating faster decision making. There would also be exciting opportunities for performance management and data analytics to identify improvements.

Although you are excited about the possibilities, it is difficult to find a good vendor. It seems each manufacturer has its own way of communicating with vendors, making it difficult for you to explain what you need. On your own, you discover that a small niche vendor seems to have a perfect cloud-based tool for your concept. The large global provider of the new planning system also has a tool, although it is server-based, less of a functional fit and much more expensive.

You sit down to plan your roadmap to champion this ground-breaking idea and identify ahead of time the challenges you may face in convincing the company to move forward.

Insights from the case: The three question framework

This disguised case presents the situation confronting the new VP of materials supply chain at HungryPet. Newly arrived in the role, the VP realizes that the ambitious new project to implement an end-to-end planning system neglects the key bottleneck of materials supply between the HungryPet factories and their ingredient and packaging vendors.

In response to this situation, the VP conceives a new, innovative cloud solution to improve collaboration between HungryPet and its vendors. The solution would improve and streamline the information flow, saving planner time and propagating supply requirements and confirmations more quickly. This would protect and enable the expected benefits of the new planning system project.

The case provides a vehicle for considering the challenges any company might face in designing and implementing a digital supply chain solution. The focus is squarely on managerial challenges, not technical questions related to digital supply chain management and Industry 4.0.

The challenges facing the VP can be broadly divided into the responses to three questions, as described in Chapter 1 in the section "The Real Industry 4.0 Challenge":

1. How to identify the business drivers and pair them with the optimal solutions to ensure the right Industry 4.0 fit?
2. How to build the business case?
3. How to identify organizational inertia, scalability and resistance to change in order to overcome implementation barriers?

Examining the information available in the case, it is possible to project the following issues underlying each question:

1 How to identify the business drivers and pair them with the optimal solutions?

One of the challenges the VP faces is to explain why the proposed SaaS platform is right for HungryPet. He must be prepared to explain what business problem the SaaS platform is solving.

The case provides sufficient context to identify business drivers that connect to the proposed SaaS platform. The significant investment in an end-to-end planning system sends a strong signal that HungryPet is considering aligning supply and demand, ensuring that rapid decisions about production and responding to the market are made a top priority. The case also mentions that the number of new product launches and promotions is increasing.

The SaaS platform is perfectly in line with these objectives. The case strongly implies that the upstream material supply chain is a bottleneck in the overall supply chain. The SaaS platform would facilitate and accelerate not only information flows to the vendors by detailing the material requirements but also the necessary confirmations from the vendors to make viable and feasible planning decisions. This rapid propagation and return of information is essential to supply chain agility in the face of volatile market demands.

The business drivers for HungryPet are reactivity to market demands, increased promotional activity, shorter product lifecycles and catalogue turnover.

2 How to build the business case?

Several avenues are available for the VP materials supply chain to craft arguments that comprise a business case for HungryPet.

The case mentions that the planners are often lower-performing employees using processes that are manual and extremely labor intensive – e-mail, Excel spreadsheets and phone calls. This creates an opportunity to formulate a business case argument around labor productivity. An integrated digital solution would reduce the repetitive, low added-value tasks in the planners' routine. There would also be less confusion and disagreement around what the correct requirements are and the corresponding confirmation. All this would reduce the time needed to complete this step in the planning cycle

The VP has two options at this juncture: One would be to present the time savings as an opportunity to lower headcount and payroll, thus reducing factory overheads; the other would be to argue that the time saved could be repurposed into higher added-value activities. This could include collaborating with vendors on deeper bottlenecks or analyzing flows to optimize safety stocks or production runs.

This line of reasoning should lead to identifying other benefits of the SaaS platform that enter into the business case. The platform can act as a digital repository of information, capturing data that was not captured easily or at all when it was in the form of e-mails, spreadsheets and conversations. This data can be leveraged to apply analytics in any number of ways – populating vendor key performance indicators (KPI) in terms of service and reactivity, measuring volatility in the upstream supply chain, capturing volatility to better size safety stocks, and the like. Taking an even broader view, this creates an opportunity to train the planners in new skills and to take advantage of the new data sources, which would increase both the motivation and added value of employees.

Combining the accelerated information flow benefit with the data analytics and KPI benefits leads to the identification of another element of the business case — better service and lower working capital. By having a more reactive upstream supply chain, the key bottleneck in the HungryPet supply chain is partially alleviated. This improvement should enable HungryPet to lower safety stocks, react more rapidly to market changes and improve promotional lead times.

When formulating the business case, it is important to consider the impacts on the vendor as well. The arguments regarding productivity, leading to lower headcounts or higher added-value employee activity, apply just as much to the vendor as to HungryPet. This allows the VP to argue that vendors should lower their prices to HungryPet and even lower projected future increases. These would be direct improvements in the cost of goods sold (COGS) of HungryPet products.

The elements for the business case, then, are lower working capital, higher supply chain reactivity, increased employee productivity, employee upskilling, data analytical possibilities and improved COGS.

3 How to identify organizational inertia, scalability and resistance to change?

After finding the right solution to connect with the company's business drivers and building the business case, the VP material supply chain's concept faces a number of challenges that are firmly in the managerial realm.

The case mentions that HungryPet is undergoing a major IT initiative to implement an end-to-end planning system and that the provider of this system has a collaborative tool that is functionally less ideal and more expensive than other options. It would not be surprising for the VP to encounter resistance from the IT department about adding a new vendor, which would entail more complexity, more interfaces, new sourcing contracts and more interlocutors.

The case implies that cloud technology is new to the company, and likely new to IT, creating a potential competency challenge for IT when they are focused on the ambitious planning project. If IT endorses the SaaS initiative at all, it will likely be to push for the suboptimal solution offered by the planning system provider. The new vendor is identified as a small, niche entity. This opens up questions regarding its long-term viability, thus creating another argument against the preferred vendor. Another aspect of being a small, niche vendor is that it may be unable to scale up to meet the volume of all of HungryPet's factories.

These dynamics of IT resistance are explored in Chapter 3 in the section "Supply Chain Digitalization: IT Management Challenges."

The existence of two vendors that have a minimally viable solution will put pressure on the VP to provide justifiable vendor selection criteria and the required functional capability. The fact that cloud technology is new to HungryPet opens the door to concerns about cybersecurity, thus adding additional layers of time-consuming scrutiny.

Although the matter of under-skilled planners presents an opportunity to build a business case, it also presents a managerial challenge. The planners may well resist changes that require them to take on new skills, particularly any that they feel may endanger their continued employment. Passive resistance is a strong possibility. The vendors might experience the same risk with their planners.

The vendors might also feel pressure regarding their IT abilities and the need to invest in capabilities to use the SaaS platform. HungryPet's sourcing department may intervene, challenging the need for this solution and seeking to prevent avoidable disruptions in the commercial relationship between HungryPet and its vendors.

What is not addressed in the case is the question of who will pay for the SaaS platform. If HungryPet is to pay for the operating expenses of the platform, the business case becomes particularly critical. If the vendors are expected to pay, the commercial relationship will be strained and could undermine the endeavor.

The key challenges that the VP materials supply chain might encounter regarding organizational inertia, scalability and resistance to change are: IT aversion to complexity, IT innovation competence, scalability, vendor selection criteria, user resistance to change, payment models, cybersecurity and destabilization of partner relationships.

A non-exhaustive summary of the different challenges and key success factors can be found in **Table 4.1**. It is a powerful demonstration of the usefulness of "The Real Industry 4.0 Challenge" three-question framework for identifying the right path forward for success.

Table 4.1: HungryPet three-question framework

How to identify the business drivers and pair them with the optimal solutions?	How to build the business case?	How to identify organizational inertia, scalability and resistance to change?

• Reactivity to market demands
• Increased promotional activity
• Shorter product lifecycles
• Catalogue turnover
	• Higher supply chain reactivity
	  − Lower working capital
	  − Improved service
	• Employee productivity
	• Employee upskilling
	• Data analytical possibilities
	  − Volume analysis
	  − Trend vs. budget
	  − Supplier evaluations
	  − Mold capacity
	• Improved COGS
	  − Smoothed deliveries
	  − Fewer line stoppages
	  − Purchase price
	• Future capabilities
	  − Advance shipment notices
	  − Quality certifications
	  − Document exchange
		• IT aversion to complexity
		• IT innovation competence
		• Scalability
		• Vendor selection criteria
		• Niche vendor risks
		• User resistance to change
		• Payment models
		• Cybersecurity
		• Destabilization of partner relationships
		• Reliance on existing standards

2 CASE STUDY | TETRA PAK: A DIGITALLY ENABLED SUPPLY CHAIN AS A COMPETITIVE ADVANTAGE

Richard Markoff and Ralf W. Seifert

Tetra Pak, a world leader in packaging systems, understood that moving forward in operations excellence meant embracing Industry 4.0 – a new and technologically driven field.

Tetra Pak was built on innovation and commitment to excellence, and it showed in the company's recent operations successes. The company began implementing Total Productive Maintenance in the 1990s, a program of relentless, data-driven reduction and elimination of productivity losses. These efforts culminated in Tetra Pak receiving the first ever Japan Institute of Plant Maintenance Global Leaders Award in 2016.

Industry 4.0, the catch-all name given to a promising, cutting-edge suite of digital innovations, seemed like the natural next step in this journey. It comprised many disparate technologies, including cloud computing, augmented reality, artificial intelligence and predictive analytics. The common thread was the combining of the physical and cyber worlds to achieve new capabilities. The possibilities were endless but daunting.

Johan Nilsson, VP Industry 4.0 Solutions & Digital Services, described the fundamental challenge facing Tetra Pak:

> "We all know too little about this topic and are limited by our imagination. We need curious leaders to lead our digital transformation."

Starting from a position of humble curiosity, Tetra Pak would have to address fundamental questions to succeed in a digital transformation. How could it learn to work as a cross-functional organization? How could it select, out of a maze of technologies and vendors, the right ones for the company and its value proposition? How would it justify the required investments and bring a large, complex organization on board? What would success even look like on this transformation journey?

Company background

"A package should save more than it costs"

Since it was founded in Lund, Sweden in 1951, Tetra Pak and its packaging innovations have become a staple of kitchens around the world.

The company was best known for its distinctive four-sided packaging container for liquids, from which the name Tetra Pak was derived. Invented by Dr Ruben Rausing, it was the first oxygen-free technique for packaging liquids. Dr Rausing claimed that he came up with the concept while observing his wife making sausages by filling a long sausage casing tube and then cutting the sausages from the tube one by one as it was filled. He applied the same approach to filling liquids. A long tube of packaging material was continuously filled, and small segments of the filled tube were severed and sealed below the line of the rising liquid. The tubes were a cleverly layered combination of paper, aluminium and polymers that gave the package both strength and resistance while still being foldable.

The result was an oxygen-free, aseptic, stackable and easy-to-use package that most people will recognize (*refer to* **Exhibit 1**). The aseptic properties of the packaging meant that a cold chain was no longer required for many products, leading to reduced logistics costs and less product spoilage. Heavy, breakable packaging like glass could now easily be replaced. These innovations were all a result of Dr Rausing's vision that "a package should save more than it costs."

From there Tetra Pak innovated into different packaging configurations, including the now-ubiquitous Tetra Brik, which launched in 1963 (*refer to* **Exhibit 2**). By 2017, there were 12 different Tetra Pak packaging systems each offering various sizes, used for dairy products, juices and nectars, ice cream, cheese, dry foods, fruit, vegetables and pet food (*refer to* **Exhibit 3**).

More than just packaging

Tetra Pak's innovative packaging created more than just an opportunity for the company to sell packaging materials to consumer goods companies. Specialized production equipment was required to fill and seal the package while maintaining the quality, integrity and aseptic properties of the package and its contents. Tetra Pak therefore also provided this equipment, including processing equipment to manufacture the product with operations like blending, heating, cooling, pasteurizing, homogenizing and drying. These processing systems could be used for dairy, cheese, beverages, ice cream and prepared foods such as soup. In addition, the company offered filling equipment specifically designed to maximize quality and efficiency in filling its packaging, as well as providing distribution and material handling equipment like conveyors, rollers and automated packing machines.

In an attempt to be a complete service provider for its customers' manufacturing operations, Tetra Pak developed software platforms to manage, monitor and automate the operation of its equipment to minimize downtime, improve line efficiency and provide end-to-end operations visibility.

Tetra Pak today

By 2017 Tetra Pak was one of the largest packaging suppliers in the world, with almost 25,000 employees and €11.5 billion in sales in over 160 countries (*refer to* **Exhibit 4**). Sales of packaging materials for diverse food types accounted for about €8 billion, corresponding to an annual production of roughly 190 billion packages (*refer to* **Exhibit 5**).

The remaining share of turnover came from equipment and services. Almost 9,000 Tetra Pak packaging lines were installed in customer locations around the world, along with nearly 80,000 processing systems. Tetra Pak had 55 factories producing packaging materials and 5 research and development centers.

Competition

Over the years, competition had increased, particularly from "non-system suppliers." These companies sold packaging materials similar to Tetra Pak's that were compatible with Tetra Pak's packaging equipment, taking advantage of the fact that Tetra Pak's patents on its innovations had expired several years earlier. Other suppliers offered Tetra Pak-type packaging with their own integrated production systems.

Likewise, Tetra Pak's spare parts business was under attack from spare parts integrators that did not rely on original equipment manufacturers' (OEM) catalogue numbers. They offered the use of image recognition to identify spare parts and replace them with non-OEM equivalents.

Lastly, Tetra Pak faced competition from manufacturers of other packaging technologies, such as PET bottles and glass. These solutions were fully recyclable; Tetra Pak's goal was to have 40% of its packaging recycled by 2020.

Organizing a digitally enabled supply chain

Context

To maintain its market leadership in the face of competition, Tetra Pak embarked on a transformation journey to create a digitally enabled supply chain that would give it a competitive advantage. Peter Prem, VP Integrated Supply Chain, explained the company legacy:

> *"We started implementing TPM (Total Productive Maintenance) in the 1990s and have received over 110 TPM awards ...this has been achieved through a top down commitment to a bottom up culture of continuous improvement, guided by a relentless focus on data driven loss understanding and loss eradication."*

Talking about digital technologies, he noted:

> "*[They] give access to more sophisticated automation, higher resolution data, and greater depth of insight/analytics into quality and efficiency losses, but it is helpful to view all of these through the same TPM lens that has guided operations excellence over past decades. It is a continuum.*"

To help shape its digital efforts, Tetra Pak established three business priorities across its own operations and those of its customers to serve as broad objectives for investments:

1. **Make a step change in quality and performance**: With non-system competitors using the same technology as Tetra Pak, leveraging the vast amount of potential data of the end-to-end supply chain to ensure that it offered superior quality was seen as an important driver.
2. **Offer outcome-based service contracts**: Tetra Pak wanted to begin offering service contracts based on measurable successful outcomes, such as increasing the operational equipment efficiency of a filling line, rather than billing per technician hour or for spare parts used.
3. **Reinvent the package**: Spurred by competition and exploding omnichannel distribution, Tetra Pak saw the package as a way to enhance manufacturers' marketing intelligence as well as the consumer experience.

The digital transformation program

To accelerate and coordinate digitalization, in 2017 Tetra Pak began its Digital Transformation Program, led by Erik Winberg. The objective was to provide leadership and direction company-wide in all digital supply chain initiatives. Erik explained Tetra Pak's motivation:

> "*Digitalization is central to our strategy and to our value proposition. We needed to make a step change in the quality and performance of the products we deliver.*"

Erik echoed Peter's description of Tetra Pak's motivations:

> "*We launched a strategic study in 2016 to ask 'What can IT do for the business?' We found that we were lacking a mobile workforce and advanced analytics. Our data treatment was really just financial analysis.*"

This led to the realization that Tetra Pak had to take steps to ensure that it remained the technology leader in food and beverage packaging, a cultural positioning that was very strong within Tetra Pak.

A Digital Program Office was set up with a mandate to coordinate all selected digital pilots in collaboration with the operational business units. This allowed Tetra Pak to maintain a consistent policy for identifying potential projects and selecting the ones to move forward on, and to ensure coherence between the different initiatives. It was critical to avoid duplication or to pursue projects that, for example, might require data that the IT infrastructure could not deliver.

Erik explained that the decision to create the Digital Program Office outside of the existing IT organization was in large part due, ironically, to an extremely successful SAP rollout that had begun in 1999 and was fully deployed by 2013. Tetra Pak had succeeded in developing a single core system and instance of SAP for the company's entire global footprint. This heavy presence of SAP led many to the perception that Tetra Pak lacked agility in implementing IT systems. Erik noted:

> "We had an SAP-first approach, where we would not consider other solutions if SAP offered a similar capability."

Functional experts placed centrally in the organization had to approve any process changes to SAP. But this rigorous IT governance approach had its disadvantages when it came to Tetra Pak's ability to break outside its current scope and imagine innovative value-added offerings for customers. Erik explained:

> "Our own IT organization didn't have the competencies to inform our technology partner selection. They didn't step forward, hence the train left without them."

The desire to find best-in-class solutions while protecting its leadership position in food and beverages led Tetra Pak into a partnership with Microsoft to develop and implement the solutions that would emerge from the digital transformation.

Building the foundation

In addition to having a coordination function, the Digital Program Office also took on key centralized accountabilities for Tetra Pak's digital efforts. Critically, Erik created a Data Science Center of Excellence (CoE) within the Program Office.

The Data Science CoE provided a centralized strategy for identifying and securing the sources of all key data needed for Tetra Pak's selected projects. The CoE hired, trained and deployed data scientists who could develop the necessary advanced analytics algorithms for the projects to succeed. It would have been impossible for the functional teams in each project to replicate this expertise. Erik explained that starting with the Data Science CoE was critical. Any digital solution would need to rest on a solid data foundation, so these competencies had to come first and had to be internalized.

Erik realized that in order for Tetra Pak's digital transformation to succeed, the Program Office needed to garner support from all levels of the company. In a coordinated effort, they approached the broad base of Tetra Pak employees to democratize the digital transformation and foster local input and participation.

For example, having chosen Xamarin as a platform for building bespoke mobile apps, the Program Office invited employees across geographies and functions to Xamarin "hackathons." These two-day sessions enabled participants to brainstorm different mobile apps that could benefit Tetra Pak. At the same time, the Program Office could assess employees' skill levels and identify potential pain points when the time came to implement the new tools.

Once digital initiatives had been identified, the Program Office did not let up on the participative approach. They organized Design Sprints, which brought together outside technical expertise in coding and user experience, as well as data scientists from the CoE, and functional experts and end users from the affected business units. These teams would spend long days for up to a week in intensive sessions, debating the key questions about the best approach for a particular digital solution.

Then, over the course of several weeks, the Design Sprint teams defined the concrete deliverable of the digital project, identified potential risks and even developed and tested prototypes together.

Explaining the power of this inclusive approach, Peter said:

> "Our family spirit of dealing with employees with a warm heart and cool head helps to garner support for the various digitalization/transformation initiatives – as does clear commitment from the top, from the CEO and every member of the executive team and every level down. Historically, we have been good at change management – set the agenda for the change, build a guiding team, find quick wins, and don't let up. Now we needed to approach the whole change agenda in two frames – agile and flexible to explore and discover, and then systematic to deploy widely and make it stick."

The three digital capabilities

Tetra Pak identified three capability pillars to its digital transformation strategy. These were three distinct capabilities that the company deemed essential for understanding, structuring and communicating the importance and potential of digital technologies to create a competitive advantage:

1. Connected workforce: Provide information at the fingertips of our workers via mobile and wearable technology

2. Advanced analytics: Discover, interpret and communicate meaningful patterns in data
3. Connected solutions: Enhance or create new customer solutions by adding digital capabilities to our products and services.

As well as being aligned with the top business priorities for the digital transformation, these three capabilities were consistent with the company's view of its supply chain. Tetra Pak maintained that for the supply chain to be a competitive advantage, it had to include not only the company's internal operations but also the operations of its customers and vendors; and it had to consider the quality and value of the packaging, from materials through to a filled product for the consumer.

Within these capabilities, Tetra Pak chose to develop specific applications. The selection criteria were based not only on return on investment (ROI) but also on the broader benefits. Peter explained:

> "I'm puzzled when people talk about business cases only in terms of ROI, NPV [net present value] and payback years. Sure, those are the hard elements that frame a business case, but the soft elements and entrepreneurial calls are equally important. At Tetra Pak we always look at both hard and soft elements of a business case in making the call whether to do something. This of course makes it harder to rank investments and choose where to put precious resources, but that's what separates good business decisions taken with long-term perspective from those taken to extract short-term value and suit a quarterly agenda."

Tetra Pak is a privately held company with owners committed to long-term sustainable profitable growth. Investments in new and risky initiatives are sometimes approved because "We have to be first." The owners expect us to establish a leadership position in all our long-term strategic priorities. The whole company understands this.

The connected workforce

Tetra Pak's extensive network offered many intriguing possibilities for connecting the workforce digitally. Not only did the company have 55 factories producing packaging materials, but it also maintained and repaired tens of thousands of processing and packaging equipment installations at customers' premises. This was fertile ground for Tetra Pak to imagine disruptive digital approaches.

The smart and connected factory

Internally, Tetra Pak invested in sensors to monitor every step in the manufacture of its packaging materials to fully capture all of the potential areas of production disruption. The amount of data was staggering. Per Dmitry Smolin, Director of the Smart and Connected Factory Program noted:

"We record, on a daily basis, one billion data points from all of our machines. For example, a laminator has 400 sensors which are constantly recording information. The different information sits in different systems in our factories, so it is not really connected and we are using maybe 1% of the information in our analyses."

In addition to equipment sensors, Tetra Pak automated all movements through RFID (radio-frequency identification) sensors and Automated Guided Vehicles that moved goods from the lines into trucks at the loading bay. All this data was collected, aggregated and displayed in an integrated Manufacturing Execution System designed by Tetra Pak to meet its specific needs.

Externally, Tetra Pak saw the complex machines it provided for clients as an opportunity to collect and leverage data in a way that could enable it to service these customers faster and more efficiently. It installed remote sensors on the equipment to collect data about a machine's operation, including hours operated, speeds, temperature, pressure and other critical data points (*refer to* **Exhibit 6**).

By 2017, over 20,000 different pieces of equipment were connected and compiled data through a cloud platform (Microsoft Azure in this case). In order to do this, the Data Science CoE had to work with functional groups to identify which data would be collected, whether it would be in batches or via streaming, how to identify it and how best to store it so that it could be properly exploited.

To complete the picture, Tetra Pak needed not only data from its machines but also data from the customer that was external to the machines. This might include quality properties of the product being filled, the ambient temperature in the factory or the air pressure provided to the machines.

Creating, structuring and managing this factory connectivity was a challenge in itself, but it was a prerequisite to enable Tetra Pak's vision for the smart and connected factory. This vision was directly linked to Tetra Pak's ambition to move its service offering to outcome-based contracts. Johan Nilsson explained that Tetra Pak's outcome-based service contracts included equipment not supplied by Tetra Pak, such as compressors or water pumps needed by the whole factory. If asked by the customer, it could even include competitors' equipment within the same factory.

Advanced analytics

Predictive maintenance and process control

Having real-time access to hundreds of discrete data points for each item of equipment allowed Tetra Pak to move forward with visible, tangible capabilities that would improve customers' performance with its machines. All data were analyzed by the Global Analytical Team at the Digital Program Office at company headquarters in Lund, Sweden.

The technical teams there, with the help of the Data Science CoE, used advanced analytics from the array of sensors to generate a virtual copy, also known as a digital twin, of a customer's production installation. With this digital twin, Tetra Pak technical experts tried to anticipate breakdowns or equipment failures before they occurred (*refer to* **Exhibit 7**). This enabled Tetra Pak to deploy technicians in a planned, controlled manner to the customer's factory for preventive maintenance. This meant less stress and unplanned production stoppages for the customer and a more professional service offering for Tetra Pak.

A centralized repository of data from external and internal sources, obtained from thousands of pieces of equipment, allowed Tetra Pak to consolidate the potential learning from the data. Advanced analytics and predictive algorithms are much more powerful with larger data pools from which to learn patterns. Having a harmonized data approach that could aggregate this data was a key element in this.

An example of the power of pooled, historical data is the way Tetra Pak resolved a long-standing, recurring quality issue on the folds of the final formed package. Combining offline data from its vendors with inline process control data from its internal factories allowed it to shed light on the possible cause of the poorly folded corners and reduce the incidence of this problem at its customers. Using machine learning and image recognition of the finished product coming off the line at speeds of up to 10 units/second, Tetra Pak could identify problems in folds on customer filling lines. It then connected these incidents with data gathered just a few seconds earlier on, for example, the conditions of packaging material being unspooled, and then with data from the Tetra Pak factory that produced the packaging material and even the raw material suppliers.

Applying machine learning to find underlying patterns in material quality specification or environmental conditions enabled Tetra Pak to fine-tune these parameters to significantly lower the number of quality incidents on packaging folds. This meant customers did not have to scrap finished products, there were fewer technician calls and production speeds on the filling lines improved.

Mobile and virtual access solutions

One powerful way that Tetra Pak leveraged its smart and connected factory data was in the deployment of field technicians to customer facilities for installations, repairs and maintenance.

Mobile applications, generated through the workshops with Xamarin, informed technicians about work assignments and provided information beforehand, so that they were prepared to solve the specific problem when they arrived on site (*refer to* **Exhibit 8**).

Once in front of the equipment, technicians used HoloLens augmented reality gear from Microsoft to call up and consult manuals and guides. The HoloLens, in conjunction with the mobile application, was connected to expert teams in Lund to help identify and resolve technical issues rapidly.

This enabled Tetra Pak to deploy technicians faster, resolve problems faster and limit customer downtime. When used in conjunction with the predictive maintenance capability, Tetra Pak could demonstrate significant performance capability in operational equipment efficiency, compared with other equipment manufacturers.

Johan stressed how critical it was to have field technicians deeply involved in Tetra Pak's efforts on the customer factory floor:

> *"Many companies struggle to implement Industry 4.0 solutions and document the savings because these improvements don't happen in the boardroom. You really need people who know the various processes well."*

Connected solutions

Tetra Pak believed that its packaging could play a bigger role than simply storing the product for customers. The package contained valuable information for the consumer, was an integral part of the product and was the way in which the consumer interacted with the consumable inside.

Tetra Pak was developing and deploying what it called the connected package. Working with interested customers, it could place a unique Quick Read (QR) code on each package. Consumers could scan this QR code with their smartphone to access Tetra Pak's customer database, which would provide them with information about the product's ingredient provenance, detailed nutritional information and more.

This turned the package into more than a container; it was now an information channel between Tetra Pak's customer and the consumer. Peter explained:

> *"The ability for packaging to take on new capabilities by being uniquely identifiable, by providing a more direct communication channel with the consumer, by enabling further expansion of ecommerce, and by gathering deeper actionable insights into consumer behavior translates into the need for an end-to-end "smart and connected" supply chain."*

Having a connected package enabled Tetra Pak to offer customers more granularity in product traceability, tracking a single product up through the supply chain to identify every step on the way and which specific ingredient lots were used. This was seen as a critical value proposition in the event of quality incidents and product recalls and in order to meet ever more stringent regulatory requirements.

The connected package might soon also offer the manufacturer more granularity in the effectiveness of digital promotions, although that day has not arrived yet. "It is a bit more visionary and less clear today," noted Erik. Johan concurred, describing connected packages as a "leap of faith that the revenue models will emerge."

The road ahead

Over the previous three years Tetra Pak had worked hard to implement a digitally enabled supply chain that supported its business priorities. But it could not stop there. Erik summed up the challenge of supply chain digital transformation:

> "Digital transformation is about catching up with technology, but it's also about the speed of change, working in a more agile way and changing the way we work, changing the solutions we deliver and ultimately changing how we are perceived by the customer."

Tetra Pak's vision moving forward was captured by its ambition of "Enhancing customer experience through digital tools." This put the emphasis on supply chain visibility, which would have to extend outside of Tetra Pak's internal activities since, as Peter pointed out, "80% of the data needed to run an effective global supply chain resides with partners."

This poses as many challenges as opportunities. For example, following the Petya cyberattack that impacted A.P. MøllerMærsk in June 2017, some Tetra Pak customers unilaterally decided to cut all connections due to cybersecurity fears.

The supply chain control tower

Tetra Pak had already had an advanced planning system (APS) in place for several years. The APS enabled it to consolidate demand from its various geographic markets, match the demand to the available capacity, and allocate production to different factories. But Tetra Pak wanted to go much further and extend its APS through an end-to-end supply chain control tower.

A supply chain control tower would work with the stock, demand and production plans internally, as well as capturing and integrating the stock and production of Tetra Pak's vendors and customers. This would make it possible, for example, to make production decisions based on the detailed availability of materials produced by vendors, not only what was in Tetra Pak's stocks. Similarly, Tetra Pak could fine-tune its production schedules based on precise information on customer production timing, not on rough demand plans.

Tetra Pak's vision for its supply chain control tower included integrating data from its transportation management system (TMS), which provided real-time information on the status of inbound and outbound shipments. The result would be a complete picture of stock, service and production in Tetra Pak's supply chain, from vendors to customers, including goods in transit.

The logistics blockchain

Tetra Pak participated in the first and most notable pilot for using the distributed ledger technology known as blockchain to improve product traceability. In partnership with the shipping company Maersk, IBM and consumer goods companies like Nestlé, the blockchain was tested as a way to track the lifecycle of food ingredients. From harvest to consolidation to processing, filling and to the shelf, the blockchain could provide a way to securely offer consumers immediate access to information on the origins of their food. It would also enable traceability to immediately identify which products had been impacted in the event of a food ingredient quality incident.

The participants deemed the pilot to be successful and it was deployed with Walmart in the United States in 2018. Tetra Pak, along with Walmart, Nestlé, Unilever and others, was a key player in this new operational blockchain called the Food Trust, which managed 1 million different products in about 50 different categories.

From prediction to cognition

Although Tetra Pak's capabilities in predicting machine failures and analyzing the sources of chronic, long-standing quality problems were significant, the company believed that it could get even more out of its data science competencies.

From a connected supply chain, which enabled data collection and structure, to predictive analytics that allowed for smarter and faster service, repairs and product quality, the next step would be to develop cognitive data capabilities. Tetra Pak saw cognitive data as the ability to use data not just to make predictions but also to make automated decisions based on advanced analytics.

A fertile ground for this would be to leverage Tetra Pak's plans for the supply chain control tower and implement "no-touch planning." Since it had data on stocks, production capacity and market demand plans, the control tower would more autonomously decide which factory would be allocated production requirements to optimize service, stock, and production and transportation costs.

Expanding the smart and connected factory

Internally, Tetra Pak planned to connect all of its packaging systems together to better manage and drive production efficiency. As Dmitry Smolin noted:

> *"We'll be able to connect information not only between the different systems within one factory, but also between factories, making our global converting base into truly one global factory. With the help of this data, we will be able to analyze issues we could not do before. We actually estimate that when we connect all the factories together, we will get access to 10 billion data points – ten times more than we have today – and we will be able to analyze 100% of those in the future."*

Speaking about these ambitious visions, Johan described them using a phrase often heard at Tetra Pak:

> *"You have to dream big, you have to start small, but most importantly you have to start."*

At the same time, he acknowledged:

> *"The culture at Tetra Pak is very much that you can do things but of course you then also have to show results."*

Exhibit 1: Original tetrahedron Tetra Pak packaging

Source: Company information

Exhibit 2: Tetra Brik packaging

Source: Company information

Exhibit 3: Tetra Pak packaging models (2017)

Source: Company information

Exhibit 4: Tetra Pak sales by geographic region (2017)

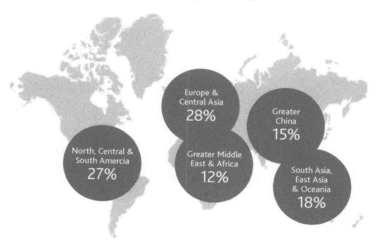

Source: Company information

Exhibit 5: Tetra Pak sales by market segment (2017)

Liquid dairy	Prepared food
56%	6%
Juice & nectars	Cheese
14%	3%
Still drinks	Wines & spirits
9%	2%
Dairy alternatives	Ice cream
7%	1%

Other 2 % (including dairy powder, carbonated still drinks and cosmetics)

Source: Company information

Exhibit 6: The smart and connected factory

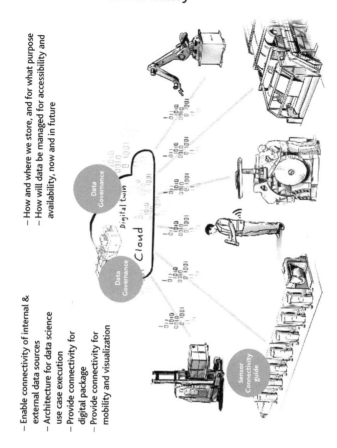

Source: Company information

Exhibit 7: Predictive maintenance and process control model

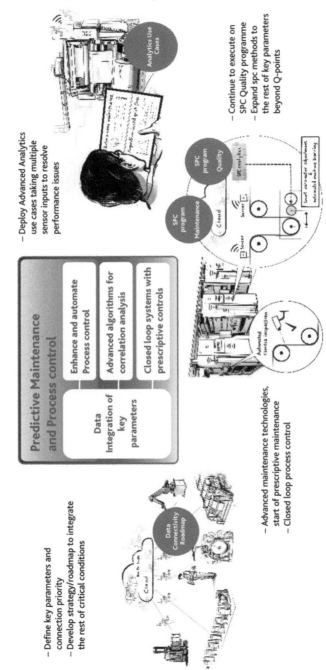

Source: Company information

Exhibit 8: Mobile and virtual access solutions

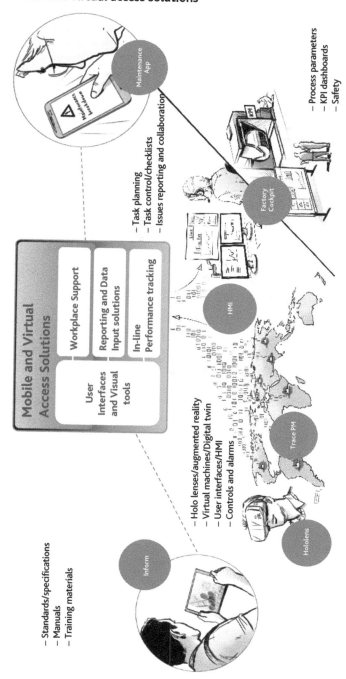

- Process parameters
- KPI dashboards
- Safety

Maintenance App

Factory Cockpit

- Task planning
- Task control/checklists
- Issues reporting and collaboration

HMI

Trace PM

Hololens

Mobile and Virtual Access Solutions

User Interfaces and Visual tools	Workplace Support
	Reporting and Data Input solutions
	In-line Performance tracking

- Holo lenses/augmented reality
- Virtual machines/Digital twin
- User interfaces/HMI
- Controls and alarms

Inform

- Standards/specifications
- Manuals
- Training materials

Source: Company information

Insights from the case: Tetra Pak's digital transformation journey

This case describes the packaging supplies and equipment vendor Tetra Pak and its digital transformation program. It details why Tetra Pak undertook this initiative, how it organized the program and identified and selected which technologies to implement, and the steps it took to overcome implementation challenges. The case structures the company's journey around its priorities – connected solutions, advanced analytics and a connected workforce. The emphasis is on the value proposition of Industry 4.0 and supply chain digitalization for both Tetra Pak and its customers.

As with the HungryPet case, a useful way to look at Tetra Pak's journey is through the lens of challenges and key success factors. Although categorization can be difficult and perhaps fuzzy at the edges, eight broad categories can be used to distinguish the different challenges and key success factors: (1) technology, (2) platforms and standards, (3) customers, (4) competition, (5) benefits, (6) management, (7) implementation and (8) people.

Looking at them each in turn illustrates how Tetra Pak was able to build and execute a successful supply chain digitalization program.

1 Technology

The key challenge in terms of technology is for Tetra Pak to determine which Industry 4.0 capabilities it would like to explore for implementation. With so many possibilities available, it can be daunting to know where to begin. The category "benefits" will clearly influence this decision – and possibly even be predominant in a publicly traded company – but a useful point of discussion is whether return on investment (ROI) is the only, or even the most important, selection criterion. Tetra Pak's development of a connected factory at the customer matched a company strategy of expanding its service offering and shifting to an outcome-based service model. This can provide competitive differentiation that goes beyond an ROI-based perspective.

Linked to the question of which capabilities to explore is which vendor to work with. Companies are inundated with vendors proposing new technologies, often with offers to pilot them at no cost in order to develop use cases to spur future sales. Tetra Pak acknowledged the challenge of breaking out of the restraints of SAP and looking for other vendors, even if it meant complications for the IT or purchasing departments. The company ended up partnering with Microsoft, even though there were doubts about Microsoft's technical abilities in some areas. The result was a productive partnership for both.

The combination of technology and vendor selection both figure when it comes to scalability – the company's ability to expand the geographic or operational scope of implementation. Even if a technology and vendor appear to be a perfect fit, it is often the case that Industry 4.0 vendors do not have a global scale or the financial resources to expand their operations.

As the case cites, cybersecurity is increasingly prominent as a consideration. It is not only malware or viruses – as mentioned in the case with the example of Petya – but also the security of confidential or proprietary data and intellectual property, highlighted for example in the hacking of Equifax in 2017 or Marriott International in 2018. Since many Industry 4.0 solutions involve cloud computing and the internet of things (IoT), the question of cybersecurity cannot be avoided. This puts the spotlight on the management dilemmas involved in seeking to follow a first adopter in Industry 4.0 implementations.

2 Platforms and standards

The more the proposed solutions are in the Cloud, or connected to another solution, the more critical the category of "platforms and standards" is. As with any new technology, the ability to integrate and interface with legacy systems and other new technologies must be explored. This will drive many choices about what data is available and what standard to use. Tetra Pak made the creation of the Data Science Center of Excellence (CoE) one of the first steps in its transformation, highlighting the critical importance of the data model to success.

When working on platforms that collaborate with other entities – be it companies, consumers or governmental departments – standards and regulations must inevitably be established and respected. They could be as basic as data attributes – such as coding or measurement standards – but they could also have regulatory implications such as data safety and consumer confidentiality laws. For example, Tetra Pak needs to consider these elements in its connected package, as well as its novel blockchain traceability project. Using an RFID chip rather than a QR code could raise privacy objections, for example.

3 Customers

When it comes to customers, a company must ensure coherence between its Industry 4.0 strategy and the company's overall strategy regarding its markets and value proposition. One of the strongest pressures in many industries is to increase agility, which may mean the ability to provide a service or product quickly but it could also mean the capacity to change the service or product quickly. There is a strong theme of agility enhancement in Industry 4.0 and, along with it, the ability to offer customization – the ability to tailor products and services to groups of customers or even individual customers.

Agility and customization are two aspects of customer expectations: What does the customer want and — even more challenging — what will the customer want and be willing to pay for in the future? If the Industry 4.0 choices are not consistent with the broader company vision of customers' expectations, there is a risk that the choices will be strictly limited to short-term ROI considerations.

If the collaboration between technological possibilities and consideration of customer expectations is fully explored, it may expose Blue Oceans — new markets or new value propositions that did not previously exist and can create entire revenue streams for a company.

4 Competition

Tetra Pak is clearly aware of the competition and sees Industry 4.0 as a way to differentiate itself in the eyes of its customers. The strategic choices the competition makes often inform the choices a company makes in investing in Industry 4.0 capabilities. In many of its new initiatives, Tetra Pak has decided to be the first adopter, positioning itself as a pioneer and trailblazer. This comes with the risk that the technology will not work, or will not be accepted, or will not bring the expected benefits. Another possibility is to be the first follower, letting the competition take the risks and then to step in quickly afterwards, having learned from the missteps of others. But clearly Tetra Pak does not want to be a laggard, trailing the competition in transforming its supply chain towards digitalization and Industry 4.0.

5 Benefits

Building the financial case for a new technology is a key challenge in many companies. Emphasizing the financial return is an understandable reaction to the potentially confusing array of choices a company faces — and it is especially hard when evaluating true innovations.

The leaders of the transformation may be challenged to provide estimates of labor productivity, in other words how much time (and therefore money) will be saved on an existing operation thanks to the proposed technology. Labor is one example of an operating cost, but other elements of operating costs are cost of goods, utilities and waste. Similarly, there may be an impact on inventories due to increased agility or changes to run sizes. Predicting the savings in these areas is often difficult, but particularly so when a company is a first adopter. Weighing against the proposed operating cost savings is the capital investment in the technology, an investment for which the company naturally seeks a return.

But the biggest challenge may be in articulating the intangible benefits of an Industry 4.0 transformation. These are benefits to the company that are not easily captured in an ROI approach. As mentioned earlier, the benefits may lie in matching the business strategy with customer expectations, but they could also be in areas that are difficult to quantify. One example might be sustainability, another corporate social responsibility. The case mentions Tetra Pak's company culture of innovation. If management deems this culture to be important, then it has to be nurtured and fostered and considered a benefit worthy of investment.

6 Management

The case highlights the importance of having the support of senior management, who provided a vision of the company's culture. Tetra Pak appointed a senior executive to lead the transformation, signaling the importance of the effort.

To that end, Tetra Pak defined and installed clear organization and governance to lead it on the journey, defining the steps, the deliverables, the accountabilities and the resources needed. Resources do not only imply money; they also include talented people and the time and attention of senior management.

These strong signals help establish collaboration between functional and technical teams. The risk is that the two types of team do not seek the best alignment between the needs of the different business functions (purchasing, planning, production, etc.) and the technical complexities and capabilities of the proposed solutions. This collaboration is also essential between the different business functions. Given the nature of the business drivers discussed here and explored by Tetra Pak, in the customer connected factory, for example, input from sales, marketing, supply chain and design all need to be considered.

7 Implementation

As with the implementation of any new digital technology, digitally enabling the supply chain is a project that must be planned carefully to ensure minimal business disruption. This includes contingency planning so that if the new capability does not work as anticipated, it is possible to return to the previous way of working or another alternative.

Some new technologies may require data to "prime the pump" of the new capability, making data migration a critical element to implementation success. Predictive analytics is a good example of this step.

Even if a technology proves effective in a pilot project and successfully scales to, for example, a factory, there is still a challenge in implementing a company-wide rollout. Differing levels of maturity, process and know-how across sites can create a barrier to successful implementation across the span of a company's whole supply chain.

Many Industry 4.0 initiatives require other actors external to the company. In Tetra Pak's case, this includes customers for its connected factories, and the blockchain traceability project will require collaboration from end to end along the supply chain. A key challenge is to work to achieve network buy-in for these efforts. This will require patience, persuasion and leading by example, as Tetra Pak is doing with Maersk and IBM.

8 People

Not to be overlooked is the challenge of aligning people in the organization and overcoming the inherent resistance to change and skepticism about new technologies. It is easy for proponents of Industry 4.0 to forget that not everyone shares their passion and excitement. Tetra Pak recognized this challenge and, apart from senior management sponsorship, implemented hackathons and Design Sprints to foster participation from the company's workforce and gain buy-in. This helped reduce the fear of the unknown that some might experience and ensure no one felt neglected or that their voice was being ignored in the transformation.

Recognizing that IT is often reluctant to adopt technologies that will increase complexity, interfaces and the number of vendors, Tetra Pak built an organization outside of IT to avoid potential obstacles.

Lastly, Tetra Pak understood the limitations of its existing talent pool and recruited data science experts to form the new CoE.

Summarizing the challenges and key success factors

The challenges and key success factors presented here are not an exhaustive list, but they serve to illustrate the many potential challenges in a successful Industry 4.0 and digital supply chain transformation. **Table 4.2** summarizes Tetra Pak's digital transformation journey.

Table 4.2: Tetra Pak challenges and key success factors

Technology	Platforms and Standards	Customers	Competition	Benefits	Manage-ment	Implemen-tation	People
Capability	Legacy systems	Agility	First adopter	Labor productivity	Vision	Migration	Resistance to change
Vendor selection	Cloud	Expectations	First follower	Inventory	Leadership	Contingency planning	Skepticism
Scalability	Data models	Blue Oceans	Laggard	Capital investment	Governance	Network buy-in (upstream/ downstream)	Fear
Cyber security	Integration	Customizing		Operating costs	Functional/ technical collaboration		Training/ expertise
	Regulatory approval			Intangible benefits	Resources	Company-wide rollout	Winners/ losers
				ROI			Recruiting

3 CASE STUDY | FAURECIA DIGITAL TRANSFORMATION (A)

Amit Kumar Singh, Yanik Cantieni, Marco Amici and Carlos Cordon

Greg Dupont arrived at Faurecia Interior Systems' Abrera plant in Spain in January 2015, eager to prove his leadership capabilities. Faurecia's management had identified Greg as a natural choice to lead Abrera as the plant manager. His mission was to assess the situation and the root causes of the plant's continuous loss-making operations, propose suitable strategic options and implement and execute the chosen options.

The Abrera plant manufactured injection molding parts for small cars, but it was facing a number of challenges. Since 2003, when Faurecia had acquired the Abrera plant, it had lost €3 million per year (*refer to* **Exhibit 1**). The financial situation was exacerbated by the fact that Abrera was operating in a small industrial cluster with essentially one customer – Volkswagen – and five Tier 1 suppliers. In addition, the Abrera shop floor operations had been plagued with inefficient processes, unpredictable downtimes and difficulties with machinery maintenance.

Greg spent his first few months trying to understand what was going on at the plant. After about six months, he received an invitation from Faurecia's head office in Paris to present his strategic options and recommendations about Abrera's future to Faurecia's board in two weeks' time.

As Greg sat in his tiny office at the plant, he realized he only had five options to present to the board:

1. Business as usual
2. Close the plant
3. Sell the plant to a local competitor
4. Turn the plant around
5. Invest in new areas of growth.

Greg knew that the board would expect a detailed financial analysis for each option, so he had work to do.

Background: Faurecia and Faurecia Interior Systems

Faurecia, a French-based corporation with around 109,000 employees globally, was the sixth largest international automotive supplier and preferred partner to major automakers around the world. It was a global technology leader in its three business areas – automotive seating, interior systems and clean mobility. The Abrera plant was part of Faurecia Interior Systems (FIS). FIS's core business was injection molding (IM). The supplier of its IM machines was Engel, its molds were designed in house, manufactured in China and surface finished in Europe.

The municipality of Abrera in Catalonia, Spain, north of Barcelona, had a population of 12,000 people and had been home to FIS's plant since 2003. The Abrera plant had around 370 employees and 65 suppliers. It mostly worked on small cars for three customers – the main ones being the Volkswagen group and Nissan. In particular, Abrera manufactured IM parts for the Seat León and the Audi Q3, plus it was involved in foaming, welding, assembling, painting and milling parts. The Seat plant in Barcelona produced half a million cars per year on 2.5 production lines.

FIS Abrera's main competitors were: SMP (Samvardhana Motherson Peguform) with two plants in the area of Abrera, Grupo Antolin, Yangfeng (located further away near Valencia, but still considered a competitor), Reydel and CK (Calsonic Kansei). The competitive rivalry among suppliers was high and price wars had led to reduced profit margins (refer to **Exhibit 2** for more details). In addition, three main trends in the automotive industry – autonomous cars, electric cars and digitalization – were having a massive impact on the manufacturing and supply chain processes. To be competitive in this complex automotive environment, FIS Abrera needed to face up to a number of challenges.

As of 2017, Faurecia's global sales were €20.2 billion. It served all major car manufacturers globally, e.g. Ford, Fiat Chrysler, Peugeot Citroen, Renault-Nissan, BMW and VW, from its headquarters in Nanterre, next to Paris (refer to **Exhibit 3**), and the 290 factories plus 30 research and development (R&D) centers in 35 countries. One in four automobiles was equipped by Faurecia.

FIS developed and produced instrument panels and central consoles, cockpits, door panels and modules, acoustic products and modules and decorative components out of wood, aluminum, plastic and glass. FIS's global sales were €5.4 billion in 2017, with 85 production sites and 8 R&D centers in 23 countries. Faurecia was recognized as number one worldwide in this segment. Its main global competitors were Yangfeng, IAC, Grupo Antolin and SMP. (Refer to **Exhibit 2** for Porter's Five Forces related to Faurecia Interior Systems.)

The Abrera plant was acquired by Faurecia in 2003, to expand into the promising Spanish market, which over time grew to become the second largest manufacturer of automobiles in Europe with more than 2.8 million units produced in 2016, representing 10% of the gross domestic product. The Abrera plant, which produced injection molded (IM) parts and components – such as cockpits and door panels – for the automotive industry, was equipped with several IM units, machinery and assembling units (e.g. for milling or clipping), as well as a basic paint unit.

The key original equipment manufacturers (OEMs) in the Spanish market were Ford and the VW group, particularly Seat. Seat, created in the 1950s by Francisco Franco in partnership with Italian car maker Fiat, but sold to Volkswagen in 1986, was the Abrera plant's main customer thanks to its geographical proximity to the Seat plant in Martorell, just six kilometers from Abrera.

Challenges at the Abrera plant

Despite having Seat as its main customer, the Abrera plant had experienced huge losses of €3 million per year since 2003 (*refer to* **Exhibit 1**). This lack of profit was rooted in the final customer – Volkswagen (VW) – which used five suppliers in the area, but only had enough orders for two or two-and-a-half decent-size suppliers. The breakeven in automotive was about €50 million in sales per plant, so VW was barely keeping its suppliers alive, despite its promises to expand and grow. This resulted in price wars among the suppliers.

In 2014, Abrera had total sales of €78.2 million and €76 million in 2015, which included product, assembly, design and tooling sales. The cost of raw materials was very high at 67% of revenues, direct labor (plant workers) was 16%, indirect labor (quality, maintenance) was 6% and manufacturing was 8%, resulting in a gross margin of almost 0%, selling, general and administrative expenses (SG&A) of 3% and earnings before interests and taxes (EBIT) of -3% (*refer to* **Exhibit 1**).

As of 2017, the workforce in Abrera – which was supported by a strong union – was 327 employees: 268 direct labor and 59 indirect labor employees. The average seniority was 15 years and the median seniority was 20 years. If Faurecia were to close the Abrera plant, it would cost more than €15 million in social costs.

There were two different production models for building cars. The American model, employed by Ford and the German carmakers, was very rigid. It required large upfront capital expenditure (CAPEX), but once the equipment was depreciated, the cost of running the plant was inexpensive. The Japanese model, which employed lean manufacturing, was flexible, based on people and required very little CAPEX. Faurecia was trying to have the best of both models. In terms of the American, it had one large machine that could handle 100% of volume and in terms of the Japanese, it had four smaller machines that could each handle 25%. These machines were meant to help improve the layout of the Abrera plant, which was old and messy.

Greg Dupont

Greg Dupont was a 30-something-year-old French engineer with a prestigious MBA and global supply chain experience in various groups worldwide. In 2015, he was the global supply chain director at Faurecia's headquarters in France. His energy, experience and commitment, along with the ability to see the bigger picture in a company as complex as Faurecia, got him a lot of praise from senior management. He delivered greatly on many projects and process improvements worldwide, all of which he had accomplished with no direct reports, just functional leadership. For instance, he led the working capital initiative that reduced the production inventory levels from 3.8% of production sales in 2013 to 3.3% in 2014.

Greg had a huge level of confidence and was very outspoken with a clear idea of what he wanted to achieve. He was an expert in lean supply chain management, spoke quickly from his heart and had very little patience. With an expanding family, and a Chinese wife, he wanted to prove that he could deliver not only in the ivory tower of the Faurecia Corporation in Paris, but also on the ground, resolving key issues directly in the field and working closely with the business. His motto was "continuous improvement, day by day." While Faurecia's top management had identified Greg as having good potential for senior leadership, it also realized that there were limitations in his attitude and experience.

Given the issues at the Abrera plant and Greg's desire to prove himself in the field, Faurecia's management appointed him to lead Abrera as the plant manager in January 2015 (*refer to* **Exhibit 4**). His mission was to assess the situation and the root causes of this continuously loss-making operation, propose suitable strategic options and implement and execute the chosen option.

The options

When Greg moved to Abrera, he spent his first few months understanding what was going on. Since he did not speak a single word of Catalan, it took some time for the team, which was governed by very senior workers with strong union ties, to accept him. As Greg explained:

> "The team's morale was pretty low when I arrived as they were the bad guys in the eyes of the group (having constantly lost 3% operating margin per year for the past 12 years), and Abrera's main customers – VW & Audi – were very demanding, always sending the team challenging messages. So, we had to break this negative spiral, and this took me a good six months, but when the first success came, it quickly turned into a virtuous cycle."

After six months, Greg received an invitation from Paris to present his strategic options and recommendations about Abrera's future to Faurecia's board. He knew that most of the board was against him, as his spectacular rise up the corporate ladder had attracted some unwanted attention from peers. Greg, sitting in his tiny office in the plant, realized he only had five options to present to the board in two weeks' time:

1. Business as usual (losing €3 million annually forever)
2. Close the plant (at a cost of €15 million), including the refurbishment of the plant (at an estimated cost of €40 per square meter)
3. Sell the plant to a local competitor
4. Turn the plant around
5. Invest in new areas of growth.

There was also another element to this: Greg knew that Mr Pizzo,[i] the Italian chief financial officer (CFO), was very much in favor of closing all non-profitable plants. From his point of view, he would prefer to get a short-term loan to cover the losses coming from these non-profitable plants, rather than continuing with the multi-year bleeding out of cash to keep them open. With a strong Sicilian character and a thunderous voice, he had addressed the Faurecia board many times to advocate for his position that non-profitable plants should be shut down, and he had recently turned his attention to Abrera.

Greg knew that Mr Pizzo would have something to say about each of the options and, given his long seniority and success as the CFO, his opinion would undoubtedly matter a lot to the board.

Business as usual

Greg pondered this option first. Despite losing €3 million annually, there was still the possibility of attracting successor business (i.e. the successor model of an existing car) without a major investment, which would enhance the relationship with VW, crucial for Faurecia's global business. In general, car models such as Seat León were redesigned every six years, plus they typically got a facelift (i.e. minor modifications to aesthetics and technology) at the midpoint of the model's lifecycle.

Greg thought that keeping the plant up and running might help capture this successor business in the future, which would improve the plant's margins and, hence, the bottom line. Seat, in fact, was due to launch a new León in 2018, so Greg played with the idea of winning this battle by holding the fort and taking advantage of FIS's strong commercial ties with VW.

In fact, keeping business as usual at the Abrera plant would have a lot of upsides: The union and labor would be happy, the community would benefit from the continuous income of the plant's employees, and VW, in particular, would be satisfied because it would mean a very high-quality supplier would continue to operate in close proximity.

---

[i] Mr Pizzo's character, ideas and actions have been introduced fictitiously to create the drama and the dilemma in order to enhance the learning.

Close the plant

Closing the plant was a very bold but attractive option, considering all the cash that had been lost in the past, with no clear indication that the situation would improve. The team's morale was very low, many of the skilled workers had already left and the plant was in need of maintenance. However, Greg was concerned about the impact on the customers, so he kept searching for a solution that would provide the parts for existing customers while at the same time stemming the bleeding at Abrera. One option was to offer the other four suppliers in the region the opportunity to pick up production of the parts, based on the highest bid, or relocating the program to another Faurecia plant in the same region.

Due to the sensitivity of this option, Greg had to do a lot of the due diligence without any help to avoid the information being leaked and, hence, possibly causing major unrest and further distress at the plant. Greg had a terrible vision of workers going on strike, with a tragic dip in morale and possibly a negative impact on productivity, efficiency and ultimately safety in the plant.

Greg fairly quickly estimated the cost of closing the plant at about €15 million. This number was a rough estimate, and he was not very confident about his analysis, so he doubted he could present it to the board. Greg assumed this option would concern the board because, as he thought, "They put me here to fix Abrera, and I would be asking for €15 million or more out of the blue."

Sell the plant to a local competitor

Ideally, a local competitor such as Grupo Antolin would be interested in the Abrera plant. Greg was uncertain about this option, which had two possibilities: a shared deal or an asset deal. Both had pros and cons, with many unknowns. A shared deal would entail Faurecia selling the plant's assets and the human resources would go with them, while in an asset deal, only the assets would change hands. An asset deal had one more complexity in that Faurecia would be responsible – actually liable – for any defective supply even after the sale of the plant's assets because Abrera would still be the contractual party to the customers and the new supplier would operate below Abrera.

Greg also doubted whether VW would agree to transferring its business to a competitor and releasing Faurecia from any responsibility. Also, this sale would most likely be at a loss, with a negative purchase price, as the plant was not profitable.

Additionally, this small movement in the market would potentially cause a huge change in the regional market; consolidating two competitors into one would reduce VW's purchasing power, which could result in repercussions for the global relationship with Faurecia.

Turn the plant around

Greg being Greg wanted to fix the plant for good, and a turnaround was naturally an appealing option, and it would be good for his career. Still, there were a lot of risks associated with this scenario, and it could either have a great impact on his career progression or be disastrous — failing in Abrera would probably cost him his job at Faurecia. Apart from the personal considerations, Greg was also concerned about the past efforts to bring Abrera up to speed; essentially, all of the previous four plant managers had tried this route without any success.

To turn the plant around, Greg explored a "big bang investment" in new technology and compared and contrasted digital and robotized manufacturing with an incremental improvement approach through progressive lean manufacturing and process improvements.

Invest in new areas of growth

Abrera focused on car interior applications, such as control panels and dashboards. The machinery at Abrera was also well suited to manufacturing components for other industries and applications such as panels for the aerospace industry. An example would be the doors of the luggage storage bins in airplanes.

Adjusting Abrera's machinery to produce these new parts would be pretty straightforward. In the end, an IM machine would work equally well for producing the cockpit of a new Audi Q3 as it would for producing the lightweight door of the overhead bin in airplanes. Given that Spain was part of the Airbus consortium, this would be a great option to grow the revenues and profits of Abrera. Greg's study of the aerospace component market, including the projected expansion of both the overall aerospace market[1] and the relative weight of Spain's participation,[2] fueled his optimism. Of course, some investment would be needed to align the production equipment and manufacturing processes, but automotive parts producers such as Abrera already had strong process controls and the flexibility to adapt its production lines, so it was a natural fit with the requirements of the aerospace industry.

What decision to make?

Greg knew that he would be subjected to the same scrutiny as any other project at Faurecia: The board would ask him for a detailed financial analysis, especially on the net present value (NPV), internal rate of return (IRR) and payback period (PB), for each of the five scenarios. This would be complicated by the large, expected impact of intangibles on all of the options, e.g. in terms of the relationship with VW and the social aspects. Brand image would surely be affected by all five options, depending on the success or failure of the chosen option. Greg's career would also be affected. *Refer to* **Exhibit 5** *for a visual comparison of the financial and non-financial outcomes of each scenario.*

Greg also evaluated the impact of each option on the most relevant internal stakeholders. For instance, he was sure the chief operating officer (COO) would be happy with any of the options, as all provided a solution to long-term pain for him. The commercial sales leadership was not expected to be supportive of anything involving a business loss, such as closure or selling to a competitor. However, Mr Pizzo would definitely not support anything other than closing down the plant. Greg was tempted to try to convince him at least to evaluate selling Abrera but, as Mr Pizzo repeatedly said, he did not believe there could be strong interest from anyone in buying an old, unprofitable plant.

Greg called Mr Pizzo to gain a better understanding of what he was leaning towards. Mr Pizzo was charming as usual and explained to Greg that "if a tooth is rotten, just take it out." It was a colorful way of advocating for the plant's closure. Mr Pizzo also said that, after talking with the Catalan government, the so-called Generalitat would be understanding about the rationale for Abrera's closing and offer retraining services to the employees who were not retiring. When Greg tried to check the other options with him, the conversation turned sour as Mr Pizzo would not even acknowledge the existence of any other solutions. As the CFO, his only concern with the closing would be the reaction of VW because it was still the largest client globally for Faurecia despite being unprofitable in Abrera.

With all this in mind, Greg had less than two weeks to come up with a solid path forward, and the challenge was made even more difficult because of his personal bias.

Exhibit 1: Faurecia financial performance 2003–2016

Income statement by year	Closing 2003	Closing 2004	Closing 2005	Closing 2006	Closing 2007	Closing 2008	Closing 2009	Closing 2010	Closing 2011	Closing 2012	Closing 2013	Closing 2014	Closing 2015	Closing 2016
Total product sales	79 602	75 266	57 997	58 212	52 930	61 109	51 050	60 560	64 443	59 926	63 917	71 326	70 994	78 048
Total raw materials & subcontracting	-53 027	-48 686	-38 073	-38 823	-35 239	-43 262	-36 676	-40 583	-42 339	-40 129	-43 260	-48 079	-47 269	-49 454
Materials & subcontracting – % P Sales	-66.6%	-64.7%	-65.6%	-66.7%	-66.6%	-70.8%	-71.8%	-67.0%	-65.7%	-67.0%	-67.7%	-67.4%	-66.6%	-63.4%
Cost of sales – direct labor	-6 455	-7 503	-6 841	-8 089	-6 139	-8 644	-8 094	-8 346	-9 343	-9 496	-9 232	-10 519	-11 861	-12 252
Direct labor costs – % P Sales	-8.1%	-10.0%	-11.8%	-13.9%	-11.6%	-14.1%	-15.9%	-13.8%	-14.5%	-15.8%	-14.4%	-14.7%	-16.7%	-15.7%
Total costs of sales – freight out	-970	-858	-548	-508	-455	-585	-1 026	-1 401	-1 397	-1 266	-1 299	-1 349	-1 406	-1 327
Freight out – % P Sales	-1.2%	1.1%	-0.9%	-0.9%	-0.9%	-1.0%	-2.0%	-2.3%	-2.2%	-2.1%	-2.0%	-1.9%	-2.0%	-1.7%
Variable costs margin	19 149	18 218	12 534	10 791	11 096	8 617	5 253	10 229	11 363	9 034	10 125	11 378	10 457	15 014
Var cost margin on P Sales – % P Sales	24.1%	24.2%	21.6%	18.5%	21.0%	14.1%	10.3%	16.9%	17.6%	15.1%	15.8%	16.0%	14.7%	19.2%
Manufacturing – indirect labor	-4 152	-4 856	-4 891	-4 993	-4 379	-3 674	-3 121	-3 202	-3 455	-3 723	-3 758	-3 698	-3 799	-3 940
Indirect labor costs – % P Sales	-5.2%	-6.5%	-8.4%	-8.6%	-8.3%	-6.0%	-6.1%	-5.3%	-5.4%	-6.2%	-5.9%	-5.2%	-5.4%	-5.0%
Manufacturing – other	-5 173	-4 618	-5 034	-5 469	-4 969	-4 548	-4 386	-4 498	-4 710	-5 513	-5 513	-6 243	-6 396	-6 591
Manufacturing costs – % P Sales	-6.5%	-6.1%	-8.7%	-9.4%	-9.4%	-7.4%	-8.6%	-7.4%	-7.3%	-9.2%	-8.6%	-8.8%	-9.0%	-8.4%
Productive equipment depreciation	-2 498	-3 025	-3 241	-3 112	-3 015	-2 618	-1 566	-1 652	-1 470	-1 227	-1 258	-1 320	-1 213	-1 239
Inventory variance – fixed costs	0	0	0	0	0	0	0	0	0	0	0	10	60	-2
Completion losses reserves	0	0	0	0	0	0	-1 300	1 600	100	1 300	400	200	0	0
Gross margin on product sales	7 327	5 720	-632	-2 783	-1 267	-2 223	-5 120	2 478	1 829	-129	-4	328	-891	3 243
Var cost margin on P Sales – % P Sales	9.2%	7.6%	-1.1%	-4.8%	-2.4%	-3.6%	-10.0%	4.1%	2.8%	-0.2%	0.0%	0.5%	-1.3%	4.2%
Total tooling sales	0	0	0	0	0	0	0	0	165	382	249	614	213	1 170
Gross margin on tooling	0	0	0	0	0	0	0	0	1	0	1	-5	-1	0
Total R&D prototypes sales	0	0	0	0	0	0	0	0	260	853	1 512	1 613	1 814	2 338
Services & royalties sales	1 795	1 402	1 877	4 059	4 498	4 037	1 558	2 101	3 510	2 836	3 484	4 598	2 992	3 662
Total sales	81 397	76 668	59 874	62 271	57 428	65 146	52 608	62 661	68 378	63 997	69 162	78 151	76 013	85 218
Gross margin	7 327	5 720	-632	-2 783	-1 267	-2 223	-5 120	2 478	1 829	-129	-3	323	-892	3 243
Total gross margin – % T Sales	9.0%	7.5%	-1.1%	-4.5%	-2.2%	-3.4%	-9.7%	4.0%	2.7%	-0.2%	0.0%	0.4%	-1.2%	3.8%
Gross margin transferred to R&D costs	-519	-623	-638	-633	-576	-644	-436	-484	-416	-418	-381	-324	-382	-448
Net R&D expenses – % T Sales	-0.6%	-0.8%	-1.1%	-1.0%	-1.0%	-1.0%	-0.8%	-0.8%	-0.6%	-0.7%	-0.6%	-0.4%	-0.5%	-0.5%
SG&A expenses	-2 057	-2 388	-2 571	-2 257	-1 914	-1 904	-1 662	-1 728	-2 046	-2 289	-2 522	-2 427	-2 319	-2 786
SG&A expenses – % T Sales	-2.5%	-3.1%	-4.3%	-3.6%	-3.3%	-2.9%	-3.2%	-2.8%	-3.0%	-3.6%	-3.6%	-3.1%	-3.1%	-3.3%
Operating margin	4 751	2 709	-3 841	-5 673	-3 757	-4 771	-7 218	266	-633	-2 836	-2 906	-2 428	-3 593	9
Operating income – % T Sales	5.8%	3.5%	-6.4%	-9.1%	-6.5%	-7.3%	-13.7%	0.4%	-0.9%	-4.4%	-4.2%	-3.1%	-4.7%	0.0%

Source: Company information

Exhibit 2: Porter's Five Forces for Faurecia Interior Systems

Threat of new entrants: Low

- Highly capital intensive (technology, manufacturing facility, machines and equipment)
- Very complex supply chain process
- Innovation and engineering intensive to meet emerging customer trends
- Reputation and reliability based on previous experiences and customer relationship
- Economy of scale and scope.

Supplier power: Moderate

- Similar cost structure
- Oligopolistic context (5 main competitors)
- Increasing level of differentiation and personalization
- Vertical integration, such as integration of engineering capabilities, new raw material (biomaterial), technologies.

Customer power: High

- Large and powerful automakers (customers)
- Large quantity order (6-year product lifetime). Considering the whole cycle, from RFQ to service parts it requires approx. 25 years (3 years of innovation + engineering + development + 6 years of production + 15 years of service parts (obligation)
- High switching efforts and costs during a product lifetime // low switching efforts and costs in between predecessor and successor product lifetime.

Threat of substitutions: Low

- No real substitutions for automotive interior components

Degree of competition: High

- Heavy cost structure and process innovation and price war
- High exit cost due to substantial investment required
- Low growth industry
- Intensifying differentiation
- Industry in transformation due to the autonomous drive, shared economy and connectivity, which is affecting vehicle interiors.

Source: Case authors

Exhibit 3: Faurecia Abrera plant identity card

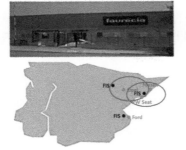

Location: Abrera, SP
Creation date: 1994
Employees: 360
Technologies: Injection, Painting, Welding
Flaming, Foaming, Assembly
Delivery: 2500 c/day
Customers: NISSAN, SEAT

Abrera plant is part of FIS.

Source: Company information

Exhibit 4: Abrera plant management team (2015)

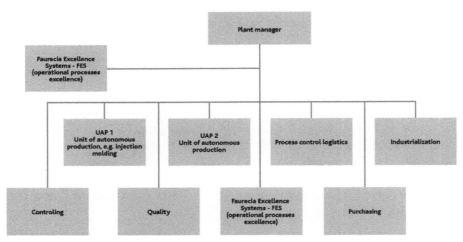

Source: Company information

Exhibit 5: Comparison forecast outcomes of five scenarios – financial and non-financial

No.	Strategic option	Yearly "high level" projected cash flows (€ million)							Potential social impact			
		2015	2016	2017	2018	2019	2020	Sum	Customer relationship	Union relationship	Labor relationship	Corporate image
1	Business as usual	-3.6	-3.6	-3.6	-3.6	-3.6	-3.6	-21.6	+	+	+	–
2	Close the plant	-3.6	-15	0	0	0	0	-18.6	–	–	–	–
3	Sell to a competitor	-3.6	-10.8	0	0	0	0	-14.4	–	neutral	neutral	–
4	Turn it around	-4.8	-4	-2	-1.6	-1.3	-1	-14.7	+	+	+	+
5	Invest in new growth areas	-3.6	-4	-4	-5	-2.6	-1.6	-20.8	+	+	+	+

Source: Company information

CASE STUDY | FAURECIA DIGITAL TRANSFORMATION (B)

Amit Kumar Singh, Yanik Cantieni, Marco Amici and Carlos Cordon

Following Greg Dupont's recommendations to the executive committee in June 2015, the board came to a decision. Despite major losses over the previous 10 years, maintaining the relationship with Volkswagen (VW) was still a very important strategic requirement for the company, and Greg's vision and leadership capability during the meeting led them to believe that a turnaround was possible. Therefore, the board jointly agreed that it did not have any other alternative but to proceed with the turnaround option.

As soon as the decision was made, there was no delay. As Greg recalled:

> *"The moment the decision was made, I went to Abrera and had rigorous meetings for one week with all the major functions in the plant. I asked the team to come up with new digital transformation ideas with a focus on increased agility and efficiency by leveraging new technologies. My motto was simple: 'Taking an innovative risk and failing is more acceptable than not doing anything.'"*

Greg explained to the board that for Faurecia to increase its agility and efficiency, the company needed to leverage technology and drive digital transformation throughout the world. Abrera, in its current circumstances, would be the ideal plant to drive a proof of concept to execution, and if it succeeded, it could be treated as a benchmark for driving digital transformation in other Faurecia plants around the world. As the cost of technology had dropped and the availability of real-time data had exploded, the opportunities to harness and analyze information were multiplying rapidly. A key driver was the need to operate at the same level as customers in terms of global information, speed of response and decision making. Equally important was meeting employee expectations for a work environment that was as modern and efficient as their private lives.

The turnaround decision: Background

The turnaround decision had major financial implications for Faurecia. However, the board realized that a digital transformation was transforming the automotive world. Increasingly affordable digital technologies, the rise of big data and a digitally mature workforce were combining to enable significant gains in an industrial environment that demanded increasing speed, quality and reliability.

The Faurecia board also knew that VW was driving the FAST initiative and had been trying to collaborate with many suppliers to meet this strategic level. The FAST initiative involved the VW Group working with its suppliers to respond to the challenges and accelerating technology changes taking place in the automotive industry. The aim was to successfully implement joint technological innovations faster than in the past and to realize vehicle projects worldwide more efficiently and effectively with the VW Group. For many years, the VW Group had consistently been Faurecia's best customer worldwide with close to 25% of product sales generated with the Audi, Seat, Skoda and VW brands.

With the above picture in mind and considering the long-term strategic need to maintain relationships with VW, it was very clear that business as usual, closing or selling Abrera to another competitor was not the right decision at this point in time, so the executive committee unanimously agreed on the turnaround.

Industry 4.0 technology options

Greg considered 11 technology options in his zeal to transform Abrera and his desire to prove his leadership capabilities:

1 Safety and security

Greg was adamant that maintaining a safe working environment in the plant was vital for the employees and the plant's productivity. Accidents cost money – the loss of trained workers, reduced production and increased insurance costs. They could also tarnish a company's brand and reputation – potentially to the point where customer trust and loyalty were eroded. By embracing a culture of safety and investing in technology to continuously evaluate the plant and manage equipment and operating procedures, many potential safety issues could be eliminated and productivity could be improved.

In addition to the social costs, workplace injuries and illnesses had a major impact on the company's bottom line. Research by the United States Department of Labor suggested that employers paid almost $1 billion per week for direct workers' compensation costs alone. The costs of workplace injuries and illnesses included both direct and indirect costs. Direct costs included workers' compensation payments, medical expenses and costs for legal services. Examples of indirect costs included training for replacement employees, accident investigation and implementation of corrective measures, lost productivity, repair of damaged equipment and property, and costs associated with lower employee morale and absenteeism.

Thus, while Greg wanted to invest in a safety management system to reduce/ prevent accidents and improve safety performance, he was also concerned about winning over the hearts and minds of the workers by ultimately improving the general level of working conditions, and automation could play a big part in achieving this. Greg realized that ergonomics was a key part of overall safety and a comfortable employee was more productive.

Video link: "Safety moment: Chemicals and dusts." Wood, November 1, 2016. https://is.gd/aPIXPY (accessed March 20, 2019).

2 Cobots (collaborative robots)

Greg felt that automotive manufacturing was a complex process, but with digitalization, quality and efficiency could be improved significantly. He thought that by having a mix of robots and cobots, complicated and repetitive tasks, such as welding, final assembly, leak testing applications and pick and place, could be optimized and automated for manufacturing. This would help the plant cut costs and price its models competitively, thereby improving its customer base and market share. However, Greg realized the need to upskill people to work in collaboration with robots and other types of automation technology. In addition, Faurecia did not have any experience with cobots; hence, it would be very risky to implement this technology. Also, it was not clear at what point robots would effectively replace humans in the plant, so Greg wanted to explore this before making a final decision.

3 Predictive maintenance

Greg found that agile manufacturing had become a key component for being competitive in the automotive sector. Research from Morgan Stanley suggested that automotive manufacturers could save US$488 billion by using predictive maintenance. By assessing in advance which equipment would need maintenance, automotive manufacturers could better plan maintenance work and smoothly convert the abrupt "unplanned outages" into shorter and fewer "planned outages." If equipment issues were detected before they actually occurred, less time would be spent on damage control.

Greg thought that by capturing and analyzing data to predict and prevent equipment failures, the plant could improve inefficiencies and increase productivity. For example, by gathering quality data from every product at different stages of the manufacturing process, together with process data from production sensors and machinery and product traceability data, Faurecia could immediately analyze the data to determine the factors that influenced product and process quality. Using this analysis, Faurecia could develop strategies to improve quality issues, including machine configuration, production modification or tool replacement. Collecting and analyzing more diverse operational data from connected plants would allow Faurecia data scientists to build better predictive maintenance models.

A predictive maintenance strategy would only be successful if Faurecia could have a computerized maintenance management system (CMMS), or some means of tracking its assets' data, the right internet of things (IoT) sensors to feed data to the CMMS, and engineers who were able to keep the system running and create value out of the data. Faurecia did not have any previous data handling capabilities; hence, it was somehow challenging and time consuming to implement this strategy.

Video link: "How to benefit from predictive maintenance." Bosch Software Innovations, April 6. 2017. https://is.gd/OjCy7Z (accessed March 20, 2019).

4 Visual communication/digital dashboard

Greg felt that Faurecia was still using paper-based checklists, which, given the available technologies, was slightly absurd. With paper-based documentation, there was no connection point, no chance to review the entire supply chain in a single readable format. By introducing software that enabled users to do exactly this within the manufacturing plant, the complete chain could be connected together and available for any user to easily review parts and material information, inspection data, build times and more.

By digitally transforming the manufacturing floor, users could be equipped with rugged tablets, smartphones or laptops to easily access information and data throughout the plant. This would allow for almost instantaneous updates to be made so the complete process could be recorded in real-time, providing greater oversight around critical issues before they escalated. This would allow maintenance engineers to simply log into the system to determine the status of a component and whether there were issues that needed resolving. Real-time on-screen monitoring of production replaced manual intervention, freeing employees for higher value added and more rewarding work.

5 Cybersecurity

With digital transformation, cyber security risks were major threats and Greg realized that he needed to be mindful of this because it could have serious implications for the company and its customers. According to the Ponemon Institute, on average, there were around 32 cyberattacks per month and the cumulative cost to an organization from cyberattacks averaged around $3.5 million annually. In addition, research conducted by Accenture, showed that cybercrime costs for organizations continued to rise as the average cost of cybercrime per organization was up about 62.5% since 2013.

Hackers could easily penetrate the IT network and steal intellectual property, stop or slow down factory production or impact the performance of cobots, which might go unnoticed during the initial production. The tiniest of variances in the performance of operational technology could cause manufacturing disruptions, which could lead to defective products (meaning recalls and reputational losses), production downtime, physical damage and even injuries and deaths.

As with any other critical risks, C-level executives and the board of directors in Faurecia needed to be engaged in budgeting for security and fostering a security culture throughout the organization. All employees had to share in security awareness and understand their roles and responsibilities in preventing cyberattacks. With Abrera losing $3 million per year, Greg saw some risk if he proposed the need for additional budget to the C-suite without showing any profits at Abrera.

Video link: https://www.youtube.com/watch?v=la2aqosRUeo

6 Machine learning

Machine learning used statistical techniques to give computer systems the ability to learn from data. As per the IDC report, machine learning was predicted to reduce costs related to transport and warehousing and supply chain administration by 5% to 10% and 25% to 40% respectively. Due to machine learning, overall inventory reductions of 20% to 50% were possible. Additionally, automating inventory optimization using machine learning had improved service levels by 16% while simultaneously increasing inventory turns by 25%.

Greg realized that by having industrial internet of things (IIOT) capabilities in the plant, there would be a huge amount of data throughout the entire manufacturing process that would need to be collected, stored and retained for data analysis. If there was any issue or defect in manufacturing parts, the team could go and check the data for that particular day, the time it was made, the shift it was made and track it all the way to the parameters of the equipment and how it was running that day. This would help them better analyze the defects, improve quality further and reduce scrap from the manufactured parts.

In 2014, artificial intelligence (AI) was still evolving and the major machine learning challenge was to find people with the technical ability to implement and understand it. For Faurecia, finding the right "data scientist" with a PhD degree and the relevant experience might cost a lot of money and time for Abrera – something Abrera's management might find difficult to afford at that time.

Video link: "Big Data and the automotive industry." Bird & Bird, July 3, 2014. www.youtube.com/watch?v=N5xJ6R7DGJg (accessed March 20, 2019).

7 Automated guided vehicles (AGVs) and radio-frequency identification (RFID)

Greg realized that the Abrera plant required high volumes of the repetitive movement of material, where very little or no human decision-making skills were required to perform the movement. He felt that new smart technologies such as AGVs could consistently and predictably transport loads of material to places in the plant where manual labor and transport were required. These vehicles could be routinely applied in 24/7 operations and could provide a superior return on investment over more conventional manual alternatives. Regardless, the AGV market was expected to reach nearly US$ 2.7 billion by 2022, at a compound annual growth rate (CAGR) of 9.3% during the forecast period 2017 to 2022, according to a report by MarketsandMarkets. Also, the technology would help reduce injuries in human delivery operations, lower the lifetime cost of non-value added transportation of materials and provide better space utilization in the factory. Greg also felt that the use of RFIDs for automatic tracking of components could simplify logistics and enable real-time management of inventory flow and quality.

8 Digital HR and communication

Greg knew that digitalization would have an impact on the workers in the Abrera plant, so it needed to be dealt with carefully. Hence, training and communication would be a key element at each step in the process. The company needed to invest in social networking and simplify the process for employees to connect to company software, thus streamlining administration. Also, Greg needed to focus on digital communication to ensure workers understood and connected to the needs for change in the factory and how this would benefit the entire ecosystem.

9 Additive manufacturing

The Abrera shop floor operations had been plagued with inefficient processes, unpredictable downtimes and difficulties with machinery maintenance. Greg felt that the manufacturing execution system could help them make the most of the shop floor capabilities, with tools that could identify underperforming and high-performance machines, and then optimize asset utilization accordingly.

3D printing was one of the options that could be used for automotive prototyping as well as tooling, while also providing an opportunity for mass customized part production. 3D printing technology was an appealing proposition for the automotive industry and additive manufacturing was increasingly getting used in this sector. The 2015 Wohlers Report stated that motor vehicles would constitute 16.1% of the 3D printing market that year. The advances in additive manufacturing that allowed for newer designs, reduced lead times and rapid prototyping could save millions of dollars. According to Machine Design, consumption of 3D printing materials by the automotive industry would reach around $530 million by 2021.

While 3D printing seemed to have huge potential, it was unclear to Greg as to what extent 3D printing could outstrip or even replace traditional manufacturing and logistics processes. 3D print technology was expensive for producing large quantities compared to traditional processes used for mass production.

10 Augmented reality

Augmented reality (AR) was another cutting-edge technology that could have been used in the Abrera plant to enhance production and maintenance and reduce the cost of design and prototyping. For example, workers at the plant could use AR glasses so that they would always have the correct manual available when carrying out routine maintenance of the manufacturing plant. This would enhance the safety and efficiency of the maintenance work, and it would also reduce Faurecia's dependency on skilled labor in the plant. Secondly, using augmented reality technology during the design stage of car making would allow Faurecia to be creative and design concept models with minimum cost. This meant many variants could be shown, modified and assessed during the early phases, thus reducing the time and cost required for the overall process. As per a worldwide market study by ABI Research, the use of AR glasses for the global automotive industry would reach 1.7 million units in 2022. The total automotive AR market was expected to have a CAGR of 177% during the forecast period and would reach $5.5 billion in 2022. However, this technology was still in its early stages of development and hardware and software developers were still grappling with issues around the wearability of the devices and the availability for mass consumer adoption.

Video link: "Internet of Things and Augmented Reality for the Automotive Industry." Transition Technologies PSC, March 21, 2017. www.youtube.com/watch?v=KtqNvJC2o6Y (accessed March 20, 2019).

11 Automatic light touch assembly (ALTA)

Greg realized that on the assembly line, the complexity was much higher. In Abrera, multiple variations of a product were usually assembled on the same line, which required a tremendous amount of flexibility. He felt that the assembly line could be performed perfectly by electric and pneumatic parts with a programmable logic controller (PLC) program. By having ALTA, which was well designed, easy to maintain, efficient, stable and accurate, they could substitute or replace manual work entirely, double the efficiency and guarantee higher quality.

The next step for Greg was to determine which options would be the best to pursue for the Abrera plant, given the key objectives that he presented to the board:

- To leverage the digital transformation to increase agility and efficiency.

- To make Abrera a benchmark for digital transformation for Faurecia.

- To operate at the same level as customers in terms of global information, speed of response and decision making. In particular, the FAST initiative of the VW group.

- To meet employee expectations for a work environment that was as modern and efficient as their private lives.

CASE STUDY | FAURECIA DIGITAL TRANSFORMATION (C)

Amit Kumar Singh, Yanik Cantieni, Marco Amici and Carlos Cordon

Greg discussed all of the digital technology options with Abrera's management before making a final decision on which options were the best ones to start with. The main criterion was to choose the options that would add the most value in terms of performance and financial improvements at the Abrera plant. As everyone was saying, "We need to go digital," Greg viewed this as an opportunity to secure the investment required to automate. Finally, four options were chosen: Cobots (collaborative robots), AGVs (automatic guided vehicles), ALTA (automatic light touch assembly) and the digital dashboard. There were three key prerequisites for implementing the digital technologies: cabling the plant, installing servers and optic fiber, and implementing a software and integration system for all machines.

The digital transformation was in motion at Faurecia and Greg knew the head of the digital transformation project at Faurecia headquarters well. He was keen to show that the digital transformation would significantly improve the Abrera plant.

Cobots

One of the chosen technologies was cobots (*refer to* **Exhibit 1**), which would perform auto clipping through standardized robotic clipping cells. The clipping cells would include two cobots, two bolt feeders that would feed the clips through vibration, a rotating table hosting the parts in a nest and a camera to check if the clips were placed properly. The main benefits for Abrera would be a drastically reduced cycle time from 5 seconds per clip to 2.5 seconds per clip and the replacement of four operators with one operator and a cobot. It would also lead to a significant cost reduction and a very attractive payback of 0.95 (in less than one year) on the capital expenditure (CAPEX), which was €108,000, of which €45,000 was for a cobot, €20,000 was for the bolt feeders, and €43,000 was for the system integration, the grippers, tools, nest and safety device. This new concept would also enable the plant to establish a leaner layout, based on standardized work, and improve the balance of the operator loads. The operations were very repetitive and often painful for the fingers of the operators who installed clips all day.

Greg appointed Lionel, a promising young technician in the manufacturing engineering department, to lead this initiative. As Lionel explained:

"The project began with me contacting some suppliers, but management quickly decided to build it internally, so I started by buying a cobot. I was the guy who put it all together. The management sent me to Kuka near Villanova during my holiday in August of 2015 to learn how to program a cobot in JavaScript. I could not believe it, after the training, I needed to implement this stuff, and Greg gave me only six months to make it work!"

As soon as Lionel returned from the training, he started developing a prototype, built the concept for the nest with simple automatic grippers and tested the cycle time. "If the cycle time was not quick enough, then we increased the number of clips, it took some trial and error."

The cobots were a relatively low-cost solution for Abrera to quickly reduce its direct labor costs. It was designed to be integrated easily, it offered high flexibility, low maintenance, was easy to implement and did not required the space nor the level of programming and engineering features that standard robots usually needed. The payback would be 0.95 years.

Before joining Abrera, Lionel had no prior work experience in the automotive industry nor in automation. He had previously worked in a pizzeria in Valencia, and he came to Abrera for the automation and predictive maintenance project with just a post-graduate education in automation and programming from Barcelona, but no real work experience. As he explained:

"I saw an ad at the university, I applied and got the job. It was an exciting project, I was given a lot of autonomy. I had to be very creative in designing the concept, and I had to improvise a lot. Of course, Greg challenged me continuously to find better solutions, to make it less expensive and to increase the output. Greg would say, 'You focus on your stuff, and I will handle the pressure.'"

Digital dashboard

Abrera decided to implement a digital dashboard as a tool to display real-time and historical data about the performance of the plant and some specific machines. In order to automatically capture real-time data for each machine, a digital manufacturing control (DMC) system (*refer to* **Exhibits 2** *and* **3**) was installed on the six injection molding (IM) machines at Abrera. The DMC was developed internally by Faurecia as a tool to monitor the performance of the equipment and the various work stations, based on some of the key performance indicators (KPIs), e.g. the efficiency performance or quality of the parts per shift (*refer to* **Exhibit 4**). It provided statistical analysis and a pareto report of non-OEE (overall equipment efficiency) and NQC (non-quality costs) in real time for quick reaction. The six IM machines were connected capturing 180 process parameters per shot, with an average of 60 shots per hour times

22 hours per day times 5 days per week, leading to more than 7 million data points collected per week. All data were saved in the Faurecia cloud.

The automatic data collection through the DMC led to much more accurate data that was instantly recorded for better traceability. It was now possible to trace the precise time a part was produced, under which conditions it was produced and with which machine parameters. With the help of data scientists, more statistical analysis could be performed (running algorithms to understand the pareto report and correlations of anomalies, such as for scrap parts).

The information provided through the digital dashboard became very transparent and was easily shared across the various functions of the plant. Operators were given an iPad so they could visualize real time KPIs. It increased the reactivity of management to make better decisions and improve the OEE and DLE (direct labor efficiency).

As part of the leadership team at Abrera, Jesus, who was the manager of the UAP1 (unite autonome de production), was instrumental in building organizational readiness for the digital transformation. As Jesus described:

> "This was a time of major changes at Abrera; it was essential to involve everyone right from the start. The employees were not used to these sorts of technologies, so they did not see the advantages for the company. To me, projecting the vision was essential. We were focused on our daily plant routines, and we were operating in survival mode. It was difficult to think and act outside of the box. The vision helped us to visualize where we wanted to be in one, two years' time."

The biggest challenge was speed. "It was sometimes demotivating to see the slow progress, but we did not give up." Daily communication about the vision and the objectives was a key part of the change management. During a decision-making meeting to go ahead with the digital dashboard, Greg said, "You need to try even when you think you may fail; unless you try, you won't know." The more employees' new ideas were valued, the more they felt encouraged to bring new ideas. "It became super contagious," said Jesus.

"We can now communicate, visualize the KPIs and execute in real time with the operators." The motivation of the employees increased dramatically. The daily top-five meetings on the plant floor became interactive. The dashboard displayed key information about the plant performance and gave continuous feedback.

ALTA (automatic light touch assembly)

The main objective of the ALTA (*refer to* **Exhibit 5**) was to roboticize the post-processing and the assembly of components. These post-processing and assembly operations involved 30% of the plant's direct labor costs. One ALTA cell cost €405,000. It generally led to a one- to one-and-one-half-year payback (depending on the project), based on six operators per day being removed and assuming two operators per shift on a three-shift model. In addition, the reduced human contact with the parts during the whole process led to higher-quality parts. ALTA was a very flexible technology for highly repetitive operations. It could easily be adapted for the production mix or for volume changes. The main functionalities of ALTA included welding, screwing, punching, fastening, drilling and clipping. According to Antonio, the plant manager:

"What fascinated me most was the fight against the machine. There was no need to push the operators to run faster; they wanted to beat the tack time of the machine. It was perceived as a game to compete with the machine, with clear targets to reach an OEE of 85%, from a low of 65%."

ALTA cell main steps for the seat program:

- Take nest
- Sprew cleaning
- Take photos of the part for traceability
- Punching
- Install rivets
- Check photos
- Record the data for traceability.

The total cycle time was 58 seconds.

AGV (automatic guided vehicles)

Besides the fact that AGVs (*refer to* **Exhibit 6**) were becoming very popular in the automotive industry, the main objective of implementing AGVs at Abrera was to save logistics labor costs, which were generally around 10% of the total direct labor costs. The operators were becoming more productive during the AGV transportation time, as they did not have to move the parts themselves anymore. Due to the increasing popularity of AGVs, the number of suppliers increased significantly and the purchase price or leasing costs decreased drastically over time. Therefore, AGVs had an attractive payback. "AGVs are now a must in the industry," according to Samuel Leduc, industrial director at Faurecia Interior Systems.

At Abrera, the AGVs picked and moved part kits from the IM machine shop, dropped them at the next station (e.g. welding or assembly), and then moved the finished goods to the TPA (truck preparation area) for dispatch to customers. By using AGVs, Abrera was able to reduce the number of forklifts in the plant by 80%.

According to Felip, the human resources and chief happiness officer at Abrera:

"A good, honest and transparent communication plan was vital. It was important to tell the employees why we wanted to launch an automation project, as it could create uncertainty regarding employees' jobs. It was incredible to see the changes in people. The employee commitment improved a lot."

Abrera management saw that its competitors were launching digital transformation strategies, and if Abrera did not do so, then there would be a greater likelihood that Abrera would disappear sooner rather than later.

At the beginning of this whole initiative, the employees were asking themselves, "How can a production line function properly without people." This was a major change, but Greg was instrumental in creating an understanding throughout the organization that "this was the way forward."

The running costs for one AGV were relatively low — rental was €239 per month and maintenance was performed in-house. Besides the financial benefits, the introduction of AGVs helped Abrera eliminate traffic jams in the plant, improve the safety of its employees and reduce the transportation time for parts.

The technicalities of the AGVs included:

- Running on a magnetic guide
- Continuously charging batteries
- Easy to maintain and replace if needed
- Equipped with an RFID (radio frequency identification) card reader
- Controlled by a database (giving instructions to stop, go, turn, ...).

Additional video links

- Faurecia Global: Interesting to get a "feel" for Faurecia's vision. https://www.youtube.com/user/faurecia
- Faurecia Digital Manufacturing: Touches a number of technologies discussed in the case. https://www.youtube.com/watch?v=ZcWyGzp1dDo
- Faurecia Digital Transformation: Provides a general perspective regarding Faurecia's strategic focus. https://www.youtube.com/watch?v=-yph00SP7uE
- https://www.youtube.com/watch?v=QA1zRw6ZgAM

Exhibit 1: Cobot

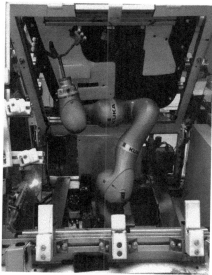

Source: Company information

Exhibit 2: Digital dashboard

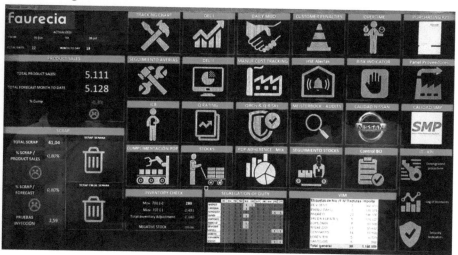

Source: Company information

Exhibit 3: Digital dashboard on maintenance

Source: Company information

Exhibit 4: Abrera operations and quality scorecard

Data subject to changes based on final review with Abrera plant manager		ACTUAL YEARLY RESULTS				TARGETS	RESULTS ANALYSIS		
		2015	2016	2017	2018	Abrera	Status & trend		Comments
Customer	PPM	25	20	18	18	15	😕		
Quality	NQC (k€)	2 840	1 561	1 278	816	816	😐	↘	Mainly due to scrap and claims
	NQC % sales	4%	2%	1.8%	1.2%	1.2%	😐	↘	
	Scrap ppm	25 000	20 000	16 000	8 000	<8 000	🙂	↘	
	% of scrap vs. sales	2%	1%	0.9%	0.8%	0.8%	🙂	↘	
Operations	OEE %	76%	80%	81%	82%	85%	☹️	↗	
	DLE %	42%	45%	46%	46%	50%	☹️	↗	

Source: Company information

Exhibit 5: ALTA cell

Source: Company information

Exhibit 6: Automatic guided vehicles

Source: Company information

Exhibit 7: Technologies/drivers & cost/saving

Concept	Drivers	Capex/ Expense (K€)	MOD (Heads/ day)	Other annual cost reduction (K€)	Pay-back (years)
COBOT: X-60 DP Auto-clipping and automatic welding	Direct labor cost improvement Quality clipping improvement	108	3		0.95
ALTA: SE 270 Shot channel injection automation	Direct labor cost improvement capab/repet process	49	1.5		0.86
ALTA: SE 270 IP assembly automation	Direct labor cost improvement Ergonomics improvement	356	9		1.04
Digital Dashboard: eTOP5, maintenance, tooling	Online information Historical data recording	15	0	Efficiency improvement	
AGV automation: Delocalized shop stock	Direct labor cost improvement Layout improvement	97	3		0.85

MOD = Direct labor

Source: Company information

Insights from the cases: Faurecia's digital transformation strategy

The Faurecia case puts into practice many ideas discussed in previous sections of the book. Like the executives at TetraPak and HungryPet, Greg carefully positioned his proposal for digital transformation in the context of business drivers.

The automotive industry was quickly ramping up digital capabilities, generating a sense at Faurecia of being left behind. Its main customer, VW Group, had the FAST initiative to help bolster the case in terms of customer demand and competitive pressures. Also of note is how the plant's difficult situation made the financial business case more palatable for Faurecia. In a vacuum, the projected ROIs provided by Greg might or might not have been sufficient to convince the board to move forward, but in a context where every option requires capital, it emerged as the most promising.

Greg cleverly combined the two realities of external business drivers and internal cost pressures to propose a digital transformation as the solution. His roadmap is a blend of initiatives around communication and digital culture, on the one hand, and cost efficiency, on the other.

The digital dashboards were a highly visible method of demonstrating to the workforce how important they were to the success of the digital transformation. Supplying workers with iPads is the sort of gesture that makes them feel valued, trusted and open to using this new information productively.

Even the efforts that clearly targeted cost efficiency – the cobots and the ALTA cell – were done with complete transparency as to the nature and motivations of the project. The workers were treated with maturity and respect, and the testimony speaks to how well this was received.

The AGVs, it can be argued, are a blend of both culture and efficiency. Although they had a payback of less than one year, they also sent a strong signal about the importance of safety and hygiene. AGVs are considered safer alternatives to human lift drivers since their cameras cover 360 degrees without blinking, and they always place their cargo precisely within the prescribed zone, thus reducing tripping hazards.

We even see in Faurecia's approach what its intentions are for the second phase of its roadmap. Case C describes how the plant collects over 230,000 data points per machine per day to help feed its digital dashboard. This could be the fuel for the implementation of predictive maintenance at a later date. In Chapter 2 we shared our view of predictive maintenance as a "killer app" of Industry 4.0, providing tangible, measurable benefits that can be appreciated by all levels of operations, from senior management to shop floor operators.

A final element worthy of consideration is Faurecia's willingness to pilot a digital transformation in a poorly performing factory. Some companies use a "lighthouse" approach of selecting a high performing factory as the location for all digital pilots. The expectation is that this creates the highest probability of success for the initiative and can serve as inspiration and a benchmark for other factories. The Faurecia case shows that there is more than one viable approach. A roadmap that balances the questions of culture, communications and payback can be successful even in challenging settings.

4 CASE STUDY | ADIDAS RUSSIA/CIS AND THE RUSSIAN CRISIS: RETRENCH OR DOUBLE DOWN (A)

Beverley Lennox, Carlos Cordon and Benoit Leleux

This case won the Supply Chain Management category in the 2016 EFMD case writing competition.

MOSCOW (RUSSIA), MARCH 2015. The Russian economy was in a tailspin. The combination of a sharp decline in oil prices, a weak ruble, the political fallout from the forceful annexation of Crimea, Western sanctions and inflationary pressures had all contributed to an economic crisis (*refer to* **Exhibit 1**). It was the "perfect storm" if there ever was one and the results were predictable: dramatically lower consumer and investment spending.

Against this backdrop, Joseph Godsey, the vice president of supply chain management and information technology at adidas Russia/CIS (which included Ukraine and Kazakhstan), and his team were preparing for a key "Strategy 2020" meeting with adidas headquarters and the Operations Excellence steering committee later in the month. Their discussion would center on what should be their priorities and the pace of implementation for the next 12 months. Five key initiatives – click-and-collect, customization, endless aisle, radio-frequency identification (RFID)-enabled stores and warehouses, and ship-from-store – would be on the table. These initiatives would mix online, offline and mobile approaches, and they would involve a radical rethink of adidas Russia/CIS's supply chain management (SCM) policies. They would also require significant investments.

Since arriving in Russia at the beginning of 2014, Joseph and his team had made great strides in improving the efficiency of adidas Russia/CIS's IT systems; and with over 1,200 corporate-owned stores employing more than 15,000 people, Russia/CIS was becoming increasingly more important to the business. In fact, over the years, adidas Russia/CIS had continuously met or exceeded expectations and had gained sufficient credibility within the organization. As a result, it was now tasked with defining the future of adidas's omnichannel retailing, a combination of digital and physical commerce that held the power to transform the customer experience into a seamless journey supported by the integration between channels on the back end.

Joseph attributed the successes his team enjoyed during his first year at adidas Russia/CIS to the entrepreneurial mindset of the organization, a willingness to take "calculated" risks and the team's ability to move fast. But Joseph was now about to take the biggest risk of his career and he was not so sure it was a calculated one. With the Russian economy taking a definite turn for the worse, was it really time to engage in major IT and SCM investments? Were Russian customers ready for such leading-edge offers? Could Russia/CIS actually become a beacon of excellence in retail IT and supply chain management within the adidas Group?

The young Adi Dassler in his shoe factory

adidas Group

In the small German village of Herzogenaurach, located 12 miles northwest of Nuremberg, Adolf "Adi" Dassler registered "Adi Dassler adidas Sportschuhfabrik" on August 18, 1949, following a family feud at the *Gebrüder Dassler Schuhfabrik* between him and his older brother Rudolf. Rudolf had earlier established Puma, which was also headquartered in Herzogenaurach and which quickly became the business rival of adidas.

At the 1954 World Cup final, when the German national football team, wearing lightweight adidas football boots with screw-in studs and the iconic three stripes, faced the unbeatable Hungarians, the Germans' victory made adidas a household name on football pitches everywhere.

Source: adidas website

Adi's son, Horst Dassler, eventually took the reigns of the company, but after his sudden death in 1987, the company entered troubled waters. It was first acquired in 1989 by French industrialist Bernard Tapie for a reported €244 million, which Tapie mostly borrowed. Famous for rescuing bankrupt companies, Tapie decided to move production offshore to Asia. A record loss in 1992 brought adidas to its knees, and ultimately, it was taken over by its main bank, French state-owned Crédit Lyonnais, which then engineered a sale to financier Robert Louis-Dreyfus and other private equity investors in 1993. Robert Louis-Dreyfus, as the company's new CEO, and his partner Christian Tourres, turned the company around and took it public in 1995.

Over time, the adidas Group (*refer to* **Exhibit 2**) evolved into a global leader in the sporting goods industry with a broad portfolio of products available in virtually every country in the world. In 2013, however, the Group reported that its sales and earnings targets for the year were no longer achievable due to negative market developments, which included the effects of a weakening currency, the ongoing softness of the global golf market and unexpected short-term distribution constraints that resulted in the transition to a new distribution facility in Russia.

adidas Russia/CIS

For 10 years, Russia/CIS[ii] was one of the most important markets for the adidas Group with constantly rising sales and profits (*refer to* **Exhibit 3**). For the five years prior to 2013, the market was growing 30% to 100% a year, with Russia often rolling out 200+ stores per year. Joseph described the pace of growth as "simply insane." In 2012, as increasing wages in emerging markets supported consumption, Russia/CIS was identified as a key growth market and one of three "attack markets" within the adidas Group, alongside North America and Greater China. The three attack markets were expected to contribute around 50% of the adidas Group total growth under the company's "Route 2015" plan, with each market targeting a double-digit compound annual growth rate.

adidas Russia/CIS, under the leadership of managing director Martin Shankland, enjoyed a great deal of autonomy. In Martin's words:

> *"When KPMG seconded me to audit adidas Russia/CIS in 1996, I felt like I had landed on the moon, and it was great. I was only supposed to stay for three months, but on the second day, I knew this is where I wanted to be. I was supposed to stay with KPMG in Russia for two years, but half way through that term, I began working for adidas. There was an incredible sense of optimism. This is where I felt I could realize myself. It was a place where I felt I could do the things that I was capable of, which, in a way, is always more difficult in a developed, established market where the rules are all worked out. adidas Russia/CIS appeared to be a place with lots of opportunity and not many rules."*

Martin played an instrumental role in moving Russia/CIS from a wholesale to an own-retail business model, which proved to be a competitive advantage for adidas in Russia. By 2012, it had about 1,000 stores in the country, with plans to open around 150 additional stores during the year, representing over 90% of the total business. In comparison, in 2008, the company had around 650 stores, representing 70% of adidas/CIS business. Competitors that did not have their own retail stores would find it more difficult to offer a seamless omnichannel experience. Conversely, Russia could leverage its own retail stores, which focused on full-price sell through[iii] and were deemed one of the main growth drivers for the next years. As Martin explained:

[ii] CIS is the common acronym for the Commonwealth of Independent States, a regional organization formed during the breakup of the Soviet Union with nine of the 15 former Soviet Republics.

[iii] The sell-through rate is commonly represented as a percentage that compares the amount of inventory a retailer receives from a manufacturer or supplier against what is actually sold to the customer. The sell-through rate is important because the longer items stay on a retailer's shelves the more money it costs the retailer (e.g. through discounts at the end of a season) because dead stock means the retailer cannot refresh products until it sells through what is in stock.

"adidas Russia/CIS was mainly a distribution business, but after the 1998 Russian financial crisis, wholesalers were left with no capital. They owed us huge amounts of money and were simply unable to repay. That forced a new era on the company. Prior to the crisis, the thinking was that relying on wholesalers and putting a limited amount of our own infrastructure on the ground would limit our country exposure. The crisis made it clear that operating a wholesale business model was anything but low risk. The good news was that the market indeed had tremendous potential and it picked up pretty quickly after the crisis.

"At that point, we focused on the brand and how it was represented at the point of sale. Initially, the general standards of merchandising, customer service, etc. were low; we wanted our brand to be presented in line with the global image of adidas. I realized that even though we knew next to nothing about retailing, we didn't know any less than our distributors. In other words, it could not get worse if we started our own retail business, so we started to open stores one by one. There wasn't any real strategy behind it, just a desire to improve the quality of distribution and the shopping experience. It was very much below the radar.

"Around 2005, we got to the stage of opening 25 to 30 stores a year and we could no longer wing it – we had to get capex approvals at the beginning of each budget year. I remember going to a meeting where I had to present to the entire board. That meeting was a chance for me to demonstrate that the capital outflow from capex was actually no worse than the wholesale discount we were giving wholesalers at the time. But it was a mindset change to accept that the retail price that we get from the consumer for our goods is our money, regardless of whether we put these goods through our own retail channel or the wholesale channel. So I showed them both models. I showed them cash outflows from capex (under our own-retail model) and from the wholesale discount. I was able to demonstrate that we were better off under our own-retail model. I tried to turn around the perception that capex was a bad thing, something to avoid. The board got the message and that was the real turning point. From then on, we got whatever capex we needed, launching a period of exceptional growth."

The Group expected European emerging market economies to benefit from robust domestic consumption in 2013. Russia, in particular, with the expansion and increasing sophistication of its own-retail activities, was expected to have a positive influence on Group sales. Consequently, adidas Global Operations, which focused on building the required infrastructure, processes and systems to support the Group's growth plans, completed a state-of-the-art distribution center in Chekhov, Russia in July 2013. The existing distribution center in Klimovsk, Russia was facing capacity and systems challenges, which resulted in a backlog of deliveries to stores and consumers in the Russian market. The switch to the new distribution center also led to inventory shortages in the country, and these combined shortages were partly responsible for adidas not attaining its 2013 goals.[3]

Though Russia/CIS had historically been one of adidas's most important markets, by mid-2014 sales and profits began to decline further amid the stuggling economy and Western sanctions imposed on Moscow over the Ukraine conflict. In August 2014 adidas cut its plans for new stores from 150 to 80 per year. Then, in March 2015, adidas announced it would close 200 shops across Russia due to the poor economic situation in the country. The economic downturn was blamed on "deteriorating consumer sentiment." Additionally, the ruble's collapse (it lost 40% against the dollar in just six months) ate into revenues and profits, particularly since most suppliers globally were paid in dollars (*refer to* **Exhibit 4**).

Joseph Godsey

When adidas's chief information officer approached Joseph about moving to Russia to lead the IT team, Joseph's first thought was, "Oh my God, my wife is going to kill me." He had heard many difficult stories about Russia and he was pretty convinced this was not the place for him. But when he broached the idea to his wife, she was surprisingly open to it. They had two little boys and were ready to transition to a new stage at that point. So in April 2014, Joseph, together with his family, moved to Russia as part of a "dream team," which was sent there based on a board-driven directive. Joseph's mandate was to motivate the Russian team to completely rebuild the IT organization, stabilize the SAP and other IT platforms, deliver a broader roadmap of initiatives and fix structural operation issues.

Joseph was born and raised in the US and had degrees in engineering and political science from Clemson University in Tennessee. From an early age, he had a clear entrepreneurial penchant. One of his early passions was technology, and while still in school, he built a website that enabled teachers and students to interact more effectively. His first job after graduating was with General Electric (GE), which took him to an aircraft engine service facility in Scotland and then to a wind turbine manufacturing facility in Germany (where he learned to speak German) for a greenfield enterprise resource planning (ERP) implementation. As Joseph explained:

> "This was where I was first introduced to supply chain. I learned to dissect supply chain processes, reorganize them for efficiency and put technology on top of them for speed."

While in Germany, he met his American wife-to-be. So, by the time GE offered to move him back to the US, he was somewhat conflicted about it. Through a series of circumstances, his now-wife was contacted by adidas about a job back in the US. The couple still had serious reservations because they had fallen in love with the European lifestyle. After researching the company, Joseph decided to also apply for a job with adidas, but in Germany, not the US. In the end, both he and his wife were offered contracts in southern Germany.

For Joseph, going from manufacturing supply chains and Oracle systems to retail and SAP systems was a big leap. As he explained, the working cultures, industries and IT systems "were polar opposites." After a couple of roles in adidas, he decided to take a parental leave and do his MBA at IMD in Switzerland, which offered a leading global MBA program with a strong industrial focus. When he finished the program, he explored various options, but quickly came to realize that he loved the fast-paced environment that adidas offered, so he returned to the company.

From a career perspective, adidas Russia/CIS was a risky move for Joseph. The IT team in Russia had been successfully running 1,200+ stores, but significant cracks were starting to show. On top of that, the market was saturated, growth was stagnant, profits were being challenged, the IT setup was nearing a breaking point and the distribution center was bursting with backlogged 2013 inventory, just to mention a few of the issues. Joseph knew the risks involved were substantial if he could not manage the situation. But the challenge was just too tempting to turn down.

> *"How often do you get a chance to make a difference in a company when you are an IT guy? Russia/CIS was a big bet for me, but I figured it mattered a lot to adidas, so I would get the right support to make things happen. And if they did happen, then I could really get my dream job!"*

Hitting the ground running: Putting out the fires

When Joseph arrived in April 2014, the challenge he and his team were facing quickly came into focus. The IT organization and systems landscape were in need of a severe overhaul. The new distribution facility was at the limit of its physical capacity and the operation throughput needs were double what the warehouse management system (WMS) could handle. This combination created a real risk in relation to the upcoming sales peak in June. According to Joseph:

> *"It was overwhelming at first. We were tasked with pushing for operational excellence, but it was as though we were looking over a landscape and all we could see were fires everywhere. The IT organization had to be completely rebuilt, and we had to find a solution for the distribution center's WMS, which was a structural sales risk. I had confidence in the*

Russian team's capabilities, but to be successful, we had to step back and look at the big picture, rather than just a small piece of it."

As part of the Route 2015 initiative, Global IT had designed a standard ERP template that it was rolling out to most markets globally. It planned to roll out the Global platform to each of the regions, but Russia/CIS was unique given the scale of the retail footprint in Russia. The Russian team insisted on many changes to the standard template to handle the unique size of the retail business in Russia. The resulting processes and system landscape were too complex for the scale of business. According to Joseph:

"The implementation of the new system initially went relatively well, but then cracks started appearing. As an example, inventory accuracy was very poor because the company was operating three distinct systems: the stores were using an ERP system for inventory; another ERP system provided a snapshot of the distribution center and the stores; and a third system provided just the distribution center's inventory."

The challenge for the team was clear: They needed to reshape the ERP, WMS and other systems so that they would be able to support the business during the upcoming peak in June and for the longer term. They had the key ingredients to make it happen: They enjoyed the Group's support and trust, and many key stakeholders still believed in the potential of Russia/CIS. According to Joseph:

"The original team on the ground in Russia was exceptionally capable and smart, so I kept it in place and added a few more resources to improve its efficiency."

Joseph and his team were able to rebuild the WMS with a focus on reliability. It had previously been inconceivable that the 25-year-old WMS could run a distribution center as big as the one in Russia, but the results spoke for themselves. They were able to get it to work with unlimited capacity, saving millions in the process. In addition to eliminating the 15 million units of mixed cartons,[iv] Joseph and his team were able to show improvements in shrinkage[v] and stock accuracy, and replenishment time was significantly reduced across all regions, e.g. Moscow's replenishment time was reduced from 6.3 days in October 2014 to 2.7 days by March 2015. And there was still room for improvement. According to Joseph:

"The team had the capability; it was just a matter of looking at the problem the right way."

[iv] A mixed carton contains several SKUs (stock keeping units) as opposed to a carton containing just one SKU.

[v] Shrinkage or loss of inventory is the result of factors such as employee theft, shoplifting, administrative error, vendor fraud, damage in transit or in store, or cashier errors that benefit the customer.

As a result of its accomplishments, the team received an award from the managing director. As Martin explained:

"IT has moved to being a leading factor on our business success, really pulling the business forward."

Once the overall IT landscape was stabilized, the distribution center was running smoothly and the IT team was rebuilt, they began working on "taking the business into the future."

Reforming IT and the supply chain

Supply chain was one of the strategic pillars of the adidas Group. The company viewed speed and agility as key to outpacing competition. In fact, it had a non-financial key performance indicator (KPI) — on-time in-full (OTIF) — that measured delivery performance to its customers and its own retail stores. The company was committed to ensuring constant product availability in the correct size and color, providing game-changing technical innovations and the latest high-end fashion products to the highest quality standards. It aimed to become close to every consumer by building and managing a supply chain that quickly responded to changing market needs and supported multiple distinct business models. To support this initiative, Global Operations initially collaborated closely with the IT function to consolidate and improve legacy structures and reduce complexity and costs for the adidas Group. Against this background, the Group made a decision in 2014 to consolidate the IT and supply chain functions. Russia/CIS was a pilot market for combining both, and in February 2015, Joseph, with his unique background in IT and supply chain and his record of accomplishments in the company, was promoted from head of IT to Vice President Supply Chain Management and Information Technology at adidas Russia/CIS.

Russia, in particular, had some unique characteristics. It was the world's largest country in terms of area with over 17 million square kilometers (*refer to* **Exhibit 5**). It spanned 11 time zones from the Baltic to the Pacific, and each region had completely different geographic, cultural and climatic features. Its infrastructure was seriously underdeveloped, which posed a number of logistical challenges, especially when it came to accessing markets outside major cities. Road density was thin, primarily because many regions were sparsely populated, with an average of about nine persons per square kilometer though most people lived in urban areas.

Prior to 2013, Russian e-commerce was the fastest growing market in Europe in 2012, with 48% of internet users making their first online purchase that year. The market was expected to triple by 2015 to $36 billion.[4] Many foreign companies shared the misconception that Russian consumers had lower expectations than their Western counterparts. In fact, consumers were asking for more than low cost and superior quality; they expected short response times and high service levels. While price was still important, reliability and speed were becoming increasingly significant factors in a company's distribution strategy.[5]

Over the past five years, income levels and consumer spending had increased by 50%. On top of this, the proportion of the population with internet access had doubled to 53%, making Russia the most populous online market in Europe. In addition to having the most mobile phones in Europe, the share of purchases made using smartphones was expected to reach 50% by the end of 2013.[6]

Joseph recognized that the adoption of these technologies in Russia had generated a boom in e-commerce and thus presented an emerging opportunity for omnichannel retailers. Furthermore, the team realized that on a competitive basis, adidas could potentially position itself in a unique space relative to its competitors in the market.

Taking the business into the future

At the beginning of 2014, adidas Group drove the company's first foray into omnichannel sales. Russia and Germany were chosen to pilot "Click-and-Collect" (C&C)[vi] whereby customers could order products online and then pick them up in store rather than have them delivered to their homes. According to Joseph:

> "Global, together with a local team, built a C&C capability and went live with the pilot program at two stores in Moscow in November 2014. At about the same time, the devaluation of the Russian ruble resulted in consumer panic, and everyone was rushing around buying everything from clothes to electronics while the currency was still worth something. Overnight the C&C demand went from an expected 10 to 20 orders per week per store to about 30% of Moscow's e-com orders converging on a few stores (about 1,000 orders per week). It was simply impractical to handle such a high demand in our standard stores and with the processes developed. As a result, they had to put a hold on the C&C initiative until they could find a solution that could handle the demand."

Joseph's first year at adidas Russia/CIS was focused on Operational Excellence – "perfecting the engine" and "controlling and reducing," which entailed fixing things, putting out fires, bringing stability to the system, reducing replenishment speed, increasing stock accuracy, reducing complexity by eliminating mixed cartons, reducing headcount, etc.

[vi] C&C proved to be a popular alternative in Russia for a number of reasons, but primarily because of the way returns were handled. When customers ordered products online and chose home delivery, they had to try the item on while the delivery person waited, in case they wanted to return it.

Now that the fires were under control, Joseph's focus switched from Operational Excellence to taking the business into the future. Compared to other retailers in the Russian market that were becoming more sophisticated on the omnichannel front, adidas Russia/CIS had nothing. As a result, it was feeling the pressure. It needed to pivot the business and develop new capabilities. According to Joseph:

> "At the end of 2014, we had hit a wall. The next level of capability in omni – ship-from-store – would provide the biggest business benefit because it would unlock working capital. To seize this opportunity, we had to act fast. The board understood the importance of navigating through this difficult situation, and it knew how essential an investment in IT was in doing this. For the first time, I felt we had a change in mindset; IT was no longer considered just a support function; we were an enabler."

Steps towards 2020

As Joseph and his team sat around the table discussing what the priorities should be for the business, he knew he had to challenge them to think about things in a different way. Rather than focus on the capabilities and their acronyms, they decided to develop a holistic plan that was tied to the consumer and, from there, figure out which capabilities they needed. Through the lens of initially providing adidas's Russian consumers with "unrivaled accessibility and convenience," Joseph and his team considered the following:

- Click-and-collect (C&C), which provided customers with the convenience of picking up their online orders at a local store, even in smaller cities. The consumer could order multiple sizes, models or colors, try them on with help from the store staff and keep only what they wanted – all for no additional cost. Going into 2015, Joseph wanted to quickly restart the rollout of C&C, but in a controlled manner, driving careful change management to ensure success. The rollout would require a POS (point-of-sale) software upgrade and a rollout of C&C to 200-plus locations at the rate of 30+ stores a week.

- Customization or "mi adidas." Initially introduced by the adidas Group in 2000 and rolled out to select stores in 2001 and later to the first e-commerce countries in 2009, this service allowed consumers to create customized footwear or apparel based on their personal specifications. Implementing this service would be complex, but it could be a big success with consumers.

- Endless Aisle (EA) allowed customers to see the full range of adidas products on an in-store digital display. Customers could see images from different angles, select sizes and colors, check inventory and purchase products. The benefit of Endless Aisle was that consumers could have full access to the entire adidas range regardless of the size of the store. It also provided a point of interaction between the sales associate and the customer, which drove service to a higher standard. And, as Joseph said, "If the item the customer wanted was not in store, it could be ordered through EA rather than the customer going next door to one of our competitors." Some efforts had already been made in this regard, but they were not working, so the team needed to completely rethink the model.

- Radio-frequency identification (RFID). This technology could support and optimize inventory management and product availability on the sales floor. It held the potential to increase sales, reduce working capital, increase retail staff productivity and drive high stock accuracy in the stores. Joseph had initiated an initial request for proposal (RFP) process, but major investments would be required to bring it to fruition. RFID was seen as one of the highest risk projects across the industry due to the complexity of change management and total system complexity.

- Ship-from-Store (SFS). This would allow adidas Russia/CIS to start trading in-store stock online rather than just trading stock at the distribution center. It would offer consumers wider and deeper product choices. Orders placed online could be "brokered" from the closest store to the consumer and the unique SKUs only available in store would be seen as available inventory online for order. According to Joseph, "This initiative could be compared to double-bypass surgery; it could kill the business if we didn't do it properly." Joseph estimated that they could implement SFS in a year or a year and a half. A multi-stage RFP had been conducted, but again, further investments would be required to move it forward.

When the meeting with his team wrapped up, the next step was to secure buy-in at the corporate level. As Joseph began to prepare the presentation for the upcoming meeting, he felt confident; he had an extremely capable team behind him and he knew Martin, who had been successful in creating a supportive, entrepreneurial culture where people were comfortable pushing the limits, was behind him. As Nina Sinitsyna, VP Business Transformation, said:

> "Martin has created an environment where you're allowed to try new things and fail; it's even encouraged. However, if you try something new, fail and give up or stop trying, that's not allowed. You cannot survive if you do not try new things. But when we talk about taking risks, we are allowed to take risks, but they must be calculated risks."

Despite Martin's support, Joseph knew there were a number of challenges that he had to be prepared to address in order to gain the support of the corporate stakeholders. In particular, he needed to answer the following questions:

- Given the economic and geopolitical turmoil in the country, was the timing right to make major IT and SCM investments in Russia?
- Were they taking on too many intersecting and complex initiatives all at once?
- Would they be able to build a team that could successfully implement and roll out the capabilities?
- How would they manage the enormous change that would be required at the retail level?
- Would they be able to manage all of this on top of the crisis?

Exhibit 1: Russian economic indicators

02 / Quarterly unemployment rate by region[1]

(in % of total active population)

	Q4 2013	Q1 2014	Q2 2014	Q3 2014	Q4 2014
USA[2]	7.0	6.6	6.2	6.1	5.7
Euro area[3]	11.8	11.7	11.5	11.5	11.4
Japan[4]	3.7	3.6	3.7	3.6	3.4
China[5]	4.1	4.1	4.1	4.1	4.1
Russia[6]	5.6	5.4	4.9	4.9	5.3
Brazil[7]	4.3	5.0	4.8	4.9	4.3

1] Quarter-end figures.
2] Source: US Bureau of Labor Statistics.
3] Source: Eurostat.
4] Source: Japan Ministry of Internal Affairs and Communications.
5] Source: China National Bureau of Statistics.
6] Source: Russia Federal Service of State Statistics.
7] Source: Brazil Institute of Geography and Statistics.

03 / Quarterly development of Consumer Price Index[1]

(by region)

	Q4 2013	Q1 2014	Q2 2014	Q3 2014	Q4 2014
USA[2]	1.5	1.5	2.1	1.7	0.8
Euro area[3]	0.8	0.5	0.5	0.3	(0.2)
Japan[4]	1.6	1.6	3.6	3.2	2.4
China[5]	2.5	2.4	2.3	1.6	1.5
Russia[6]	6.5	6.9	7.8	8.0	11.4
Brazil[7]	5.9	6.2	6.5	6.8	6.4

1] Quarter-end figures.
2] Source: US Bureau of Labor Statistics.
3] Source: Eurostat.
4] Source: Japan Ministry of Internal Affairs and Communications.
5] Source: China National Bureau of Statistics.
6] Source: Russia Federal Service of State Statistics.
7] Source: Brazil Institute of Geography and Statistics.

04 / Quarterly consumer confidence development[1]

(by region)

	Q4 2013	Q1 2014	Q2 2014	Q3 2014	Q4 2014
USA[2]	77.5	83.9	86.4	89.0	93.1
Euro area[3]	(13.5)	(9.3)	(7.5)	(11.4)	(10.9)
Japan[4]	40.0	36.9	40.5	39.6	37.5
China[5]	102.3	107.9	104.7	105.4	105.8
Russia[6]	(11.0)	(11.0)	(6.0)	(7.0)	(18.0)
Brazil[7]	111.2	108.8	106.3	109.7	109.2

1] Quarter-end figures.
2] Source: Conference Board.
3] Source: European Commission.
4] Source: Economic and Social Research Institute, Government of Japan.
5] Source: China National Bureau of Statistics.
6] Source: Russia Federal Service of State Statistics.
7] Source: Brazil National Confederation of Industry.

05 / Exchange rate development[1] (€ 1 equals)

	Average rate 2013	Q1 2014	Q2 2014	Q3 2014	Q4 2014	Average rate 2014
USD	1.3283	1.3788	1.3658	1.2583	1.2141	1.3296
GBP	0.8492	0.8282	0.8015	0.7773	0.7789	0.8066
JPY	129.58	142.42	138.44	138.11	145.23	140.44
RUB	42.298	49.205	45.933	49.560	68.303	50.737
CNY	8.1674	8.4825	8.4035	7.7417	7.4291	8.1919

1] Spot rates at quarter-end.

Exhibit 1: (continued)

06 / **2014 oil price development[1]** (in US $ per barrel)

| Jan. 1, 2014   Dec. 31, 2014 |

100

70

40

1] West Texas Intermediate Cushing crude oil.   Source: Bloomberg.

Source: 2014 adidas Annual Report

Exhibit 2: adidas Group

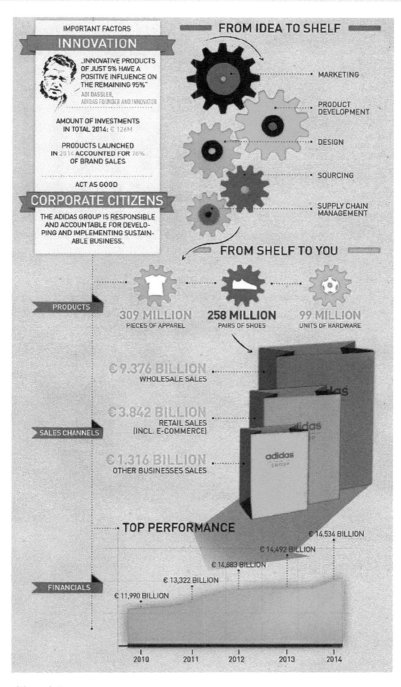

Source: adidas website

Exhibit 3: adidas Russia/CIS net sales

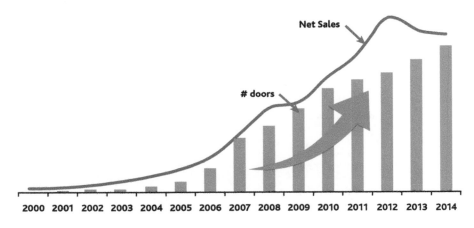

Source: adidas Russia/CIS

Exhibit 4: Supplier factories by region in 2014

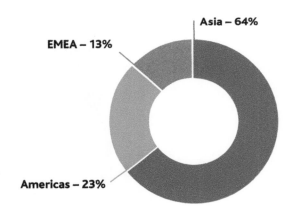

Source: 2014 Annual Report

Exhibit 5: Russia and North America compared

Source: CIA World Factbook

CASE STUDY | ADIDAS RUSSIA/CIS AND THE RUSSIAN CRISIS: RETRENCH OR DOUBLE DOWN (B)

Beverley Lennox, Carlos Cordon and Benoit Leleux

This case won the Supply Chain Management category in the 2016 EFMD case writing competition.

MOSCOW (RUSSIA), MAY 2016. As Joseph Godsey, vice president of supply chain management and information technology at adidas Russia/CIS, was preparing to relocate back to Germany to take on a new challenge at adidas Global, he reflected on all that had happened since the Strategy 2020 meeting with adidas headquarters and the Operational Excellence steering committee one year ago.

Prior to the meeting, he and his team had decided to focus on three of the five original options: click-and-collect (C&C), ship-from-store (SFS) and radio-frequency identification (RFID). Despite putting endless aisle (EA) and customization on hold in order to focus on the other three capabilities, he was still asking for a huge investment during troubled times in Russia, and it would take an enormous effort on the part of his team and significant cross-functional collaboration among many teams, both local and global, to deliver the roadmap. But, as Joseph explained:

> *"I trusted that I had an army of people behind me that would make this happen. Because it was such a bold move, everyone got on board and wanted to move the needle."*

To their delight, Joseph and his team got everything they asked for. The Russian team had gained the confidence of headquarters; hence, headquarters was willing to invest in the team's roadmap. In Martin's words:

> *"We were always respected for our entrepreneurialism, but there was always some skepticism as to whether or not we had the people here who could engineer systems and processes at the level of a world-class retailer. Very quickly, the headquarters guys came to respect the talent here and understood this would be a great place to incubate the next generation of retail processes and systems capabilities. As for Joseph, he is not just an IT guy. He has a vision for the consumer along with a joint local-global vision. And he has the capability to sell his vision, provide a plan and motivate his team to deliver solutions.*

"In the past, I was always trying to pull IT and supply chain along. Now we can't keep up with them; they are actually pulling us into new territories."

Rewind to March 2015: The lead-up to the Strategy 2020 meeting

With the crisis hitting hard in 2015, Joseph was feeling the pressure. He was seeing the profit and loss statements every day, and he knew they were at a point of survival. According to Joseph:

"We could either duck and hide and hope we would survive, or we could cut our losses and run – get rid of our capital exposure and reduce our exposure to Russia altogether, or, we could invest in the crisis."

The sliding sales in the key Russian market contributed to the adidas Group cutting its profit goals in 2014, and shareholders were pressing management to accelerate a turnaround, arguing it should have reacted faster to the collapse of Russian demand.[7] But Joseph and his team wanted to win, so he knew he had to make a strong case to the executive board that adidas should invest in the crisis so that when it was over, adidas Russia/CIS would have a strong competitive advantage.

Despite the economic and political turmoil facing the country, the roadmap he and his team had decided on would require a hefty investment to bring it to fruition. But he had to frame it in such a way that the corporate stakeholders could digest it. He needed to shift the focus from the business to the consumer. So, he thought:

"What if I could write the strategy slides and never mention the acronyms – C&C, SFS, RFID, etc. Instead, I could focus on how we can leverage our store network and online/digital capabilities to provide the ultimate convenience, accessibility and personalization for the consumer; in other words, we could provide products to the consumer whenever and wherever. Only then would I talk about what that means in terms of capabilities."

Further, he knew that the corporate stakeholders would challenge him on how the team could develop such complexity and capabilities in parallel. Typically, such programs would be run in a staged process to avoid conflicting dependencies. Also, he would be challenged on how they would implement and roll out the capabilities. During the rollout, change management would be a key obstacle to overcome. All of these elements had to be addressed.

The meeting

Joseph started by outlining what Omnichannel and Operations Excellence meant in the Russian context. As he explained:

"For the consumer, it means the right product at the right place at the right time – the ultimate experience of accessibility and convenience. For the stores, it means making their lives easier so they can better serve the consumer and ultimately drive higher sales and profitability. For the back office, it means making the end-to-end processes more efficient from a profitability perspective but also reducing our working capital needs. Also, the positive consumer experience would build long-term loyalty for the brand."

He went on to describe the team's philosophy in terms of implementing a program that would provide the ultimate consumer experience. Instead of investing one or two years in developing a program, which could be risky if it failed in the end, they planned to move as fast as possible to prototype a live model, then build it with constant iterations, learning from each phase. He explained how they could achieve business benefits (higher sales and profits and lower working capital) incrementally with a plan that leveraged change agents and decoupled dependencies between each of the omnichannel initiatives. In addition, Joseph proposed that each of the initiatives in the roadmap be "glocally" led and staffed.

He then went on to propose the three capabilities he and his team had decided to pursue:

- **Click-and-collect.** Starting immediately, they planned to upgrade the point-of-sale (POS) software in all relevant stores to accommodate the rollout of the C&C program to 200 locations at 30 stores per week. This would require a significant ramp up of staffing, particularly store change agents that would drive change at the store level to ensure store staff understood the new system and had the support they needed for a successful implementation.

- **Ship-from-store.** Despite the complexity of SFS, Joseph took a bold risk by initiating a comprehensive, multi-stage request for proposal (RFP) process prior to the meeting. The team sat through a great first round of order-management-system demos. The architecture for SFS had been developed and the plan was to align efforts and feasibility with all of the global teams in the coming weeks so that it could be quickly and cost-effectively scaled on a global basis. They proposed a phased-build plan of the capabilities over a 1.5-year period that reduced the risk exposure but scaled in business capabilities every four months. The same change agent network for C&C would be moved over to roll out SFS capabilities.

- **Radio-frequency identification**. A comprehensive RFP to find a vendor was underway for in-store processes. They had a good first round, and they had narrowed it down to three vendors. From these sessions, they also gained a solid understanding of the business capabilities and the system setup needed to succeed. RFID would not only be critical to creating the high stock accuracy required for Omni models, but it would also provide significant efficiency and sales benefit to the larger retail base. The same change-agent network would also be critical for success.

In addition to the above, Endless Aisle was put on hold temporarily to keep the focus on the C&C rollout. Once the team had time to free up capabilities, the plan was to build an EA proof-of-concept and roll it out to the first stores, leveraging the same change agent network. EA could potentially be scaled to 200-plus stores by the end of 2015.

The results: Omni-speed

According to Joseph:

> "At the end of 2014, we were stuck in a gridlock on how to realize the future of the Omni and RFID roadmaps. But we were building credibility with our Operations Excellence strategy and getting some of the foundations [i.e. RFPs for SFS and RFID] of other things in place. By mid-to end-February 2015, we had basically introduced elements of an ambitious plan and warmed the waters.

> "At the beginning of April, we confirmed we were ready (and already running) toward achieving the ambitious plan.

> "Foundational in getting corporate's buy-in was our success with Operational Excellence and convincing the steering group of the robustness of our plan."

By May 2016, the team had delivered not only the roadmap that Joseph had presented to the steering committee in March 2015 but also much more:

- POS software that would support Russia/CIS's Omni/RFID initiatives had gone live in 540 stores, and a new "lean" version had been built to work with Omni/RFID and the rollout for future stores. The first phase of the new order management system that supported SFS went live in October 2015. A further update in February 2016 allowed the movement of goods to be synched using RFID, and plans were in place for further updates in August 2016 and beyond. While the team initially decoupled each of the omnichannel initiatives, they expected to have them completely interconnected by August 2016, and SAP would essentially be reduced to a financial system for omnichannel activities.

- C&C had been rolled out to 250 stores by June 2015 and then to a total of 380 stores by February 2016. C&C orders amounted to 70% of e-commerce sales, but there were some bumps along the way that initially resulted in an unsatisfactory customer experience; for every 10 orders, only 5 were picked up because of changing consumer demand and the lack of a quality consumer experience with regard to speed. Under the Operational Excellence program, the team had worked further in 2015 on optimizing all the replenishment process steps so that 185 stores could count on next-morning replenishment from the distribution center (sales up to 9 p.m. were replenished to the stores by 8 a.m. the next morning). The same principles were then applied to the Omni models to drive excellence across all steps in the process/systems. They figured that this could result in a 20%+ increase in net profits by converting existing orders. But it also required a mindset change on the part of the store staff. To ensure the success of C&C, they engaged six strong store managers with five-plus years of retail experience to act as change agents. The change agents provided on-site training for each of the stores, on-site support for two to three days after the launch and on-call support for a month after the launch.

- The first phase of SFS had been launched in 30 stores in 12 cities by the end of 2015. By May, over 100 stores were running SFS with plans for a total of 350-plus stores by the end of 2016. In the second phase, store stock was added to available inventory online – doubling the sales for the respective stores on the program. To date, the platform had been very stable despite being hugely complex. SFS was fast and accurate; the time from order placement to pick and pack was as low as 30 minutes, and inventory was updated every 30 minutes. It constituted approximately 4% of retail sales and as much as 10% in some stores. Stores were now processing 25% of home-delivery orders in the pilot regions. In most cases, orders were delivered the next day, or within two days for faraway places, versus three to seven days previously. Additionally, SFS reduced delivery costs in the pilot regions by about 50%. And because both the distribution center and store stock were presented as part of the online inventory, it often meant the difference between a limited and full selection of sizes. As a result, they expected a 10% to 20% boost in sales due to the increased size availability. While much had been accomplished, again the focus had to be on change management at the store level. Initially, store staff resisted preparing items for shipment because they were waiting to see if they could sell them in store. But as Joseph said, "The commission was the same whether an item was sold in store or through SFS, and in fact, sales volume would increase if delivery promises could be achieved." As Joseph explained, SFS had an additional benefit, "It burns stock down, which means we can sell it at the full price rather than mark it down at the end of the season."

- RFID was launched in October 2015 in five pilot stores covering all in-store processes, i.e. sales, receiving, stocktaking, floor replenishment, etc. The result was that the 5,000-piece inventory of an entire store could be counted with 99% accuracy in 45 minutes and the average on-floor availability was 96%. An additional 100 stores had gone live by May 2016, with an eventual rollout to a total of 500 stores by the end of 2016. The team also added RFID capabilities to the distribution center. RFID was live in the packing and inbound processes and it was fully integrated with the warehouse management system. To date, the inbound results were significant with 100% accuracy of 97% of cartons. In addition, shrinkage between the distribution center and the stores was reduced by 40% by leveraging the new 100% accuracy in packing approach and rebuilt transport/store processes, which saved €2 million in profits. Plans were in place to roll out further capabilities, including stocktaking and the outbound process. Overall, RFID had resulted in leaner inventories and reduced the need for working capital. While the scale of change at the store level as a result of all these omnichannel initiatives was enormous, positive change management results had been experienced.

- A completely new EA capability had been built and piloted with 30 stores by the end of 2015, with 120 by May 2016. The team had a plan to reach 600 by the end of 2016. A significant focus was placed on staff training with the aim of creating an overall service experience to meet any customer demand. Again, the challenge was getting stores to adopt the technology.

- A new, simple handheld label printing tool was introduced for quick and easy labeling of goods (e.g. for re-pricing), which resulted in a 75% reduction in labor effort in repricing, which typically took hundreds of hours per season.

- A new "return-to-store" capability was implemented, which allowed consumers to return their online purchases to stores for immediate refund (rather than having the delivery person wait while the consumer decided whether or not to keep an item). In aggregate, stores would then need to process standard end-of-season returns, C&C remains and e-com returns. Therefore, the entire reverse logistics process was rebuilt to drive the high operation excellence standard covered in other areas. Combined, the results of other operations programs resulted in a 78% reduction in returns to the distribution center and a 67% reduction in wrong returns. In the latest SFS models, these return volumes would be reduced further as they would be consumed as available inventory for online sales.

- A new delivery model – PickPoint – that extended convenience and accessibility to consumers by providing a centralized location where they could pick up their purchases was launched. By mid-October 2015, 550 of these PickPoints had been activated in 160 cities, which resulted in PickPoint volumes quadrupling and increasing e-commerce sales by 3%.

- A reporting tool, called Adismart Reporting, was built for easy access on the floor, on the go or from a PC, and it was rolled out to all retail staff and back-office employees. This allowed one common point where stores could see their sales results, product performance, omnichannel results, operations standards, etc.

- The CRM (customer relationship management) database allowed adidas Russia/CIS to capture, process and analyze critical customer data, which would improve customer loyalty by engaging customers in ways that really interested them – through targeted campaigns. Consumers were offered a card or mobile app to track their status, and they could use it for a fast check-out process on EA in the stores.

- While Russia's business results in 2015 were still suffering from the economic and political situations (*refer to* **Exhibit 1**), the omnichannel capabilities helped amplify the business and provide support to combat the crisis. The roadmap for the future showed that the adidas CIS team would continue investing in omnichannel initiatives, diving deeper into functionalities and expanding across markets. Compared to its main competitors in the market – Nike and Sportsmaster – Adidas Russia/CIS controlled its brands and had an unmatched distribution channel with its store network. And it was confident that the omnichannel would be the game changer that would allow it to create unrivaled, personalization, accessibility and convenience for its consumers; hence, it would be well positioned to take advantage of the opportunity that the 2018 FIFA World Cup in Russia would offer.

Exhibit 1: 2015 Business results for adidas Russia/CIS

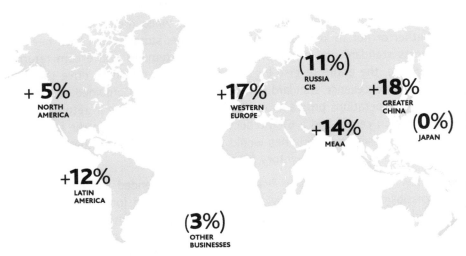

Exhibit 1: (continued)

SEGMENTAL INFORMATION I

€ in millions	Net sales (non-Group)[1]		Segmental operating profit[1]		Segmental assets[2]		Segmental liabilities[2]	
	2015	2014	2015	2014	2015	2014	2015	2014
Western Europe	4 539	3 793	909	666	1 327	1 013	145	122
North America	2 753	2 217	69	120	891	744	96	47
Greater China	2 469	1 786	866	617	465	335	146	109
Russia/CIS	739	1 098	85	173	204	226	6	17
Latin America	1 783	1 612	235	199	619	629	63	91
Japan	776	744	147	121	233	243	34	75
MEAA	2 388	1 925	664	555	633	553	77	67
Other businesses (continuing operations)	1 467	1 358	-89	-57	684	709	117	134
Other businesses (discontinued operations)	159	283	-18	19	0	139	0	37
Other businesses (total)	1 627	1 641	-107	-38	684	848	117	171
Total	**17 075**	**14 817**	**2 869**	**2 413**	**5 056**	**4 591**	**683**	**699**

[1] Year ending December 31   [2] At December 31

SEGMENTAL INFORMATION II

€ in millions	Capital expenditure[1]		Depreciation and amortization[1]		Impairment losses and reversals of impairment losses[1]	
	2015	2014	2015	2014	2015	2014
Western Europe	63	35	33	27	4	5
North America	32	32	21	18	7	6
Greater China	76	56	43	34	1	0
Russia/CIS	16	29	24	39	2	4
Latin America	30	35	22	22	2	–
Japan	13	8	10	9	0	0
MEAA	35	31	27	20	1	0
Other businesses (continuing operations)	18	20	20	17	1	1
Other businesses (discontinued operations)	4	6	4	7	0	0
Other businesses (total)	22	26	24	23	1	1
Total	**287**	**253**	**204**	**191**	**18**	**16**

[1] Year ending December 31

Source: 2015 adidas Annual Report

Insights from the cases: adidas's omnichannel journey

This case argues that crises are moments of truth when efficiency gains are most needed, thus justifying investment in omnichannel capabilities instead of retrenching. This argument is made particularly vivid by the depth of the crisis that hit Russia in late 2014/early 2015 and by the scale of adidas Russia/CIS's retail operations, among the largest globally, with oversized logistical challenges in covering the largest country in the world with limited infrastructure.

One of the keys to success in Joseph's push to invest in omnichannel capabilities was his emphasis on demonstrating the increase in revenues thanks to supply chain transformation, rather than focusing only on the cost savings. He succeeded in positioning the supply chain as a cornerstone that drives growth by focusing on the consumer desire for speed of delivery and convenience. To satisfy these expectations, multiple fulfillment strategies were necessary, e.g. distribution centers, ship-from-store, store pick-up.

A powerful argument employed by Joseph was to connect a customer expectation — ship-from-store — with a supply chain efficiency driver — RFID. Although RFID had been available for a long time, it was only in the last few years that the cost had come down, enabling its widespread implementation. It facilitated highly accurate tracking of stock over all locations. It reduced "shrinkage," whereby products "disappeared" during transport or from the store or, simply, according to store personnel, "could not be located." Given that the products that "disappeared" tended to be the ones that were most in demand, the impact on lost profits was substantial. RFID was also an important enabler for other initiatives like click-and-collect, endless aisle and ship-from-store. Thus, although RFID was complex and expensive, it would make the implementation of the other initiatives much easier and more successful.

This was particularly true for ship-from-store, which Joseph was initially going to present independent of RFID. However, its dependence on the availability of RFID was so strong that he was not able to "decouple" the two and presented them both together. Ship-from-store would allow much higher availability of products and sizes for customers at the store and online. Shoes necessitate a much higher number of SKUs than other apparel. For example, a typical fashion retailer carries an average of three sizes per product (S, M, L), whereas a shoe retailer might have up to eight sizes per product. Since this necessarily entails a large number of SKUs, no shop stocks several of each size, resulting in lost sales. As a consequence, ship-from-store would increase sales because it gave consumers access to the entire inventory across all stores.

It is interesting to put this initiative in the context of the RFID sweet spot described in Chapter 1. adidas is cited as a successful example of a company that benefited from being in the sweet spot of having moderate volumes, moderate margins and an integrated supply chain. This further demonstrates how its digital supply chain implementation was coherent with the business context.

5 SUPPLY CHAIN CAREER OPPORTUNITIES

The unexpected consequences of integration

More and more companies have complex global supply chains[8] and are evolving their management structures to maintain service levels and control working capital. As we saw in Chapter 3, sales and operations planning (S&OP) is slowly making headway to align demand and supply.

But the evolution towards end-to-end integration has had unexpected consequences for supply chain careers.

Factories used to stand separate from distribution and demand planning. Factory managers held positions of prestige, working directly with general managers to coordinate production. In an integrated global supply chain, the factory manager's role has changed, says Rachel Sheehan, former Global SVP Supply Chain Talent for multinational beauty company Coty.

It is a more matrixed role, requiring a special effort to maintain proximity to business units. It may have lost functions to mutualization, such as sourcing, new product introduction (NPI) coordination, accounts payable and production planning. The challenge, according to Rachel, is to have factory managers "feel they have a seat at the table, albeit with a modified skill set and organization design than in the past."

A career in factory management may feel less attractive. Factories are often in remote locations, while planning sits in urban centers. As Rachel notes:

> "This makes people hesitant to go into factories. And yet the factory experience is essential. The centralization of functions creates the risk that you have engineers who have never worked in a factory, don't want to work in a factory, and don't appreciate the challenges. We've created an integrated supply chain and we are more siloed than ever."

A shift from historical roots

The core competencies of supply chain management seem to be shifting away from distribution and transportation. As we saw in Chapter 3, third-party logistics providers (3PLs) have become prominent in FMCG, and the growth of 3PLs is not limited to this area. One estimate projects the 3PL industry will grow 37% between 2016 and 2022.[9] As supply management has come to encompass planning, sourcing and production, supply chain opportunities have slowly moved from their historical roots.

This has an influence on the career paths that supply chain professionals choose. A path through distribution and transportation is less desirable when distribution centers are slowly being outsourced. Yet with 3PLs still seeing cost as a key driver in being awarded business, salaries for those with logistics expertise are under pressure.

With the diminishing appeal of factories and distribution centers, many young supply chain professionals avoid production and logistics in favor of sourcing, planning and NPI coordination. Despite this, Rachel says, supply chain recruitment remains focused on engineering graduates.

However, academic institutions are stepping up. Private institutions like the American Production and Inventory Control Society (APICS) have modernized their certification programs,[10] and others are focused on planning, like the program from the Institute of Business Forecasting (IBF).[11] These certifications help professionals establish credibility and support mid-career transitions.

There has been an increase in supply chain courses. Gartner, the supply chain advisory and research company, has found that US university Master's programs in supply chain grew 67% from 2016 to 2018.[12] There are 38 MBA programs with a supply chain focus. Twenty years ago, there were virtually no academic offerings in supply chain. These programs are creating generations of professionals who specifically choose a career in supply chain.

Future-proofing profiles

But is the supply chain profession fit for purpose? As e-commerce expands and companies struggle with execution costs, demands on supply chains will grow. Companies may struggle to drive innovation with their factories more isolated from their markets and logistics outsourced.

Big data, advanced analytics and artificial intelligence (AI) will continue to grow across the supply chain – 84% of supply chain executives consider machine learning as "important and disruptive."[13] We recently met an executive supply chain recruiter who emphasized deep data literacy as a "must-have" attribute. After much fanfare, S&OP has yet to fully take hold. Only 40% of companies[14] say they have an S&OP process. Some companies are exploring outsourcing demand planning[15] altogether.

The challenge ahead

The role of the supply chain itself is in flux. In a 2018 survey, only 47% of chief supply chain officers say the supply chain is seen as important as sales & marketing or R&D/product development, according to SCM World, down from

59% five years earlier. SCM World[16] found that retaining talent and offering progressive careers are the two biggest supply chain HR challenges.

Several companies have shrunk or eliminated their supply chain Centers of Excellence (CoE), cutting off drivers of innovation, best practices and end-to-end integration.

The future may feel daunting for supply chain careers. One solution could be to focus on the emergence of shorter lifecycles, stock-keeping unit (SKU) explosions due to mass customization, and more demanding consumer behavior that requires synergies between marketing and commercial and industrial activity. Broader roles such as NPI coordination and demand planning may hold the key to compelling career opportunities.

Gustavo Ghory, chief supply chain officer at Kimberly-Clark, former VP Global Manufacturing at P&G, and current chairman of SmarterChains, concurs:

"Supply chain executives are in a unique position to integrate innovation plans for new products with executional and planning capabilities for delivery, turning the plan into a reality in the marketplace."

REFERENCES

[1] Calder, Simon. "Number of planes in the sky to more than double in next 20 years." *Independent*, July 6, 2018. https://ind.pn/2tZy9WJ (accessed March 21, 2019).

[2] "Market overview – Spain – Q3 2010." BMI Research, 2010. https://bit.ly/2OQ664z (accessed March 21, 2019).

[3] "Nine months 2013 results." *adidas Group*, November 7, 2013. www.adidas-group.com/en/media/news-archive/press-releases/2013/nine-months-2013-results/ (accessed June 8, 2016).

[4] "The omnichannel opportunity: Unlocking the power of the connected consumer." Deloitte Report for eBay, February 2014. www2.deloitte.com/content/dam/Deloitte/uk/Documents/consumer-business/unlocking-the-power-of-the-connected-consumer.pdf (accessed April 25, 2016).

[5] Vanderhasselt, E. and An Van Esser. "Supply chain challenges in Russia." Universiteit Gent, 2008–2009. http://lib.ugent.be/fulltxt/RUG01/001/392/238/RUG01-001392238_2010_0001_AC.pdf (accessed April 25, 2016).

[6] "The omnichannel opportunity: Unlocking the power of the connected consumer." Deloitte Report for ebay, February 2014. www2.deloitte.com/content/dam/Deloitte/uk/Documents/consumer-business/unlocking-the-power-of-the-connected-consumer.pdf (accessed April 25, 2016).

[7] Emmerentze Jervell, Ellen. "Investors ratchet up pressure on adidas." *Wall Street Journal Europe*, February 6, 2015.

[8] https://ourworldindata.org/trade-and-globalization

[9] https://www.3plogistics.com/global-third-party-logistics-market-reaches-802-billion/

[10] https://www.apics.org/credentials-education/credentials

[11] https://ibf.org/business-analytics-certification

[12] Dana Stifler, Kimberly Ennis, and Caroline Chumakov. "Top 25 North American supply chain graduate university programs, 2018." Gartner, August 17, 2018. https://www.business.rutgers.edu/sites/default/files/documents/gartner-2018-scm-graduate.pdf

[13] Kevin O'Marah and Xiao Chen. "Future of supply chain 2017." SCM World, October 2017. http://www.neeley.tcu.edu/Centers/Center_for_Supply_Chain_Innovation/PDFs/Future_of_Supply_Chain.aspx

[14] "APQC Infographic: The current state of sales & operations planning." *Supply Chain Management Review*. March 5, 2019. https://www.scmr.com/article/apqc_infographic_the_current_state_of_sales_operations_planning

[15] Matt Wavering. "Should you outsource demand planning." ToolsGroup blog, April 2, 2019. https://www.toolsgroup.com/blog/should-you-outsource-demand-planning/

[16] http://www.scmworld.com/home/

INDEX

The Institute for Management Development (IMD) is an independent academic institution with Swiss roots and global reach, founded almost 75 years ago by business leaders for business leaders. Since its creation, IMD has been a pioneering force in developing leaders who transform organizations and contribute to society.

Based in Lausanne (Switzerland) and Singapore, IMD has been ranked in the Top 3 of the annual FT's Executive Education Global Ranking for the last nine consecutive years and in the top five for 17 consecutive years. Our MBA and EMBA programs have repeatedly been singled out among the best in Europe and the world.

We believe that this consistency at the forefront of our industry is grounded in IMD's unique approach to creating "Real Learning. Real Impact". Led by an expert and diverse faculty, we strive to be the trusted learning partner of choice for ambitious individuals and organizations worldwide. Challenging what is and inspiring what could be.

We have made a deliberate choice to print this book on demand. Traditional offset requires printing of large quantities and the unsold copies must be destroyed.

This results in serious consequences in terms of carbon footprint: waste of paper and energy, unnecessary greenhouse emissions.

This book is printed on paper sourced by environmentally responsible suppliers to reduce its impact on our earth.

Lightning Source UK Ltd.
Milton Keynes UK
UKHW021534120920
369758UK00001B/1